PATHWAYS
TO THE HEART

OPENING THE TEACHINGS
OF THE HOUSE
OF IZHBITZ

RABBI REUVEN BOSHNACK

KODESH PRESS
5780 / 2020

Pathways to the Heart:
Opening the Teachings of the House of Izhbitz
by Reuven Boshnack

© Kodesh Press 2020

ISBN: 978-1-947857-36-0

Paperback Edition

The Publisher extends its gratitude to Rabbi Johnny Solomon for his editing and proofreading of this volume.
V. 1.2

Published & Distributed Exclusively by

Kodesh Press L.L.C.
New York, NY
www.kodeshpress.com
kodeshpress@gmail.com

נתן נחום אנגלרוד

נכד כ״ק אא״ז אדמו״ר **מוהרא״י** זצללה״ה

מראדזין

עיה״ק ירושלים תובב״א

ב״ה

אל כבוד ידידי היקר רב פעלים ויקר רוח

מרביץ תורה ויראה לעדרים

אוהב את הבריות ומקרבן לתורה

הרב **ראובן באשנאק** שליט״א

הנה כבר נודע בשער בת רבים גודל יקרת דברי רבותינו הקדושים לבית איזביצא ראדזין זצללה״ה אשר רבים וטובים מבקשים לרוות את צמאונם ממקור מים חיים. דברי רבותינו הקדושים יסודתם בהררי קודש, דברים הנובעים הישר מן המקור העליון, וחופרים לאט ובבטחה כמעין המתגבר אל עמקי פנימיותו של האדם, אשר כידוע שגלל כן נקרא הספר הקדוש בשם "מי השלוח", כלשון קדשו של כ״ק רבינו האזרחות חיים זצללה״ה בהקדמתו לבית יעקב שרבינו הרבי ר' בונם מפשיסחא "אמר עליו שהוא כמי השלוח ההולכים לאט וחופר בעומק מעמקים". ואמר בזה כ״ק אא״ז אדמו״ר זצללה״ה מראדזין אשר דברי קדשם של רבותינו הם כמעין הנובע ישר משורש עליון, וכל דבריהם מובאים ישירות מהמקור, והם כמי מעין המשפיעים הישר ממקור העליון.

אמנם דבריהם הקדושים אינם ברורים לכל דורש טוב, וצריך עיון רב בכדי להבין וללמוד מתוכם דרך לעבודת הש״י. על כן דבר גדול עשה בזה, אשר ראה לנכון להתעסק בקדשים, ולברר מקחו של צדיק, להלהיב את עיניהם ולבותיהם של ישראל בקדושה של מעלה, להאר את עיניהם ולתת בלבותיהם בינה להבין ולהשכיל ללמוד ולעשות, ולתת מקום שכל אחד יוכל להתגדר בו ולעבוד אותו ית' בקדושה ובטהרה לאור תורת רבותינו הקדושים.

והברכה אחת היא, שזכותם של רבותינו הקדושים יעמדו לימינו ולימין משפחתו, שיראה הצלחה וברכה מרובה בכל מעשי ידיו, וישיפוצו מעיינותיו חוצה להעמיד תלמידים הגונים וישרים, וישזכה שדברי קדשם של רבותינו הקדושים יחדרו לתוך פנימיותם של בני ישראל ויפעלו לטובה ולברכה אצל יראים ושלימים ומבקשי השם אשר רוצים לעלות במסילה העולה בית קל.

נתן נחום אנגלרודנכד
כ״ק אא״ז אדמו״ר **מוהרא״י** זצללה״ה
מראדזין

Congregation Aish Kodesh
of Woodmere
351 Midwood Road
Woodmere, N. Y. 11598
516 - 569-2660

RABBI MOSHE WEINBERGER

קהילת אש קודש דוודמיר

הרב משה וויינבערגער
מרא דאתרא

ב־ה

18 Adar I 5765

Some years ago, my dear talmid, Rabbi Reuven Boshnack, asked me what sefer could be most effectively used in "giving over" the depth and the sweetness of Chassidus to a new generation of American Jews, thirsting for the "Dvar Hashem." It was important that these teachings reach the minds and hearts of individuals from all different backgrounds, regardless of their lack of exposure to "Toras HaBaal Shem Tov." When I suggested the Sfas Emes, I never dreamt that Reb Reuven would undertake a project to revolutionize the method of teaching this holy sefer by providing a lucid, readable translation, while extracting a piece of down to earth practical advice from each Torah studied. In doing so, he has suceeded not only in making the Sfas Emes available for the "Hamon Am", but he has revealed the magnificent relevance of these ageless teachings at a time when they are most desperately needed.

My personal nachas is immeasurable, and my heart is filled with the Bracha that in the zechus of the great Tzaddik, R. Aryeh Leib of Gur zy'a, Reb Reuven and his family will be blessed with good health and long years, immersed in Toras and Avodas Hashem.

This letter of approbation from Rav Moshe Weinberger was from my previous sefer on Sfas Emes, and is reprinted here with his permission.

ORTHODOX UNION תורה ומצוות

ELEVEN BROADWAY | NEW YORK, NY 10004-1303
212.563.4000 | info@ou.org | www.ou.org

RABBI DR. TZVI HERSH WEINREB
Executive Vice President, Emeritus

212.613.8264 *tel*
212.613.0635 *fax*
execthw@ou.org *email*

Adar 5774/February 2014

Our tradition has many hidden treasures.

Among them are the writings of the Chassidic masters of the Izhbitz and Radziner dynasties. These treasures have remained hidden because of their unique language and profound depth. Rabbi Reuven Boshnack, who is a good friend and a veteran outreach professional, has found the language to convey this depth to all who are interested in enriching their spiritual lives.

As an educator on the college campus for the Jewish Learning Initiative on Campus program of the Orthodox Union, he has effectively opened the hearts and minds of hundreds of college students to the exquisite teachings of these Chassidic masters. In this book, he carries his work further and will certainly reach many thousands of others.

I recommend this work heartily to all who are interested in the astute and remarkably creative insights of these unparalleled mystics and thinkers. I commend Rabbi Boshnack for yet another contribution to those of our people who thirst for meaning and search for understanding. Their thirst will be slaked, and their search fulfilled, with this excellent elucidation of these sacred writings.

Zvi Hersh Weinreb

Rabbi Dr. Tzvi Hersh Weinreb
Executive Vice President, Emeritus
Orthodox Union

KOSHER
CERTIFICATION
SERVICE

Founded in 1898 as the Union of Orthodox Jewish Congregations of America
איחוד קהילות האורתודוקסים באמריקה

Introduction to the Second Edition

כ"ב טבת תש"פ

It is with thanks to HaShem, that I bring this second edition of *Pathways to the Heart* to be published . Thank you to Rabbi Alec Goldstein and the rest of the staff of Kodesh Press for all of their work, and the enthusiasm that they have shown in bringing the Teachings of Beis Izhbitz/Radzyn to a greater audience. HaShem should bless this partnership and this should be the first volume of many.

Thank you once more to my wife, Shira for her constant encouragement.

המצפה לגאולה קרובה

Reuven Boshnack
Teves 5780
Brooklyn, NY

Introductions

It is with joy and trepidation that we enter into the teachings of the house of Izhbitz. By way of introduction, allow me to share a story I heard from Rav Tzvi Hirsch Weinreb.

> *My grandfather used to daven with the Radzyner Rebbe, Reb Yeruchem Leiner (a decendant of the house of Izhbitz) in Borough Park. I remember we used to run to get there, because if we came late, we were locked out. Why? You see, in those days Borough Park was not the Borough Park that we are familiar with. The citizens of Borough Park were not used to having shtieblach on every block. The block was not zoned for a place of worship. But Reb Yeruchem, when he came to America, was already a sick man and had received dispensation to allow a minyan to daven with him. But his neighbor wouldn't let this become a big shul, so he would stand outside and count the people who'd come in. Any more than ten, and the man would call the police.*

When I heard this story, I knew it was the perfect introduction to this collection of *shiurim* on the teachings of the Izhbitzer

Rebbes. There are so many obstacles to our ability to understand the Izhbitzers' teachings, in terms of style and the profundity of their messages. But we know it's a worthwhile undertaking. The meaning that these teachings can instill in our *avodas Hashem*, the inspiration and encouragement, is worth the exertion. Despite the fact that there is something blocking the way, we run there anyway. My vision in publishing these *shiurim* is to help us get the guy out of the Rebbe's front yard and so we can enter the Rebbe's *beis midrash*; we all need to hear what the Izhbitzer Rebbes have to say.

When trying to translate these teachings into the English language and idiom, my Rebbe, Rav Moshe Weinberger told me, "You cannot just translate the words of the Izhbitzer teachings. You have to live with them, sing with them, and be with them. Then you have a chance at teaching what the Rebbe has to say." It took years until he felt that I had succeeded in bringing the Izhbitzer's fiery teachings to the black fire and white fire of the printed form.

The Izhbitzer Rebbes' teachings are profound, opening us up to the depths of the Torah and *mitzvos* in a way that touches us. Rebbe Gershon Henech Leiner explains in his introduction to his father's *sefer, Beis Yaakov,* that the most important facet of the Torah, and the Izhbitzer tradition specifically, is its relevance and how it uplifts each one of us: the relevance of every detail in Torah to each person's *avodas Hashem*.

The Title

Rav Shlomo Friefeld said, "The Izhbitzer was an avant garde psychologist." (Heard from Rav BenZion Kirsch.) The Izhbitzer teachings cut straight through to depths of the person, their motivations, their crises and their victories. Therefore, I have chosen to title this collection "Pathways to the Heart" from another quotation from Rav Friefeld, as he discussed how "there are pathways to the heart," paraphrasing *Tehillim* 84:6, and one who knows how to navigate them, will succeed in serving Hashem. It is my hope that this sefer will serve as a guide to some of these pathways in our hearts.

How to Use This Book

In each *shiur*, you will find a teaching of one of the Izhbitzer Rebbes. I've broken up each teaching into paragraphs and explained the concepts and how they flow from one paragraph to the next. You will also find the "Izhbitzer tradition," where I've provided sources for further reading on concepts which appear often in the teachings of the Izhbitzer Rebbes. Finally, each lesson concludes with practical applications, as these teachings were meant to be lived, not just read.

The Izhbitzer Rebbes

מי השלוח (*Mei ha-Shiloach*)

Rabbi Mordechai Yosef Leiner (1801-1854), the first Izhbitzer Rebbe, did not write any of his own teachings, preferring to fill his Chasidim with his teachings. The מי השלוח was written by his grandsons, Rabbis Gershon Henoch (1839-1891) and Mordechai Yosef Leiner. The teachings in this *sefer* are terse, explaining a concept in a unique style. The commentary on *Parshas Emor* is taken from this work.

בית יעקב (*Beis Yaakov*)

Rabbi Yaakov Leiner (1828-1878), son of Rabbi Mordechai Yosef, wrote many works. His teachings are relatively long, incorporating and explaining different themes and concepts. He will often clarify and illustrate his father's teachings. Only six volumes survived the Holocaust: volumes on *Bereishis*, *Shemos*, and *Vayikra* (בית יעקב), a commentary on the Haggadah, and a *sefer* on Shavuos (ספר הזמנים). Most of the *shiurim* collected here come from the sixth book, called בית יעקב הכולל which consists of teachings from the years 5621-5622. This specific book holds a special place amongst the Izhbitzer *seforim*, as many foundations of the Izhbitzer teachings can be found in it, and it was written by Rabbi Avraham Yehoshua Heschel Leiner (1843–1930), son of Rabbi Yaakov Leiner.

14

נאות דשא (*Naos Deshe*)

Rabbi Shmuel Asher Dov Leiner of Biskivitz was the son of Rabbi Mordechai Yosef. His teachings are written in a relatively simple style, usually beginning with several questions on the *parsha* or a commentary. In answering them, he reveals a fundamental teaching. The commentaries on *Parshas Acharei Mos, Behaalotecha, Devarim* and *Ki Tavo* are taken from this work.

סוד ישרים (*Sod Yesharim*)

Rabbi Gershon Henoch Leiner, son of Rabbi Yaakov Leiner, wrote on the *Zohar, Chumash, Yamim Tovim, Seder Taharos,* and on the mitzvah of *techeles.* His *seforim* on *Chumash* and the *Yamim Tovim* are written in a similar style to his father.

תפארת יוסף (*Tiferes Yosef*)

Rabbi Mordechai Yosef Leiner's *divrei Torah* explain the teachings of his ancestors, in a methodical, step by step progression, often taking us through several generations of teachings in a succinct and clear way. The commentaries on *Parshas Korach* and *Ha'azinu* are taken from this work.

Acknowledgements

As always, I begin by thanking the OU's JLIC program led by Rabbis Ilan Haber, Menachem Schrader, and Yehoshua Ross, whose program gives me the unique *zechus* of *harbatzas ha-Torah* at Brooklyn College, and the support they have shown for this project. It was there, on Thursday nights, that these *shiurim* were given along with cholent, kugel and an atmosphere of *dibbuk chaverim*, warmth, and chizuk.

Thank you to Josh Weinberg, for creating the cover to this *sefer*.

Thank you to *yedid nafshi*, Rav Judah Mischel, for his support for this project, *bechavivusa talya milsa*.

I thank my Rebbeim, Rav Binyomin Cherney and Rav Moshe Weinberger, for introducing me to the Izhbitzer *seforim* and for their feedback and encouragement for this *sefer*.

Thanks to our family, the Boshnacks and the Dubins, for their love, care, and support.

Thank you to Shira, my partner in all of our endeavors, as we walk together down the adventure we call life, may we merit to see *doros yesharim*, in the *zechus* of the *tzaddikim* of the house of Izhbitz.

המצפה לגאולה קרובה

Reuven Boshnack
Brooklyn, NY 5775

פרשת בראשית

from Beis Yaakov ha-Kollel

וַיֹּאמֶר אֱלֹהִים הִנֵּה נָתַתִּי לָכֶם אֶת כָּל עֵשֶׂב זֹרֵעַ זֶרַע (בראשית א' כ''ט). ניתן לאדם. היינו שיוכל לזרוע ממנו ולהוסיף. כי בהאדם נמצא השארה ובבהמה לא נאמר כן רק ירק עשב. היינו שאין לה השארה ולא ניתן לה בלתי לפי שעה.

Hashem said, "Behold, I have given you vegetables and seed to be sown" (*Bereishis* 1:29). The בית יעקב explains that man was given the ability to seed the ground and affect the future. Through this commandment, a person has the ability to cause his influence to remain in this world even after he has physically left it. But the animals were only given the vegetables. What is the meaning of this? The animals do not have this ability to influence the world; they only exist for the moment.

וכדאיתא במדרש תהלים (מזמור י''ט). שני דברים אין אומות העולם כופרין בהן. על הקב"ה שברא את העולם לששת ימים. ושהוא מחיה את המתים.

Based on the *Midrash Tehillim* 19, the בית יעקב gives an additional explanation about this "power to remain." There are two things with which the nations of the world agree with Israel: that Hashem created the world in six days (which is Shabbos), and the resurrection of the dead.

שבת שאינו עולה הנעלה על יד בעל אוב. לפי שהבעל אוב מעלה את האדם בזה
הכח שהיה לו בעולם הזה באיזה דבר. וישאר בהאדם תשוקה לחזור לישרא
עקימא שעיקם (עיין זה"ק בשלח נ"ד א').

Based on the בית יעקב's teaching, we can understand something
about the way the Baal Ov (someone who speaks to the dead—
see *Vayikra* 19:31) works. How does the Baal Ov speak to a
person who has died? He uses the same power that is intrinsic
to human beings which remains bound to the body, because
basically a person, even after he has died, wants to improve,
to create more, and therefore, to return to correct what went
wrong in his life. Through this power, the Baal Ov connects to
the person.

ובשבת שהאדם בנייחא אינו רוצה בזה לפי שרואה אור גדול שלא עוות מעולם.

But on Shabbos, a person is at rest and doesn't want to continue
growing. He sees through the perspective of Shabbos that
everything is part of Hashem's plan and nothing has gone
wrong. There is therefore nothing to fix, and nowhere to grow.

ובהמה גם כן לא היה לה חיים בלתי לפי שעה. לפיכך אינה עולה.

Now, we understand why we said that while an animal also has
life, it is only temporary and it does not ascend or descend. But
man's power to choose and ascend is so strong that even after he
has left the world, part of him remains to a certain degree. Man
constantly wants to straighten what is crooked.

והנה קודם המבול לא ניתן רשות לאדם לאכול מחי. כי החי היה בשלימות לפי
שלא שינו מרצון השי"ת.

כי עיקר התעלות האדם על החי הוא מפני שהוא בעל בחירה .וקודם שהשחיתו
כל בשר דרכם לא היו רוצים לדבק בהאדם לפי שהם לא היו בספק .כי מאחר
שאין להם בחירה בטח כל מה שעושים הוא רצון השי״ת. אבל האדם לפי שהוא
בעל בחירה הוא בספק. לכך לא רצו לדבק בהאדם ולכנוס בספיקות. אך אחר
שהם גם כן השחיתו אז רצו לדבק. כי גם הם כבר עוותו. ואז מה טוב היה להם
לדבוק באדם ולהשיג התעלות יותר:

Before the flood, man was not given permission to eat living
creatures. Why not? When a person eats something, he derives
strength from its life forces and nutrients, which direct the
choices that he makes. Animals don't make choices. They live
on a spiritual level of relative completion. By interacting with
humans, whose lives are dynamic, they could rise or fall from
that spiritual level. Since there was no guarantee of spiritual
elevation, the animals "did not want" to be eaten by man. For
that reason, man was forbidden to eat meat.

But after all of creation was also corrupted, through the
generation of the flood, then it wanted to attach itself, to connect
with man, as creation could then rise to a higher level.

The Izhbitzer Tradition

See (מג בראשית יעקב בית) where the יעקב בית discusses the ideas of
life force remaining in order to correct what has gone wrong.

Practical Advice

Our desire for growth is so strong, that it persists even after
we leave the world. Hashem, in creating us, bid us to fix the

present and even the future, and this is an inherent aspect of our personalities. Look for the opportunities that we have to "set straight" what went crooked. Rejoice in the power of our choices, which affect our entire world.

פרשת נח

from Beis Yaakov ha-Kollel

אֵלֶּה תּוֹלְדֹת נֹחַ **(בראשית ו' ט')**. כבד אלהים הסתר דבר וכבד מלכים חקר
דבר (משלי כ"ה ב'). כבד אלקים היינו מה שנתן השי"ת וחלק כח לכל בריה.
ובמקום הזה שם בו חסרון. כמו שנתבאר בפרשת מקץ. זה ניתן להסתר. שאין
לאדם להראותו. כי אין רצונו של מלך להזכיר שמו על אשפה (חגיגה ט"ז א')
כי יקשה מדוע לא ברא השי"ת את האדם בשלימות. מבלי יצרך עוד לבירורים.
והנה אף כי גם זה מעומק כוונת השי"ת לטובה כמו שיתבאר.

In the beginning of this week's *parsha*, the בית יעקב asks a
fundamental question. He begins by explaining a dynamic
based on a *pasuk* in *Mishlei* (25:2) that the honor of Elokim
(G-d) relates to matters that are hidden, but the honor of kings
relates to things that are visible to us. This is why the beginning
of *Sefer Bereishis* is obscure, because "it isn't appropriate to
mention the name of the king in association with garbage,"
meaning it isn't appropriate for Hashem to be associated with
the unfinished products. Even though Hashem intends for the
end result to be good, the process is not complete, and therefore
does not reflect Hashem's perfection.

וכבד מלכים היינו זה המקום שהשהשי"ת ברא את האדם. שיברר עצמו וכל
הבירורים איך יצאו לפועל. בזה צוה השי"ת לחקור ולהתבונן. וזה נקרא
בגמרא שבת (י"א א') חללה של רשות.

23

After man is created, we have the "finished product" referred to in the end of the *pasuk*, "the honor of kings is a matter worthy of evaluation." Hashem wants us to think about the world after the creation of man. It is pertinent to our lives. The *Gemara* (*Shabbos* 11a) refers to this phenomenon as the "abyss of choice." This abyss is the endless space where decisions can and must be made.

והנה כמו שבעיקר הבריאה. ברא השי״ת את העולם בהשפעת כח עצום. שיוכל לפשט ההנהגתם. עד שאחר זה הוצרך לבוא עליהם המבול.

Hashem created the world with awesome energy, and He invested people with the ability to use that energy to make their choices a reality. When the people of the generation of the flood sinned, they used that energy to create a corrupt reality. In order to free the energy from that reality, Hashem sent the flood.

מהגבהת מדות השי״ת. שהגביה מדותיו למעלה ראש. והנה לפי דעת האדם יקשה לפניו. למה לא התחילה הבריאה בשלימות כמו שנשארה אחר המבול. כמו שנתבאר שאז נטבע בלב האדם שלא יתפשט. אך זה היה בכוונת השי״ת.

Hashem wiped out the world by overpowering the choices which man made, making a world which was much more developed after the flood. After the flood, Hashem invested people with the ability to restrain themselves and not allow their hearts to go astray in the same way, rebelling against what Hashem wants.

בכדי שיהיה חיים לשעה גם לברואים שהיו וקומטו. אף שלא היה להם חיי עולם. מכל מקום גם חיי שעה נקרא טובה. ולהם לא היה שום תרעמות על דינו של הקב״ה מאחר שלא בראם בלתי על זה. ועל ידי שאלו נברא. נתבררו שאר הברואים לשלימות היותר יפה וקיים.

This limitation makes even transitory life meaningful and beneficial. This, in turn, allays the complaint of creations that live only for a set time, because Hashem created them only for this, and not for other purposes.

ואלו הבירורים ניתנו לאדם שירחיבם כפי יכלתו. וזה שאמר שלמה המלך בחכמתו שמים לרום (משלי כ"ה ג'). היינו היראה אמתית. כי שם יתגלה בהירות השי"ת בשלימות. וארץ לעמק (שם) היינו אהבת השי"ת. ואלו השנים נבראו בשיעור וגבול. ולב מלכים אין חקר (שם). היינו עד כמה יסתעף דבר השי"ת. ועד היכן יש מקום לברר.

Man's limitations create his ability to interact differently with each situation. These abilities are called *middos*, "measurements," or "boundaries." Regarding these abilities, Shlomo Ha-Melech (*Mishlei* 25:3) said, "from the heights of the heavens to the depths of the land and the hearts of kings there is no way to comprehend." The בית יעקב explains "from the heights of heavens" is about achieving true awe, being able to withdraw, and through it, finding and achieving clarity in our goal. "The land to the depths," is love of Hashem, our passion for our goal, in order to move us forward. The *pasuk* continues, "there is no investigating the heart of kings." Even within these boundaries, there is no end to the depths of work that a person can do and repair; it is a life's work to ascertain which is the correct *middah* in each situation.

מה נטע השי"ת בלבות בני אדם. לזה אין חקר וגבול. כי כל מה שיעמוק יוכל' לברר יותר. כי כל מה שיראה האדם וימצא בעצמו חסרון. יכיר במקום הזה שהשי"ת הוא שלם. כי כל החסרונות שימצא אדם בעצמו. הוא שיראה שאינו טוב נגד השי"ת. וזה נקרא חללה של רשות. היינו החלל שיוכל לקבל עליו עול מלכות שמים כשיעמיק בו לזה אין חקר.

25

We have no ability to measure the hearts of man. The more you search and discern, the more you can repair. One you have repaired what was at hand, more light of Hashem's perfection is brought into places you hadn't reached; from there you can see and repair more. This is the "abyss of choice," the empty spot where you have the opportunity to accept Hashem as king, as there is no way to reach the end.

והנה לזה ברא השי״ת את עולמו. שיברֿרו את עצמם. כי באמת היה להבריאה פחיתות וירידה במה שנבראת.

Hashem created this world so that it would repair itself with all its imperfections.

כי קודם האצילות היה כל הבריאה כמוסה בעצמותו יתברך. והיה מהנקל שיחזור לתהו ובהו. אך אחר שקלקלה והוצרכה לתקן. אז היה להבריאה חיזוק. מאחר שכבר עיותה ותרצה לתקן. כמו שמבואר בזה״ק (בשלח נ״ד א'). איך יהיה התחיה והיאך נבראו בהתחלה. ואומר שם שהבריות ירצו לחזור לישרא לעקימא. אף ששם טוב להם יותר מכל מקום ירצו לתקן ויחזרו. וכן היה כאן חיזוק להבריאה שתרצה בהוייתה כדי לתקן. וזה דאיתא במדרש תהלים (מזמור י״ט). והבהמה אפילי בחול אינה עולה. היינו לפי שלא עיותה ולא תוכל לתקן. לכן אינה עולה.

Before the world was created, it was so close to Hashem that at any moment it could return to nothing at anytime. Once the world was broken by Adam and Chava, the world became more permanent, as it screamed out for repair, and therefore the world needed to stay in existence. The Midrash (*Tehillim* 19) expresses this in its statement that even during the week an animal doesn't ascend, as an animal has no choice, no urge to be better. It therefore cannot ascend.

והנה על זה נקרא שמו נח. כמו דאיתא בגמרא ב"מ (מ"ח א') רוח חכמים נוחה הימנו. והנה הבריאה אה עד עתה היה כדברים בעלמא שאין בהם מתן מעות. ויוכל בקל לחזור. ואחר שניתן מעות אין יכול לחזור. ובאם יחזור אין רוח חכמים נוחה הימנו. והוא נברא לתקן הבריאה אחר שנתחזק הקנין. והוא יחזקו ועל זה רוח חכמים נוחה הימנו.

Now we can understand who Noach was. The Gemara (*Bava Metzia* 48a) says "that the Rabbis approved of him." (The word for "approved" is *nocheh*, which is related to the name Noach.) This phrase is also used when a person considers buying something. If he hasn't given the seller money, he can retract, but after the funds have changed hands, the Rabbis don't approve of retracting. Creation existed, but it was as if "the money" hadn't been paid. Noach came into the world after the transaction had taken place. He came to make sure the transaction was permanent, and therefore the Rabbis approve of his actions.

והנה גם בהנשמה של כל אדם מבואר בזוה"ק (בשלח נ"ד א') ובמדרש תהילים (מזמור ס"ב) על ענין כזה . שתרצה לחזור לבוראה. וכשיראה לה השי"ת כי מלא כל הארץ כבודו אז תחזור . ולזה יורדת ועולה בגוף . והנה בדורות הראשונים שקודם המבול . כאשר הרגישו את רצון השי"ת שהוא בהשפעת טובה. ובא להם תקופות בלבם. דימו בנפשם כי רצון השי"ת שיתפשטו כפי רצון לבם . ולפי שאז שלט שם הויה ככתיבתו. שמורה על התפשטות אלקותו על כל באי עולם. והם אחזו בקצה האחרון. כמו שמבואר על פסוק הוא היה גבור ציד (ומבואר במקומו). ונח היה הראשון שהתחיל לשלוט עליו השם אדני. היינו שהחל לצמצם עצמו. והגמר היה באברהם. כמו דאיתא (ברכות ז' ב') עד שבא אברהם וקראו אדון.

The Midrash (*Tehillim* 62) and *Zohar* (*Beshallach* 54a) explain that the soul, by its very nature, wants to return to its source.

27

When it sees that Hashem fills all of the world, then it returns, descending and raising the body. In the first generations before the flood, people made a grave error. They assumed that whatever happened was according to Hashem's will, and therefore they did whatever they wanted.

Each name of Hashem represents a different way by which he runs the world. Those early years were associated with "kindness," which is the source of all reality. Hence the name which was used to describe that mode of interaction was "Havaya," the four-letter name that is read, but not pronounced. The name "Havaya" literally means "to exist." We know that this name is never pronounced under normal circumstances. But one could describe the generation preceding the flood as one that "misread Hashem's name." They misread the existence of their actions as Divine approval of their actions. They read Hashem's name "as it is written." They saw the existence (as spelled out by the word Havaya) and assumed that is how He wants us to interact with Him.

Noach was the first person who submitted to Hashem's authority. As a result, Hashem began to be seen not just as the source of everything (Havaya) but also as a Master to the World. This is the root of our common practice to read the name "Havaya" as "Adnus," which means "my Master." It demonstrates that despite the fact that Hashem creates and sustains all of existence, He has demands as well. Existence is not lawless.

The Izhbitzer Tradition

See (ו) בית יעקב נח, who elaborates this concepts in greater detail. The תפארת יוסף בראשית ד"ה כבוד explains the concept of the king not associating his name with garbage. See בית יעקב ספר הזמנים הגדה של פסח בדיקת חמץ who discusses the idea of what a person's responsibilities are to repair what is in his life.

Practical Advice

The story of our lives begins with our limits; they empower us to touch that which is limitless. We seek the right amounts, the proper middos, to serve Hashem, to clarify when the right message and the right action are appropriate.

פרשת לך לך

from Beis Yaakov ha-Kollel

וַאֲגַדְּלָה שְׁמֶךָ (**בראשית י"ב ב'**). בבמדבר רבה (פי"א ס' ב') ברכתך קודמת לברכתי שמשהם אומרים מגן אברהם אח"כ אומרים מחיה המתים. כי מחיה המתים זהו ברכה דקב"ה. והאמנם כי מגן אברהם הוא גם כן ברכת השי"ת. שמגין על אברהם וזרעו. אכן העניין בזה דהנה ברכת מחיה המתים הוא נגד יצחק. וזה נקרא ברכת ה'. כי להראות לנפש מקורו מהיכן יצמח. לזה אין ביכולת שום בריה. וכדאיתא בכתבי האריז"ל כי כמה גדולים. אף שהלכו בדרך השי"ת בשלמות. ולא השיגו מקורם.

The Midrash (*Bamidbar Rabbah* 11:2) explains Hashem's promise to Avraham that "I will make your name great," as Hashem saying to Avraham, "I will place your blessing before Mine."

What does this mean? The Midrash tells us that the *bracha* of *Magen Avraham*, "Shield of Avraham," will be placed before the *bracha* of *Mechayei Ha-Meisim* "Resurrection of the Dead." Why is the first *bracha* considered Avraham's and the second Hashem's? The first one, which says that Hashem will guard the children of Avraham, is also a *bracha* of Hashem!

Furthermore, the Midrash reveals to us that the *bracha* of *Magen Avraham* corresponds to Avraham Avinu and the *bracha* of *Mechayei Ha-Meisim* corresponds to Yitzchak Avinu. So why is it called the *bracha* of Hashem?

First, we must understand what it means to be *mechayei meisim*. It is not only about resurrecting the dead. It is also about showing people what the root of their souls is, meaning what are the general and specific issues that they were sent into this word to resolve. The Arizal says that so many great people never figured out what they had to do to fix the root of their soul.

וזה דאיתא ומחוי להו יצחק הקב״ה בעינייהו (שבת פ״ט ב'). וזהי ענין תחיית המתים כמבואר בזה״ק (בשלח נ״ד א'). דבעי קב״ה לישרא לעקימא.

The Gemara (*Shabbos* 89b) discusses that in the future, it will ultimately be Yitzchak Avinu who will save the Jewish people from their *aveiros* by defending them in the Heavenly court. The Gemara says that the Jews will gratefully turn to Yitzchak and declare him to be their father. Yitzchak will respond, "Hashem is our father." From this Gemara, we see that Yitzchak Avinu's strength is to show people how Hashem is our father. It is this ability that is behind the concept of *Techiyas ha-Meisim*. As the *Zohar* (*Beshallach* 54a) says, "*Techiyas ha-Meisim* comes as a result of Hashem's desire to straighten out that which is crooked." It is evidence of Hashem's plan to redirect us and put us back in contact with our source of life, with our Father, and to return us to the point where we went wrong.

וכדאיתא בגמרא (ברכות י״ח ב') דשאל שמואל בעינא אבא. אמרו ליה אבא טובא איכא הכא. אמר להו בעינא אבא בר אבא .אמרו ליה אבא בר אבא נמי טובא איכא הכא. עד שאמר להו בעינא אבא בר אבא אבוה דשמואל הבינו.

The בית יעקב relates a startling Gemara (*Brachos* 18b) in order to explain our previous Gemara. Shmuel's father died, and Shmuel went looking for him at the cemetery. He said to the dead people, "I'm looking for Abba." They replied, "There are lots of 'Abbas' here." He said, "I'm looking for Abba the son of Abba." They responded, "We have a lot of Abbas, the sons of Abba, here too." Finally, he said, "I'm looking for my father, Abba, the son of Abba, the father of Shmuel."

כי כאשר שאל ונתן סימן באביו לא השיבוהו. כי באבותיו אין לו שייכות להתמשך אחריהם. אבל כשנשאל עליו. ונתן סימן בבנו אשר היה בחיים. תיכף הבינו. כי בזה יש לו שייכות בזה העולם יותר מכל כחו. כי אחר זה ימשך לישרא לעקימא.

When Shmuel tried to find his father, by identifying him, relating him to who his grandfather is, the dead people didn't know who he was asking for. The dead people could not differentiate between something in the past and something else in the past. Once they stopped living, there was no point of reference. However, when Shmuel said, "I'm looking for the father of Shmuel," they understood immediately, because as long as someone is alive, they are meaningful and relevant, because then one can straighten what's crooked.

וזה דאיתא בגמרא (סנהדרין צ"א ב') עומדין במומן ומתרפאין. כי עיקר התחיה שכל אחד יכיר מומו. וימשך אחריו לישרו. וכמאמר המדרש תנחומא (ויגש ס' ח') שלא יאמרו הרשעים אחרים המית ואחרים החיה. כי על ידי המום יכירו את עצמם. כי כשישאלו לאדם איזה טובה השיג ביום מן הימים לא יזכור. אבל כשישאלוהו איזה סבלנות סבל זה יזכור תכף. וזהו ברכה דקב"ה.

The Gemara (*Sanhedrin* 91b) says that when the dead people awaken, then each man will awaken with his disability. This is so they can be healed from it. This teaches us that the main point of the resurrection is for each person to recognize his defect and pursue it to correct it. The Midrash (*Tanchuma Vayigash* 8) says that this is so in order that the evil people would not say, "Hashem killed them, but someone else made people live." Therefore, Hashem said, "You shall rise the same way that you fell."

Through finding the defect, you find yourself. The Izhbitzer says that at the end of a person's life when people will be asked, "What were your good days like?" They won't remember, but when they are asked, "What travails did you traverse," they'll remember immediately. This is Hashem's *bracha*, the ability to straighten what is crooked, and to affect change.

The Izhbitzer Tradition

See *[יז] בית יעקב פרשת לך לך*, where he discusses the concept of Hashem wanting to straighten what is crooked.

Practical Advice

Think about that which is crooked in your life, and plan how to fix it, to make it straight. Rav Freifeld used to say that the times he felt most alive were when making a cheshbon ha-nefesh, a plan to straighten what is crooked. When you say the bracha of Mechayei Ha-Meisim, have in mind to ask Hashem for the ability to know what went wrong, to straighten it out, and to become truly alive.

פרשת וירא

from Beis Yaakov ha-Kollel

וַה' אָמָר הַמְכַסֶּה אֲנִי מֵאַבְרָהָם וגו' (**בראשית י"ח י"ז**). מדרש תנחומא
(וירא ס' ה') איתא. המתרגם בתורה מהו שיהא מסתכל בספר תורה כו'. ואם
שנית מה שבכתב על פה ומה שבעל פה בכתב לא כרתי אתך ברית. דברים
שבכתב הם שהשי"ת הציגם ישרים לכל נפש. ודברים שבעל פה הם שהשי"ת
נותן בינה בלב כל נפש לפי מדרגתו.

In this week's *parsha*, before Hashem destroyed Sodom, He
asked, "should I hide this from Avraham?" (*Bereishis* 18:17).
The Midrash (*Tanchuma Vayera* 5) asks an apparently unrelated
question. If a person is translating it, may he look in the Torah?
The Midrash continues, "If you have to review what is written by
heart and what is oral from a text, I have not made a covenant
with you." The Midrash explains the nature of the oral and
written Torah. Things that are written enter straight into the
soul, while things that are part of an oral tradition were created
by Hashem in such a fashion that they give wisdom to all people,
each in accordance with their level. One could make the mistake
of using an idea inappropriately by not differentiating between
situations. "Things that are oral" means that a person strives to
integrate the concept, whereas "things that are written" means
to simply accept them. When Hashem asked, "Should I conceal

this or say it directly to Avraham?" He was asking Himself whether he wanted Avraham to accept the command or to work to understand what he was being asked to do.

והנה הפיכת סדם היה נצמח ממצות מילה שנצטוה אברהם. כי הערלה רומז על זרם ורעש בחשקות עולם הזה.

The בית יעקב explains that what was hidden from Avraham was the process that was about to unfold. Sodom's destruction came about as a result of Avraham's receiving the mitzvah of *milah*. This is because *orlah* literally means "covered," being submerged by physical desires of this world that cover the true spiritual aspects of the person.

והנה אברהם היה שורש כל העולם. וכאשר הסיר אברהם ערלתו. היינו שהסיר ממנו חמדות עולם הזה. שלא יתאוה להם ברעם ורעש. אז אנשי סדום ממילא הלכו לאבדון. כי הם היו ערלת העולם. כי כל ההשפעות טובות היו ברעם ורעש וכן חשקם.

Avraham was the world's major spiritual teacher and his actions affected the rest of the world. Just as he freed himself from his gluttonous desires through circumcision, he taught the world to free itself from gluttonous desires. Since Sodom was the "capital" of gluttonous desires, it was removed from the world, like a foreskin.

והנה הקב"ה בחפצו להגדיל לאברהם לכן שלח לו כח תפלה להתפלל בעדם. ועל ידי התפלה יתנטעו בו. כי כולם נתגלגלו בדור המדבר כדאיתא בספר הגלגולים.

Hashem gave Avraham the ability to daven and influence how He runs the world. Avraham was davening for Sodom to be saved from destruction. After analysis, Avraham realized that Hashem had a greater plan unfolding. The people of Sodom would be reincarnated in the generation of the desert. They would complete their life-missions then. Avraham's attempt to stop this plan by davening that the city not be destroyed was actually not ultimately beneficial for Sodom.

ועל זה כוונת המדרש ואם שנית מה שבכתב על פה כו'. כי כח התפלה היה מהקב"ה מפורש.

This is the meaning of the idea in the Midrash, "If you review what is written by heart." "That which is written" means what you were given, but did not toil to understand. The power of *tefillah* comes from Hashem, but its application is dependent on the person.

ואח"כ הבינה שיחדול מלהתפלל זה לא השיג בלתי הארה. וזה נקרא ומה שבעל פה בכתב. היינו מבלי להתעקש נגד השי"ת.

After his bargaining with Hashem, Avraham understood to stop davening, as he felt that he had not accomplished anything. He realized he was "reading something that was given orally." Avraham was struggling with understanding how Hashem wanted him to use the gift of *tefillah* in this situation.

וזה היה בסוד בורא עולמות ומחריבן (בראשית רבה פ"ג ס' ז'). כי אח"כ כשילכו דרך זה העולם יהיה טובים :

This is the mystery of Hashem's "creating worlds and destroying them" (*Bereishis Rabbah* 3:7). The creation of the world means to live life based on one understanding and then to be able to change once that assumption doesn't work. Avraham's original use of *tefillah* was not what Hashem had wanted. This then gave rise to a new perspective.

The Izhbitzer Tradition

See (בראשית) בית יעקב, where he discusses this idea further in פרשת לך לך (כב). Additionally, the מי השלוח explains this as part of his fundamental concept that a person only rises to greatness as a result of his failures.

Practical Advice

Despite our initial understanding, sometimes after we have attempted something, we learn our earlier assumptions were wrong and a different approach is required. Only through living and trying do we gain this knowledge.

פרשת חיי שרה

from Beis Yaakov ha-Kollel

וַיָּבֹא אַבְרָהָם לִסְפֹּד לְשָׂרָה וְלִבְכֹּתָהּ (בראשית כ"ג ב'). הנה זאת נתבאר כי
כל ענין אשה הוא סייעתא וחשק.

This week's *parsha* discusses Avraham's mourning for Sarah. It
says, "And Avraham came to eulogize Sarah and to cry over her"
(*Bereishis* 23:2). A spouse exemplifies the process of completion.
The מי השלוח (פרשת בראשית) explains that the creation of a mate,
described as an *ezer kenegdo*, means a helper who is "opposing."
This means that help in personal growth, completion, comes
as a result of adversity. The interaction between two people
with different opinions and the need to compromise and find
consensus help a couple to grow as individuals as well. With
the loss of Sarah, his wife, Avraham lost his ability to grow in
serving Hashem.

והנה איתא בגמרא (סוכה נ"ב א') האי הספידא מאי עבידתיה כו'. חד אמר על
משיח בן יוסף שנהרג. וחד אמר על יצר הרע שנהרג. האי הספידא בעי למעבד.
שמחה בעי למעבד. אמאי בכו וכו'. והנה שניהם הם ענין אחד. ששניהם מרמזים
על כח עבודה שתיבטל לעתיד. כדאיתא בגמרא (נדה ס"א ב') מצות בטלות
לעתיד לבא. כי ענין שבט יוסף מורה על עבודה כידוע. והנה בעת שיסתלק יצר
הרע מן העולם אז יתבטלו כל העבודות.

38

This concept does not just occur once in the Torah. The בית יעקב gives us another example of such a funeral. The Gemara (*Sukkah* 52a) speaks about what will occur in the future, as described by Zecharia. The Gemara asks "Who was the funeral for?" The Gemara replies, either the funeral of Mashiach the son of Yosef, or the *yetzer hara*. The Gemara asks: why would we mourn for the death of the *yetzer hara*?

The בית יעקב explains both opinions are mourning the loss of a person's ability to grow and change. Moshiach ben Yosef refers to a person's ability to serve Hashem. When the *yetzer hara* is gone, so is the ability to actively serve Hashem. Without temptation, there is no struggle to serve Hashem, and, as a result, no service of Hashem. The future funeral that the Gemara speaks of is the inevitable loss of an ability to make choices and serve Hashem with them. This is the implication of the Gemara (*Niddah* 61b), which explains that in the future the *mitzvos* will no longer apply.

והנה גם אברהם אבינו עליו השלום בעת שנגמר בכל. אחר כל הנסיונות אז ניטל ממנו כל כח עבודתו וסייעתו. ולכן מתה עליו שרה הנקראת אשת חיל. והוא כח התשוקה.

Avraham Avinu, similarly, reached a point in his life when he finished the part where he was a work in progress. After he completed his last trial, the *Akeidah*, where he was commanded to bind and sacrifice Yitzchak, he had completed his development. Therefore, after the *Akeidah*, his wife, the source of his strength and his ability to complete himself, died.

כי קודם שסיגל האדם מצות ומעשים טובים. ועוד איננו שלם בכל עניניו. אז מניחו השי״ת לילך לספיקות פן ירויח. אך אחר שיגמר אז אינו מניחו. כי ברכוש גדול לא יאות להאדם להכניסו בספק.

The בית יעקב explains the same idea about our lives. Before a person gets used to doing *mitzvos*, Hashem allows him to be in a situation where he may or may not succeed, in order for him to have the opportunity to excel. However, after a person has perfected himself, Hashem does not allow him to enter into such a situation.

וזה שהתחיל המדרש רבה (חיי שרה פ' נ״ח ס' א') יודע ה' ימי תמימים ונחלתם לעולם תהיה. כי עד אברהם היה כל השפעות כאדם הנוטל בחוצפא. ואברהם התחיל לחשוב דרכיו. אז ימיו היו תמימים. שהשי״ת השגיח על מעשיו איך יתכלכלו בנחלה שלעולם תהיה:

This is why the Midrash (*Bereishis Rabbah* 58:1) of this week's *parsha* begins with the phrase, "Hashem knows the days of the perfect ones, and pays out their reward forever." This means that once a person has reached perfection, there is no longer a chance for him to engage in the risky business of *avodah*, as he could lose everything he had previously gained. Until Avraham, everything existed in a state of "chutzpah," just taking without paying for it. Once Avraham came, only then did people begin to "earn their keep in the world."

The Izhbitzer Tradition

The Izhbitzer Rebbes often talk of the processes of being and becoming an Oved Hashem and perfecting one's self. We see that Hashem makes a shidduch between the person and his circumstances, in order to create the adversity required for growth (מי השלוח ח"א, תפארת יוסף פרשת בראשית).

Practical Advice

We need to realize that our challenges are shidduchim for us from the time of creation, sent specifically for our improvement. All of our relationships, especially with our spouses, are geared for our self-perfection, as we so often are faced with opposition, all of which is ultimately for our benefit.

פרשת תולדות

from Beis Yaakov ha-Kollel

וַיֶּעְתַּר יִצְחָק וגו' (בראשית כ"ה כ"א). בזה"ק (תולדות קל"ז א') דצלי צלותיה וחתר חתירה לעילא לגבי מזלא על בנין וכו'. דהנה בזה העינן היה יצחק צריך להתעורר למעלה מכח תפלה. במקום שאין שום קטרוג מגיע.

"And Yitzchak prayed..." (*Bereishis* 25:21). The *Zohar* (*Toldos* 137a) explains that he davened and tried to deal with the spiritual setback of not having children. Yitzchak, in order to do this, had to elevate himself to a place where there was no "complaint" that could interfere with his *tefillos*.

כי בלידת יעקב אבינו נתעורר הקטרוג שהיה בהתחלת בריאת האדם כמבואר שם. כי מאחר שרצה הקב"ה לברא את האדם התעורר קטרוג. כי האדם נברא שיוכל להעלות כל הברואים למעלה בכח עבודתו. וכן חס ושלום להיפך אם יקלקל האדם יפגמו בזה כל הברואים. לכן לא רצו הברואים ליכנס לספק. ולכן היה אז קטרוג. מה אנוש כי תזכרנו (תהלים ח' ה'). וכן היה בלידת יעקב. כי לו נמסר העולם. לנהלה כולה על ידי מעשיו ומעשי בניו.

When Yaakov was born, the complaint against man's conception was renewed. When Hashem wanted to create man, a complaint was issued against him. Man can rise to the heights, and take all of Creation with him, with his ability to choose to serve

42

Hashem, but he can also fall to the depths through his choices not to serve Hashem. Therefore, Creation did not want to take a chance on man. This is the meaning of the *pasuk* (*Tehillim* 8:5), "What is man that he should be remembered?" Similarly this question was renewed with the birth of Yaakov as well, due to the awesome effect he and his children would have. Therefore, Yitzchak had to do something to get around this opposition.

והנה זה ענין כל הקנינים שכל אדם יתנהג בהם.

We see this in our lives as well. We appraise the spiritual danger as we strive for growth, but at the same time, there is the possibility of failure. A person's spiritual growth is often referred to as an acquisition. We can understand the story and drama of man's growth through the first Mishnah in *Kiddushin* which deals with marriage. As we saw in *Chayei Sarah*, people's *avodah* is a *shidduch* for them, and the way that they can marry teaches us about how they can grow as individuals.

איך יכנס בהתחלת הולדתו פירות לעולם ונכנס לספק. כי תחלה אין דעת האדם נוטה ליכנס לספק. אכן אחר שמראהו הקב"ה כי גם שמים לא זכו בעיניו. ואפילו אם אינו נכנס לספק אינו מבורר. אם כן נוח לו ליכנס לספק פן ירויח יותר. וזה נקרא קנין כסף שהאשה נקנית בו (קידושין ב' א'). כי מזה יסבול האדם וצריך ליכנס לזה באגר שלים במעשה מצות.

So how does a person begin a service of Hashem when the outcome is not a given? A person by nature does not want to enter into something whose outcome is not assured, as he thinks that there is a lot to lose. But Hashem shows him that nothing by itself is complete, and a person needs to "take a chance" in order to grow and perfect himself.

This is comparable to the method of marrying someone called *kinyan kesef* (*Kiddushin* 2a), where the relationship is transactional: "You do this and I'll do that. I'll put something down, invest something into this relationship, and you'll marry me." In this kind of situation, both parties assume they will be rewarded.

וזהו שמתרגם על פסוק קדוש קדוש קדוש ה' צבאות (ישעיה ו' ג'). קדיש בשמי מרומא עלאה בית שכנתיה. שמראה לו ענינים גבוהים משכלו שכולם הם בספק. ואח"כ מחזיר לו הקב"ה מעין עמלו בעולם הזה. וזה שאמר הכתוב מה יתרון העושה באשר הוא עמל (קהלת ג' ט') . אחרי כי הכל בידי שמים. וגם עבודת האדם יראה לעתיד שהוא בידי שמים מה יתרון העושה.

Yeshaya describes the song of the *malachim*, angels, as saying "Kadosh, Kadosh, Kadosh." The Targum translates the words "Kadosh, Kadosh, Kadosh," in three different ways. These three explanations of the word *kadosh* represent different notions of *kedushah* in the world. The first *kadosh* describes Hashem's presence in the highest abodes, the second *kadosh* means the mighty works He does here on Earth, and the third *kadosh* is that Hashem's glory fills the land forever.

The first *kadosh* describes a reality in which a person perceives what greatness is, but doubts his ability to achieve it. Hence, it refers to a *kedushah* in the higher realm, but not here. In our lives, this is expressed in the frustration whereby we can think that since everything is in the Hashem's hands, so any achievement is not truly our choice. We could easily ask, "What's the point of trying?" This is compounded by the fact that we know that in the future, Hashem will reveal Himself in such a way that we'll see that He was there with us in everything. We will be shown that there was a point to our actions. Even though Hashem is everywhere, still what we did will be called our own actions.

אכן זאת הוא יתרונו. שבאותו ענין עצמו שסבל בו בזה יושע. שיראה לו
השי״ת כי בזה נקרא מעשי ידיו. וכדאיתא בזה"ק (לך לך פ"ג א'). אי לא נתתו
בקדמיתא למצרים ולא יצטרפון תמן. לא הוי עמא יחידא דיליה. וזהו קדיש על
ארעא עובד גבורתיה (תרגום ישעיה פ"ו פ"ג) . כי השי״ת מראה לו ישועה מן
הארץ שעבד בה. כי ארץ כולל כל עניני עולם הזה. ואף כי עוד לא נשלם. מכל
מקום אין זה נקרא עוסק שלא לשמה. כי שלא לשמה לא נקרא רק בלב עקוב
(עיין ברכות י"ז א'. ובתוספות שם ד"ה העושה). וזה נקרא קנין שטר. שהאשה
נקנית בו אף שאין בו שוה פרוטה (קידושין ט' א'). כי כיון שהאדם בירר עצמו.

The *Zohar* explains that if Avraham had not gone done to Mitzraim and not been purified there, he would not have his own unique nation. This phenomenon is referred to by the Targum as "the mighty works He does here on Earth." Hashem showed His involvement in the world, that He presented us with the ability to make a difference. He made the world that our *avodah* effects. Even though a person might not have completed what he needed to do, he still is credited with having some accomplishment. It is as if he has already gotten there. This is comparable the Mishnah's case that one may marry someone with a *shtar*, a legal document testifying to their intent. Even though a woman must be married with something that has substantial worth, and a *shtar* is a document that has no intrinsic value, it talks about the process, and that's why it works. Since he has begun the process through the creation of the *shtar*, this is what is gives the *shtar* value.

אז השי"ת חותם עצמו על מעשי ידי האדם.

Then Hashem, who knows all hearts, "signs off" on his actions as a valid beginning. So too, a person's *avodas Hashem*, once begun, is invested with the value of having made an accomplishment.

וזהו חנם. כדאיתא בזה"ק (בהר ק"ח א'). זכרנו את הדגה אשר נאכל במצרים חנם. בלא ברכה. ולכן אין צריך בזה שוה פרוטה. ואח"כ כשהקב"ה חותם שמו על מעשי האדם ומראה לו שגם כל הצמצומים והעבודות הם ממנו.

There is a dimension of *kedushah* that takes place without any struggle. It is what the Jews were yearning for when they recalled the fish that they could eat for free in Mitzraim. "Free" means without any effort in *avodas Hashem*, not even a minimal effort to discover Him in that place. This is what the Targum described as Hashem's glory, which "fills the land forever. " The Mishnah describes this in terms of living with one's spouse as husband and wife, which also creates an halachic marriage. This means that it is possible to create a relationship with Hashem and connect with him everywhere.

The Izhbitzer Tradition

See (קהלת ג ח"ב) מי השלוח and (יט) בית יעקב בראשית for more about the idea of Hashem's interaction in our avodas Hashem and the comparison to kedushah and the Mishnah in Kiddushin.

Practical Advice

The בֵּית יַעֲקֹב *describes three situations in a person's attempts to bring kedushah to the world: (1) When a person works and strives toward a goal and completes a task, (2) when a person has begun, but hasn't completed it, and (3) when there is no struggle against the world. In all of these situations, kedushah is there.*

פרשת ויצא

from Beis Yaakov ha-Kollel

וַיֶּאֱהַב יַעֲקֹב אֶת רָחֵל וַיֹּאמֶר אֶעֱבָדְךָ שֶׁבַע שָׁנִים (בראשית כ"ט י"ח).
איתא בגמרא (מ"ק י"ח ב') מן התורה ומן הנביאים ומן הכתובים מה' אשה
לאיש. מן התורה דכתיב ויען לבן ובתואל ויאמרו מה' יצא הדבר. מן הנביאים
דכתיב ואביו ואמו לא ידעו כי מה' היא. מן הכתובים דכתיב בית והון נחלת
אבות ומה' אשה משכלת.

This week's *parsha* explains that "Yaakov loved Rachel, and he
said, 'I will work for you for seven years'" (*Bereishis* 29:18). What
Yaakov Avinu wanted and what he got were two different things.
So how did that happen? The Gemara (*Moed Katan* 18b) asks:
how do we know from Tanach, that Hashem makes matches
for people? The Gemara responds that in *Chumash*, Lavan and
Besuel say that the match between Yitzchak and Rivka is from
Hashem. In *Shoftim*, the Navi explains that Shimson's father
and mother didn't understand his choice of a wife, but they
declared, "It must have been from Hashem." Similarly, Shlomo
Ha-Melech says in *Mishlei* that a house and all of the riches are
your inheritance, but a great wife is from Hashem. So then how
did Yaakov get the wife that didn't love?

ובבראשית רבה (פס"ח ס' ג') מסיים. יש שהוא הולך אצל זיווגו. ויש שזווגו
בא אצלו. יצחק זיווגו בא אצלו וירא והנה גמלים באים. יעקב הלך אצל זווגו
דכתיב ויצא יעקב. והנה ענין הולך אצל זווגו. כי זווג האשה הוא עזר. שהשי"ת
שולח עזר לאדם (בראשית ב' י"ח). והנה בזה יש שני מינים אחד שהאדם לוקח
לו כפי הבנתו. ויכלכל בדעתו איך לעזור בנפשו. וזהו מי שהולך אצל זווגו.

The Midrash (*Bereishis Rabbah* 63:8) answers this question with
its statement that there are those who go to meet their spouses
and others whose spouses goes to meet them. Yitzchak's wife
came to meet him, but Yaakov went to meet his wife.

What is the meaning of seeking a spouse? The *Chumash*
(*Bereishis* 2:18) says that a spouse is an *ezer*, as Hashem has
sent the spouse to help the person. We can understand the idea
that there are two ways that a person can meet a spouse. One
way is in response to a perception of what the person needs.
This is the meaning of Midrash's statement "someone goes to
meet his spouse."

והשני היינו סיעתא שלא מדעת. וזהו גדול יותר ממה שהאדם לוקח לו מדעתו.
וכמו דאיתא בברכות (נ"ד א') הפרו תורתך משום עת לעשות לה'. זה נקרא
זווגו בא אצלו.

There is another way as well. Hashem helps people find their
spouse without their knowing or understanding what is
transpiring. The בית יעקב says that this is even greater than
when you choose your spouse. The Gemara (*Brachos* 54a
quoting *Tehillim* 119:126) states, "It is time to do for Hashem,
by breaking your Torah." He explains that "doing for Hashem"
means that it is person's job to accept that something is occurring
which is greater than the sum of his choices, it is Hashem's will.

At that point, he must go against his limited understanding of the situation and accept His will, which is unfolding. In this way we understand the Midrash's statement, "You are not going to your spouse, they are coming to you."

והנה האריז"ל מחשב זווג יעקב ורחל להולך אצל זווגו. וזווג יעקב ולאה לזווגו בא אצלו. כי הליכתו ללבן היה בשביל רחל. ולאה באה לו מאליה. וענין סיעתא שלא מדעת הוא.

The Arizal regards the relationship between Yaakov and Rachel as a person going to meet a spouse, because Rachel was the "one" who Yaakov went to Lavan in order to marry. His marriage to Leah happened without his knowledge or even his will. It was a case of being helped without knowing or even wanting.

אף כשידמה לאדם שאינו עושה מעשה טובה. ורק אח"כ יתברר לטוב זה נקרא זווגו בא אצלו.

People may think that they aren't doing something that is correct, and only afterwards do they see what transpired. This is a case of "the spouse coming to you." These two dynamics exist all the time in a person's life. There is the situation that you'd like to happen, and then there are things that happen to you that you don't necessarily want, but they happen anyway. The thing that you'd like to happen is "when you go to your spouse." The thing which you weren't going to do, but it happens is "your spouse comes to you."

וזאת נקראת אם. כמו שמצינו באדם הראשון שקראה אם כל חי (בראשית ג' כ') כי חוה היתה באה אצלו. כמו שכתוב ויבאה אל האדם (שם ב' כ"ב)

וכמו שנתבאר בספר מי השלוח (פרשת בראשית) כי ניתנה לו לעזר שישמע לדבריה. אף במקום שלא יראה לנפשי כטוב.

This relationship is referred to also as the "mother." In the same way Chava was called "the mother of all life," as she was brought to Adam. Adam was supposed to listen to her, even when her advice didn't seem positive to him.

...וכן רבקה היתה זווגו בא אצלו. לפיכך בברכת יעקב נהגה רבקה אותו למעלה מדעתו.

Similarly, Rivka was also a wife who came to Yitzchak and was the "mother" to Yaakov. She arranged for Yaakov to get the *brachos* without either Yaakov or Yitzchak knowing about it.

וגם ענין זווג דיעקב ולאה. כי כל בני לאה לא היו נושאים חן כל כך על כל הגוון כמו בני רחל. ואף שאח"כ נתבררו שהם גדולים מאד. מכל מקום האדם אינו רוצה להכניס עצמו בספק. ועל זה איתא בזוה"ק (ויצא קנ"ד ב') מהכא דסאני בר נש עדיין דאמיה. כי האדם רוצה לילך בטח בכל דרכיו. אך לאדם שטוב לפני הקב"ה. מזמין לו מעשה שאינה טובה על הגוון. ורק אח"כ יברר השי"ת כי היה למעלה מהשגתו:

We also see examples of this concept with the children of Yaakov's marriage to Leah. These children didn't immediately find favor in everyone's eyes, as opposed to the children of Rachel. However, at the end of the story we see their greatness.

People usually do not want to put themselves in a situation where they are not assured of a positive outcome. However, for a person someone to do *teshuvah*, Hashem arranges their lives in a way that it doesn't look good on the outside; and then they can do *teshuvah*. Afterwards, Hashem clarifies how that was good, only it was outside of their understanding.

The Izhbitzer Tradition

See מי השלוח פרשת בראשית and בית יעקב הכולל פרשת חיי שרה, which discuss the concept of spouses as עזר כנגדו as well as the dynamics of adversity existing to constantly refine a person and advance him in terms of serving Hashem.

Practical Advice

There are so many times that we end up in situations that are the opposite of what we wanted, or what we intended. Yaakov Avinu went to go find Rachel, but instead ended up with Leah. Hashem was teaching Yaakov Avinu and all of the Jewish people about situations that aren't what you wanted, but are what you need to grow as a person. Were Yaakov to only have married Rachel, we wouldn't know how to appreciate all of those situations that were not what we wanted.

פרשת וישלח

from Beis Yaakov ha-Kollel

וָאֵחַר עַד עָתָּה **(בראשית ל"ב ה')**. בבראשית רבה (פע"ה ס' ה') שעדיין לא
נולד שטנו של אותו האיש. וכדכתיב והיה בית יעקב אש ובית יוסף להבה ובית
עשו לקש (עובדיה א' י"ח).

Yaakov's message to Eisav was, "I lived with Lavan and
remained there until now" (*Bereishis* 32:5). The Midrash
Bereishis Rabbah 75:5) answers the implied question of what
was he waiting for. The Midrash says that Yaakov was waiting
for Yosef to be born before he left. Why? Yosef was the "secret
weapon" against Eisav. Ovadia (1:18) prophesied that "Eisav is
compared to straw and Yaakov to a fire, Yosef is a tongue of
flame that can ignite the straw." This teaches us that Yosef is the
one force that can beat Eisav.

כי אש הוא מברר בעולם הזה. למי שאומר שיש לו רכוש מכחו ועוצם ידו.
כדכתיב ואש לא אמרה הון (משלי ל' ט"ז). ובהתעטף הקב"ה בזה הלבוש אז
יתבטלו כל הרכושים. וזה דאיתא בגמרא (שבת קי"ט ב'). אין הדליקה מצויה
אלא במקום שיש חילול שבת. כי שבת רומז לה' הארץ ומלואה. ולפי
שהוא יתנגד לזה יתברר באש. כדאיתא בויקרא רבה (פ"ז ס' ו') שכל המתגאה
אינו נידון אלא באש.

53

Let's understand Yaakov, Eisav, and their relationship. Fire, through its ability to burn and destroy everything, reminds us that, despite our talents and strength, they are not what define success. Things that are acquired through them are not really acquisitions. The *pasuk* in *Mishlei* (30:16) tells us that fire does not distinguish between wealth and poverty. The Gemara (*Shabbos* 119b) also explains that desecration of the Shabbos brings the outbreak of fires. Shabbos reminds us that Hashem owns everything, and whatever we have is only what He has given to us. Desecrating Shabbos brings fire, which teaches us this forgotten concept. On a similar note, the Midrash (*Vayikra Rabbah* 7:6) also teaches us that anyone who is arrogant is judged with fire. Fire helps us see the truth; it burns through self-deception.

ולהבה שולט למרחוק. ובית עשו לקש כי הקש הוא הקל יותר נגד האש. כי בהריחו אש מיד ישרף. וכמו כן בעולם יעקב אבינו הוא הקורט והמובחר שבכל התבואה ועשו הוא רק הקש. אכן כל זמן שלא נגמר הבירור אז התבואה צריך להקש. וזה שכתוב מעט מעט אגרשנו וגו' (שמות כ"ג ל'). אבל לאחר הבירור יכלה הפסולת. ולכן שלח לו מרכושו כדי שיתן בו קיווי שעוד יש לו תקוה ולא יפרוק עולו. ולזה המתין עד לידת יוסף הצדיק. כי יוסף הצדיק הוא המחזיק והמגביל שלא יפול נפש מישראל החוצה חס ושלום. כי מדתו הוא פשוטי מצות. ובזה יש לכל נפש מישראל אחיזה.

Yosef is called a flame that can set things on fire from afar. Eisav is called straw, the thing that is burned up immediately.

Straw is used to protect grain while it grows. The grain is the purpose of growing the plant. If Eisav is the straw, then Yaakov is the grain, meaning his connection with Hashem is the goal, the purpose of the whole world. After the grain has grown, it is separated from the straw, which is then thrown away. The knowledge of this comparison is what pushes Eisav away from *kedushah*. Since he is the master of this world (and Yaakov is the master of the next world), Eisav thinks, "What is the point of repairing the world, if it will lead to my ultimate rejection?" This is why the *yetzer hara*'s mission in the world is to exclaim, "What is the significance of man that he should be remembered?" His essence is "The futility of it all!" The *yezter hara* is the "angel" of Eisav, who also proclaims, "Behold! I am about to die! Why would I need the *bechorah*!"

The answer to this dilemma is Yosef, who is compared to a leaping flame that can raise up this world. It is specifically Ovadia, the convert from Eisav, who reveals this prophetic teaching to us. Yaakov sent Eisav all sorts of gifts, things of the physical world, to demonstrate how the physical world could be lifted up, so that he should have hope and not rebel against Hashem.

Now we can understand why Yaakov waited until Yosef was born. Yosef's strength will assure that no Jew will fall out of the realm where the fire of Yaakov can touch him. The flame of Yosef means that a person can perform *mitzvos* in this world and elevate it.

ולזה היה ההבטחה בחלומו על מדתו של יוסף הצדיק. שלא ידח שום נפש מישראל. וסלם עם השם הויה הנצב עליו בגימטריא יוסף. וכן גם הבהמות ששלח לו בגימטריא שלשה פעמים יוסף. בהצטרפות שני שמות הויה ואלהים. שהוא בגימטריא יב"ק.

Yaakov's dream of a ladder with its head in the sky and feet on the ground is about Yosef. The special quality of Yosef is the ability of the Torah to reach out of the heavens down to the world, so that no one will be left behind.

The Izhbitzer Tradition

The בית יעקב further explains the fight against the depression of Eisav, the power of Yosef, and the role of Ovadia the Ger in בית יעקב וישלח (מ"ח כ"ו).

Practical Advice

Many times in life, we feel the depression of Eisav creep over ourselves. These Eisav-thoughts speak of the futility of life, and depressing thoughts which inhibit personal growth. Yaakov Avinu waited for Yosef to be born, so that we would have the strength to continue fighting for growth and meaning when we feel we are unable to to fight any more.

פרשת וישב

from Beis Yaakov ha-Kollel

וַיֵּשֶׁב יַעֲקֹב בְּאֶרֶץ מְגוּרֵי אָבִיו **(בראשית ל"ז א')**. שיר המעלות בשוב ה' את שיבת ציון היינו כחולמים (תהלים קכ"ו א').

The *parsha* begins with the phrase, "and Yaakov dwelled in the place of his fathers" (*Bereishis* 37:1). In order to understand it, the בית יעקב cites the *pasuk* from *Tehillim* (126:1), "A the song of ascents. When Hashem returned the captives of Tzion, we were like dreamers." The בית יעקב reflects on the fact that in this *parsha*, Yaakov returned from his exile.

הנה השי"ת הציב גבולים בעולם הזה. והכל מכוון נגד טובות השי"ת שישפיע לנו לעתיד.

Hashem created borders and differentiated between places in the world, corresponding to the good that He will do for us in the future.

אכן בשר ודם הנותן לחברו תבנית טובה איזה טובה אשר הכין בעדו. אין בהתבנית שום חיים. אבל כשהשי"ת נותן לאדם ומראהו תבנית הטוב המוכן לו. אז גם בהתבנית יש חיים נצחיים. אם כי אין דמיון לערך יקרות החיים המוכנים לעתיד.

57

The word *Tzion*, in addition to referring to Yerushalayim, also means an "image, plan, or summary." What is the significance of this relationship? When you show someone else a plan, it may not be clear to that person how the plan will work. But when Hashem gives us such a plan, it has life in it, even if there is no comparison between the plan and its materialization.

וכן אף בשוב ה' את שיבת ציון. אז יכירו שכל הטובות שהיו להם בעולם הזה. הם כחלום נגד הפתרון לכל מה שהכין הקב"ה בשביל ישראל לעתיד לבוא.

In the prophecy of David Ha-Melech, stating that Hashem will return the captives of Tzion, all of the good that is hidden in the plan (*tzion*) and prepared for us will become apparent for all to see. David Ha-Melech continues that we will be like dreamers. Just as a dream pales in comparison with its interpretation, the life that Hashem has prepared for us in the future is so much greater even than the revelation of good in this world.

והנה בזו הסדרה מראה השי"ת לנו. איך ממעשי האבות נעשה דברי תורה קבועים לעד.

In this week's *parsha,* by the story's focusing on the childre, we see how the actions of the Avos become *divrei Torah* for the future. Yaakov dwells in the land in which his forefathers lived. Then his children experience challenges in their lives similar to those of their father. This is the idea in the Midrash that the acts of the fathers are a sign for the children: *Maaseh Avos Siman La-Banim.*

כדאיתא בגמרא (שבת י' ב'). אסור לאדם שיתן שלום לחבירו בבית המרחץ
כו'. ואמר רבא בר מחסיא. אמר רב חמא בר גוריא אמר רב שרי למימר
הימנותא בבית הכסא כו'. כי בית המרחץ מורה על בירורים. שהאדם צריך
לברר את עצמו ולרחוץ מגלולי עולם הזה.

The process of transformation from the acts of the Avos into
divrei Torah that become constants in our life is highlighted
by a Gemara (*Shabbos* 10b) that quotes a teaching, that it is
forbidden to say "*Shalom*" to someone in bathhouse. The
Gemara continues: but Rav Chama bar Guryea says that you
can mention *emunah* even in a bathroom. Let's understand
the implications. A bathhouse is a place where people clean
themselves from the dirt of this world; therefore it reminds us
of the process of refining ourselves and working through our
life's challenges.

אסור להשען ולבטוח באיזה מדה. שעל ידה יבטח בהשי"ת ולומר שעל ידי זה
נאחז בו. כי בעולם הזה אין דבר שלם שלא יצרך לבירורים.

What is the nature of this prohibition? It is forbidden to assume
that any one characteristic is the answer to all of our problems,
and through it Hashem will save us. There is nothing in the
world that doesn't require us to work through it. This is the
middah of Yaakov Avinu, who didn't use one specific approach
and say it is Hashem's will that I do this and only this. Rather he
looked at the situation and as a result saw what Hashem wanted
him to do.

ורק הימנותא מותר. היינו שהקב"ה נקרא נאמן. כי נאמן מורה שיבטח בהשי"ת
שלא יעזבנו.

In relating to the "the bathhouse," which is about the process of self refinement and *birurei ha-middos*, we cannot say we have reached completion (one may not say *shalom*). We can say that we are sincerely engaged in the process of *avodas Hashem*. Hashem guaranteed that there will be a positive result to our exertion, and we know that Hashem is reliable. Hence, the *halachah* is that we may say "*emunah*."

ועל זה מורה שמו גם כן באלו המאמרים. רבא בר מחסיא. היינו שנכון לבו בטוח בהשי״ת שהשם מחסהו. ואמר בשם רב חמא. היינו בעוד שהאדם מחומם בילדות. ובר גוריא רומז על ילדות. אז אסור להשען על מבטח שהוא בשלמות.

It is particularly appropriate that it was Raba bar Machsya who taught these teachings, for he had focused his heart to rely on Hashem. The name Machsya means "to be under his care."

Similarly, "It was stated in the name of Rav Chama," which means when a person is fired up (*chama*) during his youth.

"Son of Guryea"– a *gur* is a youth. "Youth" implies that the person has not reached maturity or fulfillment. A person who is always young knows that he is always in the middle of a process, and therefore it is forbidden to rely completely upon any *middah* or assume that it is fully developed.

ונסמך לזה (שם). ואמר רבא בר מחסיא אמר רב חמא בר גוריא. אמר רב הנותן מתנה לחבירו צריך להודיעו. שנאמר לדעת כי אני ה׳ מקדשכם. כי כל הטובות שהשי״ת נתן והכין לישראל. הציב ציונים גם בעולם הזה. למען יוכר מה הכין השי״ת לנו:

The בית יעקב explains another teaching which follows the previous one. Rav Machsya said in the name of Rav Chama son of Guryea, in the name of Rav, that a person who gives a present to his friend has to tell him. He proves this by quoting the *pasuk*, that tells the children of Israel that Hashem gave the Shabbos, in order "to know I am Hashem, Who makes you holy." Hashem sets up boundaries and markers in this world in order for us to see all that Hashem does for us.

The Izhbitzer Tradition

Many Izhbitzer teachings speak about the fundamental avodah of birur ha-middos. See (ויישב 7) בית יעקב בראשית, which examines these ideas in greater detail. See (ויישב ו) בית יעקב בראשית, where he discusses the concept of Tzion and the return to Tzion.

Practical Advice

The challenge of birur ha-middos is making a person's dreams come true, to return the "Tzion" to real life. It is through these choices that we establish who we are and what we are really capable of. This week we learn of the choices of Yaakov Avinu's children, as they emerge as adults and choice makers. We see Yosef's dreams, and the road that follows in their materialization. We follow in their footsteps as we make our choices, becoming who we must become as well.

פרשת מקץ

from Beis Yaakov ha-Kollel

וַיְהִי מִקֵּץ שְׁנָתַיִם יָמִים וּפַרְעֹה חֹלֵם (בראשית מ"א א'). זה שאמר הכתוב
ויאמר לי עבדי אתה ישראל אשר בך אתפאר (ישעיה מ"ט ג'). הנה נמצא שני
מיני הנהגות. איך הקב"ה מנהג עם ישראל. ואיך מתהלך בקרבם.

"And it was at the end of two years, and days, and Paroh dreamed
a dream" (*Bereishis* 41:1). The בית יעקב explains this language of
"years and days" by using a *pasuk* from *Yeshaya* (49:3): "You
are my servant, Israel, in whom I will take pride." Based on this
pasuk, there are two ways that Hashem interacts with us: He
guides us, and He dwells amongst us.

יש הנהגה שנקראת ברזא דבן. ויש שהשי"ת מנהג ברזא דעבד. כדאיתא בזוה"ק
(בהר קי"א ב').

We can also say that Hashem interacts with us as a father to a
child, or as a master to a servant.

והנה מההנהגה שהוא ברזא דעבד מזה לא יצמח שום דבר שיצרך לסבול ממנה.
כי העבד יעמוד תמיד במצב אחר לא יעלה למדרגה עליונה ולא ירד ממצבו.

This way of relationship as a servant has neither pain nor joy coming from it. Quite simply, the master tells the servant to do something, and he does it. He is a servant and remains a servant. The servant knows not the joy of closeness nor the pain of distance. But he is not discouraged by failure, as he always remains a servant; nor he is he empowered to be more, because, as we said, he always will remain a servant.

אך הבן לפי שהולך כל פעם למדרגות עליונות. והנה זאת ידוע כי אין הקב"ה משפיע רק למי שיצמא לה. ועיקר הצמאון הוא כשאדם מכיר את חסרונו. ולזה השי"ת משפיע.

However, since the son always tries to find favor in his father's eyes and wishes to draw closer, and Hashem relates to us in accordance with our desire for closeness, the relationship changes all the time. What is the main thing the son should want? To be able to recognize the things within him that separate him from his father.

כדאיתא במי השלוח (לקוטי הש"ס שבת פ"ח). על מאמר הגמרא ואמר רבי יהושע בן לוי בשעה שעלה משה למרום. ולכן אין אדם עומד על דברי תורה אלא אם כן נכשל בהן (גיטין מ"ג א').

Similarly, this relationship is what the מי השולח described when he explained the Gemara (*Gittin* 43a) that a person will only stand in Torah if he has previously failed. The מי השלוח explained that it is through those failures that a person can recognize what he is lacking and contribute to the formation of a whole person. Similarly, when Moshe ascended to receive the Torah, and the *malachim* sought to destroy him for trying to "steal" it from them, he responded to them, "What lack do you have that you need to fill through the Torah?"

והוא כי יראה לו השי"ת כי באלו הדברי תורה שהיה לו לא היה די בו לעמוד נגד יצרו. וצריך להוספות אור התורה. וכל זה הוא מרזא דבן. כמו שכתוב בניו מומם (האזינו ל"ב ה').

When Hashem opens our eyes to see what we need to repair, he shows us that the Torah that we had was not enough to fight against the *yetzer hara*. He shows us that we need more of the Torah's light. Moshe Rabbeinu said this clearly in the song of *Haazinu* (32:5), that "Hashem's children have *mumim* (deficiencies)." This doesn't sound positive at all, but the truth is that it is an amazing kindness to be able to recognize one's deficiencies, rather than allow the defense mechanisms of the yetzer hara to cover them over. The operative word is children, not servants. In order to advance and grow, we must find the lack and repair it.

והנה כל זה הוא קודם שנתברר לב ישראל. אבל לעתיד כשיברר הקב"ה את קץ שנתים ימים. והוא השני טובות שנבראו באלו השני ימים שנכפלו בהם כי טוב. היינו כל מיני טובות אכילה שנבראו ביום השלישי. וצורת אדם בהתנשאותו שנברא ביום הששי. וכשיראה הקב"ה מה שצפון באלו השני טובות ולא נטו ישראל מרצונו אז ישתברו כל מיני תקיפות שנראו כמקטריגים שמצדם יוצרך סבלנות וזהו ישראל אשר בך אתפאר:

Now let's return to the beginning of the *parsha*. Yosef's exodus from jail came as a result of Paroh's dreams, which happened at the end of "two years." The בית יעקב explains that this *pasuk* is talking about the end of two years connected to two specific days. This chasm between the two dynamics of child and servant exist only in this world. It is only our broken hearts and view of reality that make us believe that there are two different ways.

In the future, Hashem will clarify the years and day. What are these days? The two days of creation when creation was described twice as being good; on the third day, "good food for eating" was created and man was created on the sixth day. Both days are days in which the beginning of the process of development was begun but will not be completed until the end of days. In the future, Hashem will reveal all of the potential that was invested in these two days. Then, we'll see that despite the fact that it seemed that there was a diversion from Hashem's will, it really was all part Hashem's plan, which will be developed in its entirety. The imperfect world is the source of criticism, for those who don't have patience to wait it out. However, Hashem says that "I will be adorned through Israel," meaning that Hashem expresses His knowledge that ultimately He will be proud of the development of the Jewish people when they achieve their long awaited perfection. Ultimately Hashem's servants will become His children.

The Izhbitzer Tradition

The מי השלוח and the בית יעקב explain the concept of knowledge of flaws as a fundamental point of a person's growth. See בית יעקב בית יעקב לך לך לך (יז) and הכולל לך לך.

Practical Advice

Many times in life, we have no clue where things are going. Our impatience to be someplace oftentimes discourages and depresses us. In last week's parsha, we left Yosef rotting in an Egyptian prison, and his life didn't seem to be going in the direction of his dreams. But in the end we see that there is a story unfolding. This is why the parsha can begin with "in the end."

פרשת ויגש

from Beis Yaakov ha-Kollel

וַיִּגַּשׁ אֵלָיו יְהוּדָה (בראשית מ''ד י''ח). אמר אלהי ישראל לי דבר צור ישראל
מושל באדם צדיק מושל יראת אלהים (שמואל ב' כ''ג ג'). אמר אלהי ישראל
היינו שהשי''ת הציב דברי תורה בהם כח ואומץ לפעול בלב אדם ברצון
השי''ת. אך לזאת נאמר בלשון אמירה שהוא לשון רכה (מכילתא יתרו פי''ט
פ''ג). לפי שהשי''ת רצה שכל מה שיסגל האדם יקרא על שמו ויגיע כפיו. לכן
נסתר חוזק של הדברי תורה ונראה לפעמים כי אין חס ושלום בכחם לפעיל.

"And Yehuda approached…" (*Bereishis* 44:18). The *Zohar*
explains that, in his encounter with Yosef, Yehuda also
approached Hashem. The בית יעקב explains this *pasuk* with
the words of the Navi (*Shmuel* II 23:3), "Hashem, G-d of Israel
spoke (אמר), the Rock of Israel said (דבר) to me, Rule over man.
The righteous man rules with awe of Hashem, G-d of Israel."

Regarding the first part of the *pasuk*, "Hashem spoke" (אמר),
the בית יעקב explains that אמר means that even though Hashem
gave the words of Torah the power to affect a person's heart,
they were given in a soft way because Hashem wanted us to be
able to benefit from our own choices. Therefore Hashem hid
the strength of the words of Torah, so that sometimes they don't
seem to have an effect.

ועד שיתראה כי יעשה הכל מדברי תורה. וזהו עיקר הגלות .

People are placed in this situation so that they can realize that everything is from words of Torah. This is the point of exile.

שמדת יוסף הצדיק היה לזווג ולחבר את ישראל לאביהם שבשמים ברזא דיסוד. ולפעמים שדברי תורה אינם מפורשים בכח הפועל. וזה נקרא שמדתו של יוסף הצדיק הוא בגלות. ולכן כל זמן שהיה ארונו של יוסף במצרים לא היו יכולים לצאת. וכאשר ירד יוסף למצרים הלכו כל ישראל בגלות.

The attribute of Yosef is the ability to attach the Jewish people to Hashem, no matter what. This is indicative of the power of the words of Torah. However, in order for people to be able to make their own decisions, words of Torah must not be given their full power. In fact, the opposite is true, that we can rationalize and project our will into the Torah. Therefore, we see in the last several *parshios* that Yosef is in exile. Furthermore, as long as Yosef's coffin was in Egypt, the Jews could not leave, and once he descended to Egypt, the Jews were in exile.

לי דבר צור ישראל זה מדבר בבעל תשובה. שאף שנראה שזה האדם עבר על מצות ה'. עתיד הקב"ה לברר שבאמת מעולם לא עשה מה שלא יחפוץ בו השי"ת. אכן שלזה האדם היו מפורשים הדברי תורה בהתגלות בבחינת דבור. וזהו לי דבר צור ישראל. שמהאמירה נעשה דיבור. והוא שקבוע בלבו כל כך אהבת ה' שכל מה שעשה לא היה רק רצון השי"ת.

We return to the words of the Navi, "The Rock of Israel spoke to me." The words are referring to the phenomenon of *baalei teshuvah*. Even when we go against what Hashem wants, Hashem will ultimately show us how everything was all according to

His plan. Therefore the word "דבר" is used, which indicates the words of Torah being experienced in a much more frontal way, which can be difficult for a person. But as אמר becomes דבר, people will discover the profound love of Hashem. They will begin to see that everything that happened to them in their life was really what Hashem wanted, because Hashem loves them.

וזה הענין היה ביהודה. שנפסק הענין לשני פרשיות מקץ ויגש. ואף שהענין הוא אחד. כי בפרשה דלעיל מניה התייאש יהודה את עצמו. אחר שראה שהשי"ת מנהג עמו מדה במדה. לכן דימה כי הוא מעומק רצון השי"ת שיענש. ואך בכח הזה הלך עתה. כי יפה צעקה לאדם בין קודם גזר דין בין בין לאחר גזר דין (ר"ה ט"ז א'). עד שהראה לו השי"ת כי עד עתה לא היה עליו שום כעס .ועמידתו בפחד היה לפני אחיו. וזה רמז על לעתיד. שיראה השי"ת כי מעולם חסנו בצלו כמו שכתוב והי' כאשר לא זנחתים (זכריה י' ו').

We see this idea expressed in Yehuda's life. There are two *parshios* devoted to Yehuda, *Vayigash* and *Mikeitz*. In *Mikeitz*, we saw that Yehuda had given up on himself. He believed that because of the circumstances which he was experiencing, Hashem was treating him in accordance with what he deserved. Therefore he believed that it was truly Hashem's will that he was being punished.

At this the beginning of this *parsha* we read, "Yehuda drew close...." The *Zohar* explains that Yehuda approached Hashem through *tefillah*, despite the fact that he felt all was lost. But then Hashem showed him that He was not intent on punishing Yehuda at all. Suddenly, Yehuda was really standing before his brother Yosef. In a moment, the *middah* of Yosef, of connection to Hashem began to shine; it was revealed that the entire episode was orchestrated by Hashem for Yehuda to recognize His profound love and guidance. This was a glimpse of the future, when we will see that we never left Hashem's shadow, and He never left us.

The Izhbitzer Tradition

The בית יעקב explains this concept in further depth in (ו) ויגש and the מי השלוח explains the transformative power of divrei Torah in כי תשא (א ח:א-ב).

Practical Advice

So often, we feel that our lives aren't going anywhere. We think that we are in control and we have wasted our choices. Often times, we blame ourselves and convince ourselves that we are worthy of punishment. We learn from Yehuda never to stop davening for help. Even more, we learn from him never to give up, hoping that the time will come when our adversaries will be revealed to be our own brothers, and we will recognize that our worst mistakes were really guiding us down the road to fulfill our destiny.

פרשת ויחי

from Beis Yaakov ha-Kollel

בְּךָ יְבָרֵךְ יִשְׂרָאֵל לֵאמֹר יְשִׂמְךָ אֱלֹהִים כְּאֶפְרַיִם וְכִמְנַשֶּׁה (בראשית מ''ח כ'). עניין שתחילה בירך יעקב אבינו את בני יוסף בפרט. ואח״כ כלל אותם בברכת יוסף בין ברכת השבטים.

Yaakov Avinu said to his grandchildren, "Through you, the Jewish people will be blessed. They will bless their children, 'Hashem should make you like Efraim and Menashe'" (*Bereishis* 48:20).

דהנה איתא בספר יצירה. שנים עשר מנהיגים בנפש זכר ונקבה. ושנים עשר שבטי י-ה. היינו כמו שהשנים עשר מנהיגים בנפש זכר ונקבה כולם יצרכו לאדם לפעמים שיצרך להשתמש בזה ולפעמים בזה. כן השי״ת משתמש בשבטים.

In *Sefer Yetzirah*, we find the following quotation: There are twelve leaders within each person, male and female. These are the twelve tribes, and each person requires them all, sometimes this one, and sometimes a different one. Similarly, Hashem sometimes uses some *shevatim* versus other *shevatim*, depending on the situation.

ובעת שהשי"ת חפץ להרבות את ישראל. אז משתמש במדת יוסף. והנה ישראל
מצדם אין בכחם להתפשט. כי תוכן כוונתם אינו בלתי אחד. ומזה לא יבא
להתפשטות מאחר שהם נכללים תמיד באחדות האמיתי. ולכן היה מהצורך
להכניסם בגלות. כי שם יוכלו להרבות. כדאיתא בפסחים (פ"ז ב'). לא הגלה
הקב"ה את ישראל לבין העכו"ם. אלא כדי שיתוספו עליהם גרים. כי באחדותם
לא נמצא רק כוונה אחת.

When Hashem wants to expand the Jewish people, he uses the
middah of Yosef (of Efraim and Menashe), since the Jewish
people cannot increase on their own. The status quo of the
Jewish people, when left on their own is to be connected to the
unity of Hashem. In the face of this close connection, there is
no place for expansion. The Jewish people needed to enter exile
in order to expand.

אך נגד האומות יוכל כל אחד להתפאר במדרגתו לבדו. ומזה יתפשטו.

Once they were in exile, they were not overwhelmed and
overshadowed by the strength of Hashem's unity. Their
individual attributes could shine, and they could expand.

וזה שקרא יוסף בנו הראשון מנשה כי נשני אלהים את כל עמלי ואת כל בית
אבי (מקץ מ"א נ"א). ואח"כ קרא שם השני אפרים. וכפי הראות היה מהצורך
לקרוא להפך. תחלה אפרים כי הפרני (שם מ"א נ"ב) . ואח"כ כי נשני. אלא כי
עיקר הריבוי בא משכחה.

Yosef called his first child "Menashe," meaning (*Bereishis* 41:51)
"He caused me to forget my father's home." He called the second
child Efraim (*Bereishis* 41:52), which means "to increase." The בית
יעקב says he thinks that this should have been reversed. Yosef's

mourning should have been mitigated by the increase in his family. However, growth can only come as a result of forgetting.

כי העומד נוכח המלך פנים בפנים לא יוכל להתפשט.

When someone stands before a king, the enormity of the experience inhibits his own growth and self- expression.

לכן קרא שם בנו הראשון מנשה. כדי שיהיה מקום להתרבות. ורק ברך יעקב אותם תחלה בפרט כדי שיתרבו ישראל.

Therefore, Yosef thanked Hashem for allowing him to forget, to feel distant from his father's home so that he could have the room to increase. This is why Yaakov blessed them, Menashe and Efraim, individually, so that the nation of Israel could increase.

ואח"כ בברכת השבטים לא יחשבו בפני עצמם. אלא שנכללו בברכת יוסף. כי בכל מקום שנחשב לוי לשבט לא יחשבו הם בפני עצמם. כדאיתא במדרש תנחומא (ויחי ס' ט"ו). כי לוי רומז על עבודה. אז כל ישראל כאחד. לאחד שם ה' הגבור והנורא. לכן כשמחשב השבט לוי. שוב אין להם מקום להחשב לשני שבטים:

Afterwards, Menashe and Efraim were counted and blessed with Yosef. Any place where Levi was counted as its own tribe, Efraim and Menashe were considered subsumed by Yosef. This is because Levi means "clarity in *avodah,*" the strong feeling that we know what Hashem wants. This clarity prevents the distance required for growth. This closeness shows itself as all of the Jews united, serving the one Hashem, Who is great and awesome. Therefore when we count Levi there is no place to count Menashe and Efraim.

The Izhbitzer Tradition

See (מ"ט) בית יעקב ויחי for a more in depth discussion of this concept.

Practical Advice

In the post Chanuka days of darkness, it's so easy to forget the warmth of the Chanuka light. The darkness of forgetting presents us with the chance to make our own light. Take these moments of darkness, not to complain why they are lacking in the inspiration of previous days of light, but as an invitation to shine on your own.

פרשת שמות

from Beis Yaakov ha-Kollel

וַיַּעַן מֹשֶׁה וַיֹּאמֶר וְהֵן לֹא יַאֲמִינוּ לִי וְלֹא יִשְׁמְעוּ בְּקֹלִי (שמות ד' א'). והשיב משה אמת כי לבות בני אדם הם ביד ה'. אך הגוף יש לו הסתרות שיוכל להסתר לבלתי שמוע כמו שנאמר ביחזקאל שניבא על עצמות היבשות ושמעו. כן לא היו להם הסתרות.

The *parsha* begins with Moshe Rabbeinu saying to Hashem that "the children of Israel won't believe me, nor will they listen to my voice" (*Shemos* 4:1). What does this mean?

The בית יעקב explains that Moshe Rabbeinu was saying, "The body has the ability to conceal Hashem's message from our soul, so that we cannot hear what Hashem is telling us." When the body is weakened, the person can hear the message a lot more clearly. For example, in Yechezkel's prophecy, he spoke to dry bones, which heard his message very clearly. The body was reduced to dry bones, and there was nothing stopping the message from getting through.

אך כאשר ניבא אל בני ישראל לא שמעו.

But when Moshe spoke to B'nei Israel, they didn't listen.

והשיב לו השי״ת מה זה בידך ויאמר מטה. היינו שנדמה לך שבחכמה נאמרו
דבריך. כי מטה רומז על חכמה וחיים.

So Hashem asked, "What is in your hand?" Moshe responded,
"a staff." The בית יעקב explains that the meaning of the staff,
the word *mateh*, is to turn to either side, to choose. Hashem
asked Moshe, "Do you truly believe that your actions are guided
through wisdom and life?"

ויאמר השליכהו ארצה באם כל דבר שאינו מה׳ אז ויהי לנחש. ואז וינס משה
מפניו. היינו שהראה לו כי למה נס. הלא צדיק גמור אינו בולע (ברכות ז' ב').
ועל כל פנים גם בך נמצא דבר מה נגד רצון השי״ת.

Hashem told Moshe, "Throw your staff to the ground." What
does this mean? Hashem was demonstrating to Moshe how all
of reality could turn against Hashem. The staff becoming a
snake (much like the snake from the Garden of Eden, which
rebelled) demonstrates this point. Even the most holy choices,
which Moshe thought were well intentioned, can have an
element of rebellion against Hashem. Moshe ran from his own
staff, because Hashem demonstrated to him that there was
something rebellious even in that.

ואז אמר לו שלח ידך ואחז בזנבו. היינו כי הראה לו אף שזנב הנחש. ששם אף
דעת הנחש נקטן. ושם אין שום טובה. מכל מקום מרצון השי״ת משם יצמח כל
טוב. כמו שכתוב והביט אל נחש הנחשת וחי (חקת כ"א ט').

Then Hashem told him, "Send forth your hand and hold it by
the tail." Hashem showed Moshe Rabbeinu that even at the tip
of the snake, where the effects of knowledge are felt the least,

and there does not seem to be a glimmer of good, if Hashem wills it, good can bloom from there. This is what happened in *Bamidbar* when the B'nei Yisrael were bitten by serpents. They were commanded to look at the copper snake and thus live.

כי במקום שגם דעת הרע אינו. שם השי"ת שולט בכל טוב והראה לו אף שישראל לא שמעו אך כשיבא מעט התעוררות בלבם. אז כביכול גם השי"ת יחתום בלבם שישמעו.

In the place where there is knowledge, there is no evil. Hashem promised Moshe that even if the people don't listen now, with just a little of awakening, they will.

ואף שנראה שאמר משה דברים נגד השי"ת . הראה השי"ת מקום זכות אשר כוון לאמת. כי איזה פעמים לא יאמינו לו .ולא ישמעו בקולו. כדאיתא בספר מי השלוח (פרשת שמות).

Even though if it looks as if Moshe fought with Hashem, Hashem used this opportunity to reveal a source of merit. Even though there would be many times the people didn't believe him and didn't listen to him, with some of Hashem's wisdom, they would listen.

The Izhbitzer Tradition

בית יעקב שמות (נה-סג סד), מי השלוח שמות (חלק א ד"ה לך ואספת) See *which discusses these concepts in further depth.*

Practical Advice

Hashem revealed to Moshe Rabbeinu that we are all the tails of snakes. We all have the potential to fall and then in the same moment turn around and climb to the highest places. But we don't believe in ourselves. So Hashem taught us this lesson through Moshe Rabbeinu. At first, we won't listen, but in the next moment, we can turn ourselves around.

פרשת וארא

from Beis Yaakov ha-Kollel

וָאֵרָא אֶל אַבְרָהָם אֶל יִצְחָק וְאֶל יַעֲקֹב בְּאֵל שַׁדָּי וּשְׁמִי ה' לֹא נוֹדַעְתִּי לָהֶם (שמות ו' ג'). בזה"ק (וארא כ"ב א') מתחיל. בטחו בה' עדי עד כי ביה ה' צור עולמים בטחו בה' עדי עד הוא כי האדם צריך לבטוח בה' בכל ענין. כי מאתו יתברך לא יצא דבר שהוא לפי שעה בלתי דבר קיים עדי עד.

Hashem said to Moshe that He appeared to Avraham, Yitzchak, and Yaakov with the name of קל שקי, but He never made known His name of יקוק to them (*Shemos* 6:3). The *Zohar* (*Va'era* 22) introduces this week's *parsha* with the *pasuk*, "Rely on Hashem forever, because with the two letter name of יק he created worlds." The בית יעקב explains the phrase "rely upon Hashem," in the following way. A person must rely on Hashem; that what Hashem has made is not only for the moment, but will last forever.

ואם האדם יראה כי ניטל ממנו איזה טובה. אז יבין כי לא היה קנינו בה בשלמות. ולא היה מעומק לבו. וכמו שנתבאר בספר מי השלוח (לקוטים מכתובים משלי פט"ו פכ"ב) על פסוק הפר מחשבות באין סוד. כי ביה ה' צור עולמים. באלו השתי אותיות ברא הקב"ה את עולמו. כדאיתא בזה"ק (וארא כ"ב ב'). ואלו השתי אותיות הם כולל שם הויה ופירושו הם אותיות ו"ה. וזה עתיד הקב"ה לפתוח לנו כשיושלם השם והכסא.

79

When a person sees that he lost something, he must understand that he really did not own it. The מי השלוח explains that when a person wants to accomplish something and he cannot achieve it, he must understand that even though he was inspired to do it, this thought was not totally his. Even though he thought he had it, it didn't belong to him in the depths of his heart.

The בית יעקב explained that this relates to the statement "Hashem created the world with the letters of י and ה". The Zohar explains that י and ה mean potential, and the letters ו and ה mean the explanation and development of that potential. יand ה mean an idea, and ו and ה mean its explanation.

והנה מה שנאמר כאן באל שדי. כי שם ש-די הוא המגביל כל התפשטות ומגדירם. כדאיתא בגמרא (חגיגה י"ב א'). אני הוא שאמרתי לעולם די. לפי שהיה מרחיב והולך. ובזה השם נראה אל האבות. כי כל התגלות להאבות היה על ידי לבושים. כמו שנתבאר בפרשת בשלח. על פסוק ויצעק אל ה' ויורהו ה' עץ.

Therefore Hashem's explanation that He appeared to the Avos as קל שקי means that He withheld the ו and ה from working. The Gemara explains that the name שקי means, "I told My world to stop expanding" in the same way. By explaining that he appeared to the Avos as קל שקי Hashem communicated to the Avos, but did not reveal Himself completely.

והנה כשיתראה איך הש"ית לעתיד. אז יקרא השם בשלמות. וזהו ושמי ה' לא נודעתי להם. היינו שיוכר גם לעיני אדם בזה השם. כי באמת מצד השי"ת גם עתה אין הפרש בין השמות. כי מצד השי"ת כל מה שהאדם יחפוץ יושע. אך מצד האדם מבין השי"ת.

"But My name יקוק I did not make known to them." To Hashem, there is no difference between using one name or another. However, from the perspective of a person, this choice of names has great significance. This distinction informs what is understood about the way Hashem rules the world and how to serve Him at that time.

כי אף שהוא מתפלל על זה הדבר. אכן באמת בעומק לא יחפוץ בזה. כדאיתא במדרש תהלים (מזמור צ"א). מפני מה מתפללין ישראל בעולם הזה ואינן נענין. על ידי שאינן יודעין בשם המפורש. כי זה הוא שם המפורש. שהשי"ת יהיה מפורש בישועתו נגד האדם. וזהו ההפרש לעת עתה בין השמות מצד האדם. כדאיתא בגמרא (ברכות ל"ג ב'). משל למלך בשר ודם שהיו לו אלף אלפים דינרי זהב. והיו מקלסין אותו בשל כסף. כי כסף מורה שאינו רק דמיון לאור יקרותו אשר על זה מורה זהב.

The בית יעקב further explains how this affects us. Even though a person davens to meet Hashem based on his understanding, Hashem really doesn't want to meet him in this way. The Midrash asks, "Why does a person daven and isn't answered? Because they don't know the entire four-letter name of Hashem." The "entire four-letter name" means what Hashem's "real name" is. The Gemara describes the difference between the different names by means of a parable. A king has thousands of gold coins, and a person praises him for having silver coins. The silver coins only resemble to the gold coins in terms of their shape, but there is no comparison in value.

ולכן אסור להלל להשי"ת יותר מכפי הנסדר. כי איך יערב לבב אנוש להלל לה' כפי תפיסתו. הלא אולי יאיר לו ה' יותר.

81

Therefore, it is forbidden to praise Hashem more than what is in the Siddur. How could people have the chutzpah to try to praise Hashem according to their own understanding? Maybe Hashem will enlighten them more and make their previous understanding meaningless. Their previous understanding was only partial at best.

דהנה הני תלת דאמרינן. אי לאו דאמרינהו משה רבינו באורייתא. ואתו אנש כנסת הגדולה ותקנינהו בתפלה. לא הוינן יכולין למימר להו (שם). כי אלו השלשה היו לפי תפיסת האבות. כי כל מה שהכירו שבחו. ועל קדושתם חתם השי״ת. שזה אין יכול שום ישראל לאבד. וזה נקבע בלב ישראל בשוה. וזה מיתר לשבח.

A question might be: if Hashem didn't appear to the Avos fully, how did their ways of serving Hashem get passed down? The בית יעקב explains that the phrase, "Great, Mighty, and Awesome" in *Shemonah Esreh*, used to describe Hashem, would be inappropriate if it wasn't written in the Torah. However, this is what the Anshei Knesses HaGedolah put into the davening, despite the fact that we shouldn't be able to say them.

However, because the Avos perceived Hashem in a limited way, Hashem gave us the ability to recognize Him as "Great, Mighty, and Awesome." Hashem affixed the *kedushah* of the Avos to the Jewish people in a way that it cannot be lost. Therefore, it is permissible to praise Hashem in this way.

וכמו דאיתא בזה״ק (ויחי רכ״ה ב'). וישתחו ישראל על ראש המטה כו'. ישראל לדידיה קא סגיד. היינו לפי תפיסתו. וזהו דאמרינהו משה רבינו באורייתא. היינו שיוכר הכרה בולטת לכל ישראל. ואתו אנשי כנסת הגדולה ותקנינהו בתפלה. היינו שאף שיהיו ישראל בגלות לא יוכלו לאבד זאת ההכרה. וזה מותר

לשבח. ולכן נתקן מפי אנשי כנסת הגדולה לומר שמונה פעמים אמת בגאולה
(עי' זה"ק ויקהל רי"ז א') להורות ע"ז. שלא יאובד משום נפש מישראל זאת
ההכרה:

We can see this concept as well in the *Zohar* (*Vayechi* 225b)
that when Yisrael bowed on the head of the bed, he bowed in
his own way, meaning in accordance with his understanding.
Then Moshe Rabbeinu and the Anshe Kenesses HaGedolah
confirmed that this concept exists always in the Jewish people at
all times; even in exile we cannot lose this understanding. Hence
they put the word *emes* eight times into the *brachos* of *Geulah* in
Shacharis to show that no Jew loses this understanding.

We now come full circle to the beginning of our piece. Since
the Avos only were given a partial understanding of Hashem,
we might think that this new revelation would take the place
of what was given to the Avos. However, the *Zohar* (*Vayakhel*
217a) tells us we can rely on what Hashem revealed to the Avos
as well in our *avodas Hashem*.

The Izhbitzer Tradition

The מי השלוח in לקוטים discusses the difference between in inner
and outer accomplishments in avodas Hashem.

Practical Advice

There are times in life that we look back and realize that we didn't
have the whole picture. If we only knew the whole story, it would
make our choices look small or silly. However, Hashem tells us
that whatever we did, it was true and formative in becoming who

we needed to be. Hashem appeared to us in that way, so that we would react in the way we did and ultimately become who we needed to become.

פרשת בא

from Beis Yaakov ha-Kollel

בֹּא אֶל פַּרְעֹה (שמות י' א'). בזה״ק (בא ל״ד א') לך אל פרעה מבעי ליה מאי בא. אלא דעייל ליה קב״ה אדרין בתר אדרין. לגבי תנינא חדא עלאה תקיפא. דכמה דרגין משתלשין מניה. ומאן איהו רזא דתנין הגדול. ומשה דחיל מניה ולא קריב אלא לגבי אינון יאורין ואינון דרגין דיליה. אבל לגביה דחיל ולא קריב. דהנה הקב״ה צוה למשה להעמיד על התבוננות עיקר צמיחת כחו.

The *pasuk* says that Hashem commanded Moshe Rabbeinu, "Come to Paroh" (*Shemos* 10:1). The *Zohar* (*Bo* 34a) comments that it should say, "Go to Paroh." Why does the *pasuk* say "come"? This means that Hashem brought him down into the deepest chambers of reality until he reached a great crocodile, from which many levels of *tumah* come. Who is this crocodile? Paroh. But Moshe was afraid and did not come closer o the crocodile's rivers. The בית יעקב explains that the world could be equated to many rivers (the *sefiros*, the pathways that Hashem created to sustain the world, which are in order: *keser, chochmah, binah,* and *daas,* representing the intellect, and the lower seven: *chesed, gevurah, tiferes, netzach, hod, yesod,* and *malchus*) that had been infested with "crocodiles," due to the great crocodile, Paroh. Moshe was afraid to try to clean up those rivers (remove the perversion of Paroh from the world), but Hashem encouraged Moshe to continue, to enter the rivers, and clean the crocodiles from them.

ושם כח ישראל יסתיר כחותיו. ומזה ירא משה. כי פרעה טען כי מדת הלילה גדולה ממדת היום. כי יום מורה כי כל נפש יביט לבלתי יעשה מעשה רק שיהיה רצון השי"ת. ופרעה טען כי מה יפעלו מעשי אנוש ומחשבותיו נגד רצון השי"ת. ולכן הוא יעשה מה שלבו חפץ וזהו רצון הבורא.

However, Moshe Rabbeinu doubted his ability to do so. Paroh believed that the essence of night was stronger than the essence of day—the clear revelation of Hashem's will and the inability of anyone to do anything save what Hashem wants. Paroh said it is impossible during the day to do anything but Hashem's will. Therefore, everything that occurs must be what Hashem wants.

כי היתכן השי"ת יחפוץ בדברים קטנים כאלו שאדם יוכל להשיגם. ולכן בטח כל מה שיעשה בעולם הוא רצונו.

Is it possible that Hashem is concerned with such trivial matters of man's daily life? Whatever man wants to do, surely that is what Hashem wants.

לזה נקרא מדתו לילה. ולכן טען כי זה הוא גדול מאד. והנה משה ירא מאד בהתבוננו זה. כי הבין כי כחו יצמח מערב הראשון.

This way of thinking is distorted. The notion that "I can't go against Hashem's will because it is so pervasive" becomes "Hashem's will is so pervasive that everything I do must be His will. This distortion is called "nighttime." Moshe Rabbeinu was afraid of this idea; it is so twisted, but it also makes a certain amount of sense. בית יעקב explains that this is the case because night was the first thing created when Hashem created the world.

כי השי"ת ברא תחלה ערב. כמו שכתוב ויהי ערב (בראשית א' ה'). ואח"כ ברא יום. כי באמת עומק דעת השי"ת אין להשיג. אך כי השי"ת יחפץ שהאדם יבין ולא יסור מבינתו כל מה שביכולתו. והנה מזה ירא משה מאד איך יערב לגשת לסתור דעתו זו. כי באמת פרעה היה במעלה גבוה מאד.

This point is incredibly deep. Why would Hashem create the world in a way that we could have such a distortion of truth? We are incapable of understanding. We only know that Hashem wanted it that way, but we don't understand why. However, we can only function based on our understanding and not employ Paroh's "nighttime" approach. Moshe was afraid how he could go against this idea, due to its seeming truth.

כי נבוכדנצר נקרא רישא ופרעה נקרא גלגלתא דשליט על מוחא (לקוטי תורה שמות). והוא נגד ספירת כתר בקדושה. ולכן כשחפץ השי"ת לסתור דעתו באלו שלשה מכות אחרונים.

Let's understand this concept more deeply. The Arizal says that Nevuchadnetzar was called the "mind" and Paroh was the "skull" that rules the mind. What is the meaning of this statement? Paroh's spiritual nature is described as the skull, this is parallel to spiritual attribute of "Keser," whose simple meaning can be defined as "what Hashem wants." Hashem wanted to contradict this Paroh-night-idea by using the last three plagues to prove him wrong.

שהם נגד כתר חכמה בינה ירא משה. כי בנסתרות גם ישראל לא נשלמו.
כדאיתא בספר מי השלוח (חלק ראשון). וגם הם מה יוכלו לעשות בנסתרות
הלא אין להם בחירה. והראה לו הקב"ה כי מעשיהם הנגלים יבררו גם את
הנסתרות. מאחר שהם עזרו לרעה לכן מגלגלים עליהם את הכל.

This is what scared Moshe Rabbeinu. Since Paroh's claim
made sense in a certain way, this means he had control of
the intellectual "rivers" supplying reality (these are known as
the *sefiros* of *keser, chochmah, binah,* and *daas*). He polluted
Hashem's "river of Keser," which is the supply line into this
world of "what Hashem wants" with his claim of "whatever
happens is what Hashem wants." These higher attributes, or as
the *Zohar* calls them, "rivers," are harder to reach. Israel does
not have such control over them due to their abstract nature.

ובישראל לפי שבמקום שביכולתם משמרים את עצמם. לכן מהראוי שהשי"ת
יברר מעשיהם. וגם בנסתרות יעיד עליהם השי"ת כי לבם מזוכך. וכן בכל
מכות התרה לו בשנים. ובשלישית לא התרה בו. כי מאחר שהוא רע בשתי
הקצוות. אז גם באמצע הוא מלא רע.

So what can Israel do then to perfect their intellectual attributes?
They do the best that they can. and In accordance with their
efforts Hashem will consider it as if they have repaired even the
deepest, most hidden parts of the world and themselves (the
highest sefiros). We see this idea in the *makkos*, the plagues,
which come in sets of three. Each *makkah* is the "removal of a
crocodile from a river," the removal of the Paroh-like thought
from the river of the world, the impurity from a *sefirah*. But
while the first two *makkos* of a set are dealing with *sefirah* of
the lower seven *sefiros*, the last *makkah* of the set accesses a

sefira which that is too ethereal and supernal for us to purify, to "remove its crocodile from the river." Hashem does that one based on the actions that were performed in the lower world. Therefore, Hashem warned the Mitzrim for two out of the three of each set of plagues, as the lower two were within a person's capabilities, whereas the last one was not so a warning was of no use.

והנה בהמכות הראה לו כי לא נמצא בו שום כח טוב מראש ועד סוף. ועשר המכות הם נגד עשר הספירות. אך בררו ממטה למעלה ושלא כסדרן.

Through the *makkos*, Hashem demonstrated that there is no power besides Him. The ten *makkos* are analogous to the ten *sefiros*. Each *makkah* undoes the perversion that Paroh had created (however the *makkos* are not in the exact order of the sefiros that we listed above).

מכת דם הוא נגד ספירת מלכות. כי מלכות הוא חיבור המאחד וכולל הבריאה. ועיקר חיבור הברואים הוא על ידי השפעה וכח הדיבור שאחד משפיע לחברו. והראה לו איך הוא כח השפעתם. כי היאור היה כח השפעתם. וראה כי דם הוא. ודם הוא הפך מהשפעה שהוא כח המשחית. בראש כל מרעין אנא דם (ב"ב נ"ח ב'). כי רומז על כעס ופירוד.

The בית יעקב explains what the error of the Paroh and the Mitzrim was in each *sefirah*, how they had polluted it, and how the "crodocdile was chased out."

This is not the place to discuss the *sefiros* in depth, but we will discuss each *sefirah*, as it pertains to us, in a way that simple people like ourselves can understand. The *makkah* of blood is parallel to *sefirah* of *malchus*. *Malchus* is the connection between all of reality and the spiritual worlds. Our reality has a common denominator that through *malchus*, Hashem gives life to all of it. Hashem showed how He is the source of the world's existence. In Egypt the people looked at the Nile as their source of life. What is the significance of it becoming blood? Inside the body, blood is the essence is life, but outside the body it signifies death. Changing their perception of the Nile from a vehicle that Hashem uses to sustain life, to the source of life itself is to "take blood out of the body" which means to make it dead.

צפרדע הוא נגד הוד כי הוד הוא הפנימית הנמצא בכל דבר. כמו שנתבאר במי השלוח (חלק ראשון). והראה כי כל דיבורם אינם מפנימית. לכן מקרקרים כצפרדעים בלי כוונה פנימית.

The plague of frogs is parallel to the attribute *hod*, the essence in all things. Hashem showed Moshe that frogs are not filled with any deep substance. They make noise like birds, chirping away without meaning.

כנים הוא נגד יסוד. כי ספירת יסוד בה נמצא עיקר ההשפעה. ועיקר השפעה הוא כשאדם מעצור עצמו לבל ישפיע לריק. אז יוכל להגדיל השפעתו במקום הצורך. כי משם שדי המורה על צמצום יבא פרה ורבה. זהו ספירת יסוד ברזא דצדיק. וכנים הוא הפך מזה. כי בבריאה קטנה נמצא מהירות במעשיה. ולכן לא יפעול עם כל מהירתו וכמו שנתבאר במי השלוח (חלק ראשון פרשת וארא).

The plague of lice is parallel to the *sefirah* of *yesod*, representing the giving to all reality. The name of Hashem, *Shakkai* (which represents the *middah* of *yesod*), when translated, can mean "enough." Hashem created the world through restraining its growth. Similiarly, the *middah* of *yesod* means that through restriction, one increases the ability to expand. Lice demonstrate this property the most, as they are the smallest creation but most powerful in their ability to increase in size.

ערב הוא נגד נצח. כי נצוח הוא באם האדם יש לו סדרים בלבו יכול לנצח. והם כל מה שרצו להרע לישראל רצו כל העם יותר ויותר. עד שלא בצעו זממם. וכל זה היה ברצון השי״ת. כי מה שהקב״ה מצילנו מידם אינו על ידי ששולח להם מחשבות טובות עלינו. רק מרדיף ומטריד ומגביר עליהם כל כך מחשבות רעות אחד על חברו עד שלא יבצעו זממם. וזהו ערב בלבול חיות רעות נגד מחשבותם.

The plague of *orev*, wild animals, is parallel to the *middah* of *netzach*, "victory." When a person has clear goals and priorities, it enables him to triumph. *Orev* means a mixture, as the plague consisted of a mixed group of wild animals. Egypt consistently planned Israel's downfall, but as these plans increased, they became so complicated that they were thwarted. This was all part of Hashem's plan. Hashem saved us not by engendering good will to Israel. Rather He created such anxiety about Israel in their hearts, that they could not achieve their plan. This is meaning of the mixture of animals, each representing worrying, confusing, trying thoughts that Hashem sent the Mitzrim.

דבר הוא נגד גבורה. כי גבורה הוא שהאדם יכיר גבורת השי״ת. וזאת היא הגבורה האמיתית. וכל מה שהאדם מכיר כי רק השי״ת נותן לו כח זה נקרא גבורה. והמצרים רצו בהפך. שאחזו כל דבר בכל כחם. ואמרו כחם ועוצם ידם עשה להם את כל. ולכן לפי שאחזו כל דבר בכל כחם. אז הוציא השי״ת את כחו מזה הדבר ונשאר גוף מת. והראה להם מה אוחזים.

Pestilence is *gevurah*. The point of *gevurah* is to recognize Hashem's might as the true strength in the world. A person needs to recognize that only Hashem makes him strong. The Egyptians wanted to believe the opposite was is true. Their cattle were the possessions that convinced them that their physical achievements held the secret to success. This belief was misplaced. By killing all of the cattle. Hashem showed that the thing that they believed would demonstrate their strength was really dead even when it was alive.

שחין הוא נגד תפארת. כי לישראל נתן השי"ת גוונין להתפאר בהם. והגוונין המה ממדותיו יתברך. אבל האומות יתפארו בדברי הבל לכן יבושו. וזהו מכת שחין שנאמר בו. ולא יכלו החרטומים וגו' (וארא ט' י"א).

Boils are comparable to *tiferes*. The *Zohar* explains that beauty can mean "lots of colors." The בית יעקב explains that when we say that Hashem gave us many colors to make ourselves beautiful, we are thinking about the many attributes of Hashem that He gives us the ability to imitate. However we can readily misunderstand this idea; that it only means the physical colors to beautify one's self. The *pasuk* says that because of the boils, the magicians were embarrassed to stand in front of Moshe. It was those boils, the colored marks on the outside of the body that were counteracting Paroh's misrepresenting *tiferes*. The Egyptians would beautify themselves with colorful things, thinking this is the only use of the colors and beauty.

ברד הוא נגד חסד. כי חסד הוא השפעה שהאדם ממשיך מהשי"ת. והראה להמצרים איך ימשכו השפעתם כי חרד בזרם ושטף.

Hail is *chesed*, the blessings that come from Hashem. Hashem demonstrated how the Egyptians took his blessings and revolted against him continuously.

ארבה חשך ומכת בכורות הם נגד כתר חכמה בינה. וכלם נקראים על שם חשך.
כי טענו שבחושך יש יתרון מאור כמו שנתבאר.

Darkness, locusts, and the plague of the first born are parallel to
keser, *chochmah*, and *binah*. All of them are called "darkness,"
as the Egyptians believed that darkness was better than light.

והנה ארבה היא נגד בינה. כי בינה הוא שימצא דרך ארץ וסדר בלב. והוא
מכח מלך שנמצא בלב כל אדם כידוע כי הלב נקרא מלך. וזהו כי ארבה לא
נצרך למלך. כי מלך אין לארבה ויצא חצץ כלו (משלי ל' כ"ז). כי נטבע בו
כח הזה והמצרים טענו כי גם להם חקים טובים בקביעות. והראה להם השי"ת
הלא הארבה טוב מכם. מכל מקום רק ישראל הם מכלכלים מעשיהם ומשפטם
בבינה ולא אתם.

Arbeh, "locusts," parallels *binah*, the faculty through which we
arrive at proper conduct and order in the heart. The king has a
place in the heart of his subjects. *Mishlei* says that locusts don't
have a king, rather they swarm by instinct without a locust
leader. Similarly, the Egyptians believed that they had all of
the rules they needed; They were already perfect! Hashem, in
sending the locusts, demonstrated that even locusts are better
than Egypt. Israel is sustained by their *binah*, their ability to
discern, as opposed to the Egyptians.

חשך הוא נגד כתר. כדאיתא בתקוני זהר (תקונא שבעין). כתר עלאה אף על גב
דאיהו אור קדמון אור צח ואור מצוחצח. איהו אוכם קדם עלת העלות. והוא כי
סתר דעתם והראם כי ישראל יונקים למעלה מהשגתם.

Darkness is parallel to *keser*, Hashem's will. *Keser* is described
in the *Zohar* (*Tikkunim* 7) as light that is so bright and refined

that it is dark. This concept light-that-is-dark is so incongruous it represents all that we do not understand. After creating this light, Hashem used it as the beginning of the creation of the world.

ומכת בכורות הוא נגד חכמה. כי אותיות השניות שבאל"ף בי"ת מיחידית עשירית מאות הם אותיות בכר. שמאז תתחיל החכמה לצאת. ובזה כחש וסתר דעתם והראם אשר רק בישראל נמצא חכמה ולא בהם.

The plague of the first born is parallel to the *sefirah* of *chochmah*. The "second series" of letters of the Aleph Beis, meaning the second in the ones, the tens and hundreds (2=ב ,20=כ ,200=ר) are the word בכר. This "secondness" is descriptive of the revelation of *chochmah* in the world. It is the wisdom that describes how Hashem created the (knowable) world. The death of the *bechor*, the first born, was demonstrating that, despite the fact that the Egyptians thought it was the center of wisdom in the world, Hashem showed them that they were not.

The Izhbitzer Tradition

See בית יעקב הגדה בדיקת חמץ *,where he discusses the chametz that is out of reach, parallel to avodah in the higher middos of Chochmah, Binah, Daas, and Keser.*

Practical Advice

Sometimes we need to have the world moved around to understand what our direction needs to be. We need to clarify where we are and what we need to do. There is yet a deeper part of ourselves that we cannot regularly access, and don't know how to perfect. Through our avodah, doing what we need to do, Hashem promises us that we will contact the deeper parts of ourselves that are now out of reach.

פרשת בשלח

from Beis Yaakov ha-Kollel

**וַיְהִי בְּשַׁלַּח פַּרְעֹה אֶת הָעָם וְלֹא נָחָם אֱלֹהִים דֶּרֶךְ אֶרֶץ פְּלִשְׁתִּים כִּי קָרוֹב
הוּא וגו' (שמות י"ג י"ז).** ויקח משה את עצמות יוסף עמו כי השבע השביע
את בני ישראל לאמר פקד יפקד. בשמות רבה (פ"ג ס' ח') מסורה היא בידם
מיוסף שבלשון זה אני גואלם. לך אמור להם זה הסימן. והנה אחרי כי משה
ואהרן היו הגדולים שבדור. למה היו צריכים לסימן של פקד יפקד. וגם ענין
הסימן מה הוא. הלא כלם ידעו זה. ואם יבא אחד בסימן זה מה יועיל.

There is a *pasuk* in our *parsha*, "When Paroh sent out the nation,
Hashem didn't allow them to go along the way of the Plishtim,
even though it was more direct" (*Shemos* 13:17). Moshe took
Yosef's bones because Yosef made the children of Israel swear to
do so, saying, "Hashem will surely remember you and take out
of Egypt." The Midrash (*Shemos Rabbah* 3:8) says that the words
pikod yifkod are a code that Hashem will use to notify the Jews
that they are being saved. The בית יעקב asks: What is the benefit
of using code words that everybody knew them?

אך ענין הסימן היה מי שיבא הפקודה בתוך לבו. וזאת הפקודה בא ללב משה
רבינו בעת שהרג את המצרי. כי בכל אומה יש נפש אחד שזה עיקר שורשם.
וכשיבא עתם ליאבד מן העולם יכנוס זה הנפש לתוך ישראל. וממילא גם כחם

96

בהטוב שחלק להם הקב"ה גם זה הכח יכנס לתוך ישראל ולא ישאר שם שום
קדושה וממילא יתבטלו. ואז גם הקב"ה שש במפלתן.

The בית יעקב explains the meaning of this Midrash. It was not
that the person who would save the Jews would say *pikod yifkod*.
It means someone who will surely redeem. Moshe Rabbeinu
began the Jewish people's redemptive process when he killed
the Egyptian man. Nations rise and fall, both physically and
spiritually. Often when a nation is conquered, its people and
land become absorbed into the conquering culture. Nations
have a spiritual existence as well, just as people have souls.
When it is time for a nation to stop existing, then the Jewish
people collect its spiritual essence. The nation's holiness, its life
force and vitality, are gone, and then the nation will physically
fade away.

כדאיתא בזה"ק (נח ס"א ב'). מה שהקב"ה אינו שש במפלתן של רשעים הני
מילי עד לא מטו זמנייהו. אבל כשבא עתם גם הקב"ה שש במפלתן. כי כשיאבדו
בלא עתם היינו כשיעיקו הרבה לישראל. אז אין הקב"ה משגיח להמתין עד
שיכנס טובתם לתוך ישראל רק בפעם אחת. ומה שלא יוכל להתברר מניח וילך
לאבדון לכן אינו שש.

The *Zohar* (*Noach* 61b) explains this dynamic further. Hashem
does not rejoice in the premature downfall of the wicked.
When a nation disappears before its time, this lack of *kedushah*
hurts Israel. Hashem does not always wait for its vitality to be
absorbed by Israel. When this happens Hashem is "not happy
with the downfall."

כי יחסר מעט טובה לישראל. כי ענין אבידתם הוא שהשי"ת ימשיך מדתו מזה
הטוב שהם נאחזים בו. וממילא גם מתוך לבות ישראל ישתרש זאת הטובה

97

והאומות ממילא יאבדו ואז הקב"ה אינו שש. וכמו שאמר הנביא על מעי למואב ככנור יהמו (ישעיה ט"ז י"א). היינו שדאג על טובם. והנה במצרים היה גם כן בלא זמנא (זה"ק נח ס"א ב'). כי באם נשתהו שם לא היו יכולין להגאל. כי הם בכשפיהם סגרו. וענין כשוף היינו עקשות וחוצפא כלפי שמיא. והיינו לפי שארצם היה משופע כל טוב. עד שאין עבד יכול לברוח ממצרים (מכילתא יתרו פי"ח פי"א).

As Israel has lost out on something, Hashem brings good into the world from that of the nation it was attached to, places it into the hearts of Israel, and the other nation fades away. It was not Egypt's time to be destroyed, but if Israel would have stayed longer, then they would not have been able to be saved from the corruption wrought by the magic of the Egyptians. Magic is brazen disobedience of Hashem, its users are upstarts seeking to undo the rules of nature. It was the magic of the Egyptians that made the land so good that no slave would leave from Egypt.

וענין שתפסו חכמינו ז"ל לשון עבד. היינו שאפילו עבד שהיה במצרים. לא היה ניחא דעתיה לברוח להיות חפשי בארץ אחרת. כי היה טוב לו להיות במצרים תחת עול. מלהיות חפשי בארץ אחרת. ולכן כשגאלם הקב"ה לא השגיח על כל טובם שיאבד ישישרש מלבות ישראל. לכך לא אמרו מלאכי השרת שירה (מגילה י' ב'). והנה עיקר הטוב והקדושה שנמצא בקליפת מצרים היה בתוך זה המצרי. ומשה רבינו הרגו בלא זמנא. דאיתא בזה"ק (משפטים קי"ד ב'). להפריש ערי מקלט למאן דקטיל בגין ההוא מצרי דקטלת במצרים ועל כן לא היה יכול להורגו רק בשם המפורש (שמות רבה פ"א ס' ל'). לפי שעוד היה בו קדושה. וממילא כשנהרג בשם המפורש גם לו היה תיקון. כמו שנאמר ויטמנהו בחול (שמות ב' י"ב). זהו קבורה. וקבורה היינו תיקון. כמו שנתבאר ועל זה נולד מזרעו בין ישראל ונהרג על פי בית דין. כי בן שלמית בת דברי היה בנו (מדרש תנחומא שמות ס"ט). כי בכל אומה יש מלך וכהן ואחר שיש לו כח

במדינה (עיין זה"ק יתרו ס"ז ב') כמו שנתבאר בספר מי השלוח (חלק ב'). כי בישראל נמצא מלך וכהן גדול וצדיק יסוד עולם.

Even a slave in Egypt would not want to leave, honestly believing that it was better to be enslaved in Egypt than to be free anywhere else. So when Hashem freed the Jews, the slave would not pay attention to any good that would come to the Jewish people. When Moshe killed the Egyptian, all of the spiritual essence of Egypt was in that Egyptian, as he was called "the Egyptian." Since Moshe Rabbeinu killed this Egyptian, a greater spiritual drama was playing itself out before him. This Egyptian was not merely a task master, but the spiritual center of Egypt. Moshe killed him before his time, causing that spiritual energy to be released into the world. (The *Zohar* says that Moshe was given the mitzvah to set aside cities of refuge because he killed that Egyptian before his time, and the cities prevent an accidental murderer from suffering the fate of dying before his time at the hands of the vengeful family.)

Since it was before this man's time to die, the only way Moshe Rabbeinu could kill him was with Hashem's name. Through use of the Name, the spiritual energy left the body of the man and returned to its source. Furthermore, this explains why Moshe hid his body in the sand. Moshe buried him, indicating that the lost energy found its way home, just like the body that was taken from the earth returned to the earth. The Midrash tells us this Egyptian's son was the *mekallel*, the person who cursed Hashem's name, who was the child of Shlomis bas Divri, at the end of *Parshas Emor*.

Every nation has a person who embodies the spiritual personality of the nation. This Egyptian was that person.

והנה בעוד שזו הקדושה נמצאת תחת ממשלת האומות נקרא נחש. כדמפרש
בזה"ק בגין ההוא מצרי דקטלת במצרים דתמן הוה נחש הקדמוני. ונחש הוא
דבר שמצמצם הקדושה שלא תתפשט. וכמו דמצינו ביריחו דישבה בה רחב.
ונתכנסו בה שבע אומות והיתה סוגרה של ארץ ישראל . כדאיתא במדרש
תנחומא (בהעלתך ס' י'). וכתרגומו של ויריחו סגרת ומסגרת (יהושע ו' א').
ויריחו אחידא הות בדשין דפרזלא ומתקפא בעברין דנחש. היינו גם כן שבעוד
שהיה הקדושה תחת יד האומות נקרא נחש. ורחב היתה זאת הקדושה. לכן
נשבה יהושע אח"כ (מגילה י"ד ב') שהוא היה הכובש של ארץ ישראל. ולפיכך
כאשר באו המרגלים של יהושע בחזרה. ואמרו שהיא היתה מפחדת מפניהם.
ומזה הבינו כי נתן ה' את הארץ בידם. אף כי לא ראו רק אותה. אך הבינו מזה
כי היא היתה עיקר כחם. וכאשר היא אמרה להם שיכבשו את הארץ הבינו שכל
הארץ בידם. וגם במצרים היה עיקר אמונתם במה שראו שהרג את המצרי. וזה
היה הסימן של פקד יפקד. היינו מי שיבא הפקודה לתוך לבו.

The *Zohar* refers to this imprisoned holiness, calling it "a snake."
Moreover, it describes the Egyptian who was killed as the
primordial snake. What does it mean by that? The first snake
in Gan Eden, which constricted the realm of *kedushah* through
its actions, caused the fall of mankind. A snake is something
that reduces holiness so that it cannot spread out. The Jews that
knew when Moshe killed the Egyptian, this was the sign that
Moshe would surely redeem, as he liberated the holiness that
was in "the Egyptian."

The Izhbitzer Tradition

See (ל) בית יעקב שמות, where he discusses the concept of pikod yifkod in terms of a promise of Geulah.

Practical Advice

Pikod yifkod is not a code word. It's a way of life. It's a feeling which permeates the personality, the ability to redeem the fallen, uplift the downtrodden, and revive the hearts of the depressed. We see this ability on many levels, historical, spiritual, and emotional. Can you be a pikod yifkod person? Can you lift up the spirits of those around? What role can you play to raise up your world?

פרשת יתרו

from Beis Yaakov ha-Kollel

וַיִּשְׁמַע יִתְרוֹ כֹהֵן מִדְיָן חֹתֵן מֹשֶׁה אֵת כָּל אֲשֶׁר עָשָׂה אֱלֹהִים לְמֹשֶׁה וּלְיִשְׂרָאֵל עַמּוֹ כִּי הוֹצִיא ה' אֶת יִשְׂרָאֵל מִמִּצְרָיִם (שמות י"ח א').

"Yisro, the priest of Midian, father-in-law of Moshe, heard about all that Hashem did to Moshe and Israel, His nation, when He took the Jewish people out of Mitzraim" (*Shemos* 18:1). The בית יעקב asks what is the significance of the fact that Yisro heard this?

כי מציון תצא תורה ודבר ה' מירושלם (ישעיה ב' ג'). ציון נקראו דברי תורה שאינם נקבעים בלב האדם. ואינו מרגיש טעמם ועושה אותם רק כציונים. ונראים עליו כמשא ומכל מקום מתגבר על לבו ועושה אותם. מזה תצא תורה. היינו שיישאר בלבו רשימה שיתחזק גופו להבין לאמתם איך יפעלו בהאדם.

In order to understand this concept, the בית יעקב explains the *pasuk* (*Yeshaya* 2:3): "From Tzion, Torah will come forth and the word of Hashem from Yerushalayim." What is the difference between these the Torah of Tzion versus the word of Hashem from Yerushalayim? Tzion refers to pictures, two dimensional images, as opposed to real life. A person who lives with Torah in the limited way of Tzion labors to keep Torah despite the fact

102

that he doesn't feel its relevance. From Tzion, there can come forth Torah, when a person accepts upon himself to accept the Torah despite its seeming distance from him. Yeshayahu tells us that ultimately a person will reach Torah as something relevant.

ודבר ה׳ מירושלם . ירושלם היינו יראה שלמה הטבועה בלב האדם. מזה יבא גודל תקיפות בלב האדם. ותקיפות נקרא דבר ה׳.

In the *pasuk*, "The word of Hashem from Yerushalayim," Yerushalayim means "full of awe." When a person perceives something clearly, it gives him strength.

וזה דאיתא במדרש תנחומא (יתרו ס׳ ג׳). לץ תכה זה עמלק. ופתי יערם זה יתרו. כי האדם צריך לגרש תחלה כל מיני לצנות מלבו. כדי שיהיה הלב פנוי ויוכל לקבל דברי תורה. וכדאיתא בזה"ק (בשלח מ"ז ב׳). מאן דמזמין אושפיזא ביה בעי לאשתדלא.

This is what the Midrash means by quoting *Mishlei* that "A scoffer is beaten, and the fool learns." This *pasuk* refers to Amalek (the scoffer) and Yisro (the fool). It means that people need to get rid of the scoffing from their hearts, so that they can receive the Torah. The *Zohar* says that a person who wants to host guests must prepare for them. How is this preparation done?

והנה גם עתה רצה הקב"ה שלא יעסקו ישראל עוד בעסק יציאת מצרים. כי יציאת מצרים הוא שהאדם יוצא מתרגולו שנרגל בדבריו עד שנכפף תחתיהם. כי זה היה ענין מצרים שאין עבד יכול לברוח ממצרים (מכילתא יתרו פי"ח פי"א). כי היתה ארץ מבורכת כגן ה׳. והורגלו בדברים טובים. עד שהיה טוב להם להיות עבדים במצרים ולא שרים בארץ אחרת.

Hashem wanted the Jewish people to stop dealing with the exodus from Mitzraim. Let's understand what Mitzraim means. The *Mechilta* (*Yisro* 18:11) explains that no slave was ever able to leave Mitzraim, as it was a beautiful land like Hashem's Garden and a person would rather be a slave there than a prince in another land. This means that Mitzraim represents being enslaved to a set of behaviors, even to good ones. The slavery of Mitzraim means the slavery of habituation, even to be a slave to good things, that a person cannot see any other way of life. The misery of servitude is one thing, but to favor it over anything else is something entirely different.

וכל זה הוא סור מרע.

Escaping from this type of servitude is this first step of a person's growth. We were enslaved to Mitzraim; even after leaving Mitzraim, it still followed us. We needed to be free from it.

אבל עתה היה בחפץ השי"ת ליתן תורה לישראל. ועסק יציאת מצרים היה כנגדו דבר קטן לכן שמע יתרו. כי בעת שהשי"ת מוציא כח חייתו מאיזה ענין אז הגר שומע אותו. ועל ענין זה נאמר בנבלה לגר אשר בשעריך תתננה (ראה י"ד כ"א). כי יצא החיים ממנה ואז יקבלה הגר. אבל ישראל שומעים תכף בעת החפץ :

Hashem wanted to give us the Torah, not just take us out of Mitzraim. Just getting away from Mitzraim is something small compared to receiving the Torah. Therefore, Yisro heard about leaving Mitzraim. Hashem, so to speak, tossed the idea out to the side, where Yisro picked it up.

This is why the Torah (*Devarim* 14:21) says give a *neveilah*, an improperly slaughtered animal, to the *ger* (which in simple meaning refers to a non-Jew who lives amongst you, but here means to a person who is going to convert). When Hashem takes the life out of a concept, it becomes a *neveilah*, something which is dead, bereft of life. Hashem changed the focus, and therefore the Exodus from Mitzraim became lifeless, something that could go to an outsider. As a result, Yisro heard of leaving Mitzraim, and he drew close to Hashem.

The Izhbitzer Tradition

See (יב) בית יעקב יתרו and בית יעקב הכולל וישב, בית יעקב, which further explores these ideas.

Practical Advice

Often times in our personal growth we don't realize that previous victories and struggles are impairing us from growing further. We need to move on and grow further. Don't dwell excessively on the past. It happened, it was real, but be wary of how it influences you now. Ask yourself, "Why am assuming that the way it was must be the way it is now?"

פרשת משפטים

from Beis Yaakov ha-Kollel

כִּי תִקְנֶה עֶבֶד עִבְרִי (**שמות כ"א ב'**) . איתא במכילתא (משפטים פכ"א ב').
בנמכר בבית דין על גניבתו הכתוב מדבר .והנה מתחיל באמצע הענין ולא
התחיל כי יגנב ואז הבית דין מוכרים אותו.

This week's *parsha* discusses the laws of the *eved Ivri* (Hebrew
servant). The *Mechilta* (*Mishpatim* 21:2) describes the
background of the story in the *pasuk* of the thief who was sold
for stealing. However, the *pasuk* starts the story in the middle.
The בית יעקב asks, "Why does it do that?"

אכן ענין חטא הגנבה הוא בשורש נפשו למעלה מכל תפיסת גבול עולם הזה.
וכדאיתא בלקוטי תורה (פרשת בראשית). כי אדם הראשון חטא בעץ הדעת
קודם שבא לעולם העשיה .ומה שבא לעולם הזה הוא שנמכר בגגבתו. כי עיקר
הגנבה הוא מה שידמה לאדם כי יש לו איזה קנין. הן ברכוש והן בעולם הבא.
לכן העונש מדה במדה.

The Torah does not speak about the theft, only about the
punishment. The בית יעקב explains that the first theft happened
at the very beginning of history. It took place when Adam Ha-
Rishon ate from the tree of knowledge. This all took place in a

106

supernal realm, the Garden of Eden. His punishment, which is having to enter into this world, is tantamount to being sold into slavery for his theft.

What is theft? It is a delusion of ownership; the thief believes that he owns something that doesn't belong to him. Of course, this is a fallacy, as Hashem owns everything.

כי החטא והעונש ממקום אחד הם. כי החטא עצמו הוא העונש בעולם העליון. ולכן נסתר מאדם הראשון ונכנס לספק וניטל ממנו התקיפות. כי מצד הראוי היה לו לאדם תקיפות היותר גדול שבכל העולם.

The sin itself is its own punishment. By accepting the delusion of ownership of something which he didn't own, he lost his ownership over that which he truly should own. This loss of ownership manifests itself in a sense of ownership over one's self as well. When people feel that they are not in charge of their lives, they lose the zest for living and clarity of purpose. Through this, man entered the "world of doubts," a world view of ambiguity and ambivalence.

כי כמו בעת שהסמיכה היתה נוהגת היה תקיפות להבית דין. וכדאיתא בגמרא (ר"ה כ"ה א') אתם אפילו מזידין. וכל זה היה כי הסמיכה היתה בהשתלשלות עד משה רבינו עליו השלום. והקב"ה סמך את ידיו עליו. כמו שכתוב ושכתי כפי עליך (כי תשא ל"ג כ"ב). ואם היה נמצא טעות אף באחרון שבנסמכים. אז גם לרבו היה טעות והסתר שסמך אדם כזה שיוכל לטעות. וממילא היה מגיע עד משה רבינו שסמכו השי"ת. אבל בהכרח זה היה ברצון השי"ת ואין בו טעות. כי השי"ת צופה ומביט מראש ועד סוף.

Therefore the slave is sold by the Beis Din. When there were Battei Din, they had the confidence to resolve the ambiguities of life. The בית יעקב quotes the Gemara (*Rosh Hashanah* 25a) that says that Beis Din can declare a new month and set up the calendar, even if they know that they are wrong about when the new moon actually occurred. This is because they have an unbroken chain of *semichah*, which goes back to Hashem giving *semichah* to Moshe Rabbeinu. If one of the people with *semichah* made the mistake of giving *semichah* to someone who erred, the judgment of the person who gave *semichah* to him is also called into question. This continues all the way back to Moshe Rabbeinu, to whom Hashem gave *semichah*. However, it must be that this error was what Hashem wanted. Despite the error, there is a sense of clarity that the world is not running in a helter-skelter way.

וכל שכן אדם הראשון שהיה יציר כפיו של הקב"ה. אכן לפי שנכנס להסתר ונדמה לו שיש לו איזה רכוש לכן ניטל ממנו התקיפות. וכמו שיתבאר בפרשת ויקרא.

Adam Ha-Rishon, who was Hashem's handiwork, originally felt this clarity as well. But when he stole, he fell into delusions of ownership. This delusion was accompanied by the constant fear that he was missing something.

וזה ענין המכירה כפי חסרונו. כן יוטב לפני העבד גם כן. כי הוא לא יוכל לקבל מחייתו מהשי"ת פנים בפנים רק דרך אמצעי. ומכל מקום השי"ת יאיר לנפש מישראל אף שהוא בתכלית המרחק. ועל זה ובשבעת יצא לחפשי חנם. היינו בעת שהוא עומד לפני השי"ת אז אין שום רשות שולט עליו. וכמו שנתבאר בספר מי השלוח (חלק שני).

This is why the *eved Ivri* is sold based on his his inability to make restitution. But it is for his benefit as well. The slave cannot receive his sustenance from Hashem directly, only through an intermediary, his master. However, there are times that Hashem shines a light into the soul of every Jew, even despite their distance from Him. This is why the *eved Ivri* goes free in the seventh year. This is when he stands before Hashem and no one else can rule over him.

כי בעת שהאדם עומד לפני השי"ת נגלה לו התקיפות. מאחר שהוא יציר כפיו של הקב"ה ומזרע האבות ודאי לא יעבור רצונו. כי אדם הראשון נסתר ממנו היחוס שהיא יציר כפיו. כי באם היה היחסו נגלה אז לא היה שייך שום עבודה. וכמו דאיתא בקידושין (ע"א א'). תאנא עוד אחרת היתה ולא רצו חכמים לגלותה. אבל חכמים מוסרים אותו לבניהם ולתלמידיהן פעם אחת בשבוע. ואמרי לה פעמים בשבוע. אמר רב נחמן בר יצחק מסתברא כמאן דאמר פעם אחת בשבוע. כדתניא הריני נזיר אם לא אגלה משפחות. יהיה נזיר ולא יגלה משפחות. אמר רבה בר בר חנה אמר רבי יוחנן. שם בן ארבע אותיות חכמים מוסרין אותו לתלמידיהן פעם אתת בשבוע. ואמרי לה פעמים בשבוע. אמר רב נחמן בר יצחק מסתברא כמאן דאמר פעם אחת בשבוע. כתיב זה שמי לעלם. לעלם כתיב. כי הכל ענין אחד. כי שם אדני מחייב עבודה. ומשם הויה יבוטלו כל עבודות מאחר שהשי"ת מהוה הכל. וזה צריך להסתיר. וזה גם ענין היחוס כי בהתגלותו יתבטל עבודה :

When people stand before Hashem, they develop strength of character and have clarity in life; they recognize that they are the creations of Hashem and the children of the Avos. It is this knowledge that keeps them from going against Hashem's will. In order to preserve a person's ability to choose, Hashem hid Adam Ha-Rishon's *yichus*, his identity and lineage from him.

In this way we can understand the Gemara (*Kiddushin* 17a), which discusses that both matters of *yichus* and the names of Hashem are transmitted in secrecy, and only once or twice a year. There are two four-letter names of Hashem. The name Havaya, which is never pronounced except on Yom Kippur by the Kohen Gadol, and the name of Adnus, which is said instead. The name of Adnus—which we say when we see Hashem's name —is a recognition that we must serve Hashem based on our decisions and not with the overpowering clarity of knowing Hashem, which is represented by the name Havaya.

The Izhbitzer Tradition

See מי השלוח חלק ב פרשת משפטים which also discusses the story of the eved ivri.

Practical Advice

We hear the story of the eved Ivri, we hear the story of our lives! When we say Shem Adnus ("My Master") we realize that we are here in this world, in effect, sold as slaves. We have left Hashem's presence because of our presumption. We forget who we are, and we forget who Hashem is. We relate as servants, but not as children of the Avos. We call out to Hashem, and yearn for days of illumination, that we may leave our slavery and remember who we are!

פרשת תרומה

from Beis Yaakov ha-Kollel

וַיְדַבֵּר ה' אֶל מֹשֶׁה לֵּאמֹר. דַּבֵּר אֶל בְּנֵי יִשְׂרָאֵל וְיִקְחוּ לִי תְּרוּמָה (שמות כ"ה א'-ב'). בשמות רבה (פל"ג ס' ד'). רבי זכריה פתח לך ה' הגדלה והגבורה והתפארת והנצח וההוד. הנה אלו השבחים אמר דוד המלך. בשעה שראה שהתנדבו ישראל לבית המקדש. והחל להתבונן בכח נדבתם מאין הוא.

The בית יעקב explains the beginning of this week's *parsha*, which deals with the collection of materials for and construction of the Mishkan—the travelling place in the desert to bring *korbanos*, and draw close to Hashem—by quoting the Midrash that David Ha-Melech was astounded by the collection taken up to build the Beis Ha-Mikdash. He declared, "To You, Hashem, is greatness and strength! Beauty, eternity, and splendor!"

What does this mean? David Ha-Melech began to think about the question of *nedivus ha-lev*: "How can you donate anything to Hashem? He owns everything!" This same question is: "How can you create a place for Hashem in the world if He is everywhere? How can we daven if everything that happens is what Hashem wants, and how do we serve Hashem if we are the way he wants us?"

וסדר זה השבח. לך ה' הגדלה היינו מה שספר גדולת ורוממות השי"ת שזה נקרא שמים. ומזה לא יוכל לצמוח נדבת לב באדם. כי מאחר שהאדם רואה כי הכל מה' הוא מה יוכל להתנדב. אך מצד מדת השי"ת הנקראת גבורה שנקראת ארץ והוא צמצום אורו יתברך. וידמה להאדם כי כחו עשה לו את כל. ומזה יצמח נדבת לב.

It is for this reason that David Ha-Melech exclaimed, "To you, Hashem, is greatness." David Ha-Melech thought, "When a person speaks of Hashem's greatness, it is impossible to come and give of one's self. When a person sees that everything is from Hashem, what can he give? However, when Hashem acts from the aspect of strength, He hides the fact that He is there, and then people can believe that it is their own strength that causes their achievements." This is where it is possible for people to give of themselves, as they believe that they can achieve.

ובעת שיצרך לאדם נדבת לב אז מדת הגבורה יקרה ומתגברת מאד. ומזה יבא לו נדבת לב. ועל ענין זה לא מצינו שמשה רבינו ינדב. מפני שאליו היה מפורש אור השי"ת תמיד. והנה הנביא מתאר את כבוד ה'. האוכל בשר אבירים ודם עתודים אשתה (תהלים נ' י"ג). והנה באמת להבין איך זה הוא שבח לפני כבוד השי"ת. אך המאמר יורה כי מצד בריאת השי"ת כל הברואים שום. מאחר שעל ידי כלם נעשה רצונו בעולם. כי עיקר ענין תפלה אינה באה מהתבוננות השכל. רק מידיעת החסרון.

When people need to be able to give of themselves, then Hashem acts with the attribute of strength, and the circumstances require that each person be able to call upon his inner wellsprings. Moshe Rabbeinu never gave anything to the Mishkan because he felt Hashem's Presence everywhere. David Ha-Melech described Hashem's glory as the defeat of the mighty. From Hashem's point of view, everyone is the same, merely instruments to bring His will into the world. However, *tefillah* is not contemplation of the thought that Hashem is everywhere, but the person's knowledge of what is missing in himself.

וכן כל הברואים מכירים מה שחסר להם. והשי"ת עונה להם. אך זה ההפרש בין אדם לבהמה. כי האדם מרגיש שיש לו בורא להשען עליו. וכי הוא ימלא בקשתו.

All of the creations realize that they are lacking. Hashem fills their lack, but only mankind recognizes that it is their Creator who will answer their request.

וזה הוא ענין נדבת לב. היינו ידיעת החסרון והכרת אור השי"ת. ומאלו השנים ביחד יתחייב עבודה ונדבת הלב. כי מידיעת החסרון לבדו לא יתחייב עבודה. וכמו כן מהכרת הבורא לבדו. ואלו השנים הם גדלה וגבורה. גדולה הוא הכרת רוממות ה'. ומזה לא יבא עבודה ונדבת הלב. כי מאחר שהאדם מכיר כי השי"ת הוא הבורא והפועל כל. איך יצמח בלבו לעשות שום מעשה הלא לא תקרא על שמו. וכן מגבורה שהוא צמצום והסתר גם כן לא יתחייב עבודה. אך מאלו השנים יתחייב עבודה ונדבת הלב.

This is what giving of one's self means, that people recognize both Hashem's Presence, and where Hashem creates a void. When only thinking of Hashem's Presence, a person will feel that there is no purpose in trying to do anything because Hashem is everything! If one only thinks on Hashem's concealment then there is no relevance to their actions either.

זה דאיתא בשמות רבה (פל"ד ס' א'). שדי לא מצאנוהו שגיא כח כו'. אלא שארד ואצמצם שכינתי בתוך אמה על אמה. היינו אף כי השי"ת מרומם מכל עולם הזה. מכל מקום ירצה נדבת הלב מאדם ותעלה לפני כסא כבודו.

This is the implication of the Midrash's (*Shemos Rabbah* 4:13) statement that despite the fact that Hashem fills the heavens, He constrains himself to the area of an *amah* by an *amah* (approximately 60 cm x 60 cm) so that we can serve Him. Despite the fact that Hashem is everything, He wants to deal with each person in accordance with his own circumstance.

והנה בזו הסדרה נתקשרו עשרת הדברות במעשה המשכן .(עיין זה"ק במדבר קי"ז ב'). כי שורש הבריאה הוא מדברי תורה. כמו דאיתא בזה"ק (ויקרא י"א ב'). עשרה עשרה הכף בשקל הקדש. עשרה עשרה למאי קא אתיא. אלא עשרה למעשה בראשית. ועשרה למתן תורה.

In this week's *parsha* we connect the Aseres Ha-Dibros with the Mishkan and with its creation.

At the *chanukas ha-Mishkan*, the word "ten" is mentioned twice for each Nasi's offering. The *Zohar* (*Bamidbar* 117b) asks why it is that the word "ten" is mentioned twice. The answer is that ten is for creation and ten for giving of the Torah. We know that the entire world is created based on the words of Torah. We see an interesting dynamic between the ten of creation and the ten of the giving of the Torah. This concept connects with the idea that we have been discussing. Hashem created the world, with ten utterances that He uses to maintain and sustain it, implying his "Greatness" but then He asks us to change the world by commanding us with the Ten Commandments, implying His "strength."

דהנה מצד קדושת אבותינו הנקבע בנו. לא יוכל שום נפש מישראל להפסיד. וזאת הקדושה היה שורה עלינו אף כשהיינו במצרים. וכמו שכתוב ואנכי ה' אלהיך מארץ מצרים (הושע י"ב י'). שאף גם שם היה השי"ת עמנו. אך מצד

114

האדם יכול להפסיד. ועל זה רומז המאמר אנכי ה' אלקיך אשר הוצאתיך מארץ מצרים. ונגד זה נצרך למעשים ופעולות.

Similarly, within a person's life, there are two *kedushos*. One is the *kedushah* of the forefathers that is ingrained with a person, and which no person can lose. This is the *kedushah* that has always dwelled within us, even when we were in Mitzraim. Therefore, Hoshea said, "I am Hashem, your G-d from the Land of Mitzraim." I am Hashem, Who dwelled with you there in Mitzraim. No matter where you are, I am Hashem.

This statement "I am Hashem" corresponds to the ten statements that Hashem used to create the world. There is a second *kedushah*, which is created by man's efforts to rise above their circumstance. Hashem said at the giving of the Torah, "I am Hashem who took you out Mitzraim." With this commandment, Hashem gave us the ability to do *mitzvos*, and to create a *kedushah* of our own. This corresponds to the Ten Commandments.

ולזה נתקשר בזו הסדרה ויקחו לי תרומה. הוא שהאדם ירים דעתו וימשול בשכלו על גופו. כי אף שנקבע בו קדושה צריך להרימה ולהחזיר כל טובו לבוראו ועל ענין הזה רומז מצות מעקה. כי בית מורה על קביעות. שנקבע ביה טובה בקביעות. ומזה יצמח תקיפות לאדם. ולזה צריך להגביה עיניו למעלה להפסיק השפעתו במעט צמצום שיחזירו לבוראו.

What does *terumah* mean? It means, "lift up." It tells a person that he should lift up his mind and allow it to rule over his body. Even though Hashem gives us a spiritual level which is immutable, it is still our duty to exert ourselves and achieve. This is also the meaning of the mitzvah to place a *maakeh* (fence) on the roof of house. One message of the *maakeh* is that, despite the feeling that a house gives of stability and confidence, a person must strive for more. How do we do that? By placing a fence, which means the creation of boundaries, we are able to channel ourselves properly.

וזה דאיתא בתקוני זהר (תקונא שיבסר ל"א ב'). תרומה תרי ממאה. כי הוא רומז לשני נוני"ן. הנו"ן כפופה והפשוטה. כי נון מורה על נ' שערי בינה. ומהפשוטה יוכל להסתעף שיכנס למקום שהוא נגד רצון השי"ת. וזה הכפופה שהאדם כופף וממעט מעט שלא תתפשט כל כך.

This is the meaning of the *Tikkunei Zohar*'s (*Tikkun* 17 p. 31b) statement that *terumah* is two portions of 100. This means that the number 100 can be broken up into 2x50. The letter *nun* has the numerical value of 50. Chazal often refer to understand as having "fifty gates," which associates it with the letter *nun*. However, there are two *nun*'s, the bent *nun* נ and the straight *nun* ן. Each of them has a different implication in terms of a person's understanding. The straight *nun*, also known as a stretched-out *nun*, means that we can "stretch out" and feel as if we have all of the answers. This stretching out contains an element of arrogance. In contrast, the bent *nun* means to bow over, in humility.

והנה מזה בא קדושת המשכן שנשאר בקביעות בין ישראל. כי המשכן היה התחלות המקדש. ובבית המקדש היה קדושה קבועה. כי שם לא ברכו רק ברכה אתת (תמיד ל"ב ב'). והוא אהבת עולם. כי יוצר אור לא היו צריכים לברך. כי הארות אור ה' היה מפורש לפניהם. אך אהבת עולם היו צריכים לברך. כי אהבה הוא נדבת הלב. על זה היה צריך גם שם לברר:

We spoke earlier of two *kedushos*, the inherent *kedushah*, and the *kedushah* that we create ourselves. The two *kedushos* discussed in our *parsha* are the *kedushah* of the Beis Ha-Mikdash, and the *kedushah* of the Mishkan. The word Mishkan means "dwelling," while Mikdash means "sanctify." The *kedushah* of the Mishkan is the *kedushah* that will dwell with us, never to depart. In contrast, the *kedushah* of the Mikdash begins as a result of the construction of the Mishkan. It is for this reason the Gemara (*Tamid* 23b) says that in the Mikdash only the *bracha* of *ahavas olam* was said, and the *bracha* of the "creation of light" was omitted. When we speak of the creation of light, we are referring to the relationship with Hashem as described by the ten statements with which Hashem created the world. This interaction is one of inherent *kedushah*. The *bracha* of *ahavas olam* describes the giving of the Torah, the paradigm of *kedushah*, which is created by our efforts.

The Izhbitzer Tradition

See בית יעקב שמות תרומה (ה) *and* (ה) מי השלוח (חלק א) פרשת תרומה, *which deal with similar concepts.*

Practical Advice

A common question is, that if Hashem makes existence the way He wants it, then why should we need to do anything? This parsha is that of Terumah, the imperative to raise up the world. Despite the world's innate perfection, through the parsha of Teruma, and commandment to build, we are spurred on to create more.

פרשת תצוה

from Beis Yaakov ha-Kollel

וְאַתָּה תְּצַוֶּה אֶת בְּנֵי יִשְׂרָאֵל וְיִקְחוּ אֵלֶיךָ שֶׁמֶן זַיִת זָךְ (שמות כ"ז כ). שמן וקטרת ישמח לב ומתק רעהו מעצת נפש (משלי כ"ז ט). הנה סדרה זו מתחיל בשמן וסיים בקטרת. וזה מורה על שמן וקטרת.

"Command the Jewish people that they should collect pure olive oil" (*Shemos* 27:20). The בית יעקב explains this *parsha* with the *pasuk* from *Mishlei* (27:9): "Oil and incense make the heart joyous, as does the advice of the soul of your friend," since this *parsha* starts with oil and ends with incense.

וכי מאלו השנים יבא שמחת לב האמיתית. שמן מורה על יראה. כי מורה על אור השי"ת. ובעת שיתגלה אורו יבא יראה עצומה. וכן כל היראות יתחייבו מהכרת אור השי"ת. ולכן ברכה ראשונה שבקריאת שמע הוא יוצר אור. ועל ידי שהאדם מכיר גדולת אור השי"ת. יוכל להיות טפל לשכינה ונעשה מרכבה לשכינה. כי באם אינו מכיר אור השי"ת בשלמות. אז ידמה להאדם כי יש לו איזה כח פעולה או כח טובה. ועל כסא כזו לא ישב השי"ת. כמו שנאמר היתברך כסא הוות (תהלים צ"ד ו). היינו באם הכסא מצד עצמה אומרת שיש לה איזה כח אז לא תחובר להשי"ת.

True joy comes from the balance that oil and incense teach us. Let's understand. Oil means awe, because it is used for

118

illumination. Awe comes as a result of recognition of Hashem's rulership over the world. In order to reach this understanding, we must be capable of looking at the world. When there is no light, you can't see anything. Therefore, the first *bracha* which we make before *Shema* is *Yotzer Or*, "Who creates light." Hashem gives us the illumination to investigate the world. When we recognize Hashem's greatness, how He created and sustains the world, then we have the opportunity to recognize and connect to Hashem. A person who believes that he has an importance separate from Hashem has created a false understanding that leaves no room for Hashem.

אכן קטרת מורה כדאיתא בזה"ק (שמיני ל"ז ב'). קטרת קשיר כלא כחדא. והוא שבמקום שהאדם מכיר לו שאין לו שום כח במקום הזה. אז השי"ת חולק מכבודו ליראיו. וזה נקרא קטרת. וכן כל צבאי מעלה כל אחד נברא וניתן לו כח מאת השי"ת. והוא מפני שמכיר שאין בכח הזה רק השי"ת. ולכן במקום הזה ניתן לו כבוד מהשי"ת. וזה ישמח לב האדם באם מכיר גדולת השי"ת. ועל ידי זה הוא מקבל טובה ואז הוא ברורה וישמח לבו.

Incense (*ketores*) conveys the idea of connection, of being one with Hashem (*Zohar* 37b). In fact, the word *ketores* in Aramaic means "to connect." What is the nature of this connection? It is when a person recognizes that he has no independent strength, only the strength necessary to accomplish his tasks, which Hashem has given to him. This is why the *malachim* have such great power, as they absolutely recognize Hashem. This notion of connection—the strength that comes as a result, and the thought that a person is not required to accomplish everything alone—is cause for joy. This is the joy that oil and *ketores* create.

והנה לשון ואתה שנאמר למשה רבינו רומז. כי אצלו היה אלו השנים יחד שמן וקטרת. וכמו דאיתא בזה״ק (תצוה קע״ט ב'). והנה בארון היה כל המדות חצאין. שמורה כי כל הבריאה צריכה להתאחד. ולכן לא נתפרנס הארן לגבהו. כמו שנתפרנס לארכו ולרחבו בלוחות. כמו דאיתא בגמרא (ב״ב י״ד א'). כי היה צריך להתאחד בו מעשים ורצון של ישראל עם הסכמת השי״ת. ומשה רבינו עליו השלום היה נגד זה החצי אמה שלא נתפרנס הארון לגבהו. כי הוא היה חכמת כל ישראל.

In this week's *parsha*, the first word in the first *pasuk* is "you." The Midrashim explain that the word refers to Moshe Rabbeinu. He incorporated both aspects of the oil and the incense, he embodied the selfless connection, and being filled with Hashem's light. Similarly, we see this concept from the fact that the *aron*'s measurements were two and a half *amos* long, by one and a half wide, by one and a half tall. What is the meaning of these halves? They tell us that we need to move towards unity in the world. A half is on its way to becoming a whole, but it isn't there yet. The Gemara *(Bava Basra* 14a) notes that Moshe Rabbeinu corresponded to the idea of idea as he was the wisdom of the Jewish people.

כמו שנתבאר בספר מי השלוח (פרשת תצוה). ועל ענין הזה נשארו שני שבטים ומחצה בחוצה לארץ. כי אצלם נאמר ומקנה רב היה לבני ראובן ולבני גד (מטות ל״ב א'). והוא שהיה להם קנין רב בהשי״ת שלא נצטרכו לקדושת ארץ. ומאחר כי שני שבטים ומחצה נשארו בחוצה לארץ. בררו על כלם שיש להם קנין עצום בקדושה.

The מי השלוח writes about the two and a half tribes outside of Israel, who are described as having a lot of possessions. Of what relevance is a lot of possessions with regards to the land of Israel? He explains that possessions refer to the fact that they possessed such a connection to Hashem that they didn't need to live in the land of Israel. Since these two and a half tribes stayed outside of Israel, they demonstrated that they had a great connection to spirituality, that they didn't need the life line of holiness that Eretz Yisrael is.

כי כן הוא החבור באחד עם חברו יתחבר בשנים וחצי. כמו שנתבאר בפרשת תרומה. כי לדבר אחד יביטו בשותפות. כמו המלך והפרט שיביטו לחיים בשותפות. והמלך ממשיכו לטובת הכלל והפרט ממשיכו לטובתו.

When two people get together, they become more than the sum of their parts. That is how this great *kedushah* that these tribes had came about. We see this idea from the fact that the *pasuk* initially speaks of two tribes, but then the Torah describes two and a half tribes. Similarly, when there is a partnership between a king and his subjects, the king's influence extends to each of his subjects and each subject's work benefits the king.

והנה כל הגבולים שנגבלו הקדושות כגון עשר קדושות הן (כלים פ"א מ"ו). הם מצד אהרן הכהן. אבל מצד משה רבינו עליו השלום הוא מאחד כלם.וכלם מבוררים שהם אחוזים ודבקים בה'.

The בית יעקב explains this dynamic between the whole and parts, in terms of the difference between Moshe Rabbeinu and Aharon Ha-Kohen, whose role it was to make peace between differing parties. When the Mishnah (*Kelim* 1:6) describes the different areas, this tells us there are differences to be resolved. This is an example of the world view of Aharon Ha-Kohen.

However, Moshe Rabbeinu's work was not to make peace between differing parties, but to uplift and unify all of them.

וְעַל זֶה רוֹמֵז מַה דְּאִיתָא בְּתַעֲנִית (י"א ב'). שֶׁשִּׁימֵּשׁ מֹשֶׁה כָּל שִׁבְעַת יְמֵי הַמִּלוּאִים בְּחָלוּק לָבָן שֶׁאֵין לוֹ אִימְרָא. שְׁמוֹרָה שֶׁאֵין גְּבוּל מְיוּחָד נִגְבָּל.

The Gemara (*Taanis* 11b) also makes note of this concept when it remarked that Moshe Rabbeinu served during the inaugural days in a simple white robe with no border on this. Moshe had no boundaries like that robe. Without a boundary, he could unite all of them.

כִּי נִיתַּן לוֹ הוֹד לְמֹשֶׁה וְהָדָר לִיהוֹשֻׁעַ (סִפְרֵי וְזֹאת הַבְּרָכָה פִּיסְקָא שנ"ג). הוֹד הוּא הַפְּנִימִית. וּבִפְנִימִית כָּל יִשְׂרָאֵל זַכִּים וּמְבוֹרָרִים. אֲבָל הָדָר שְׁמוֹרָה עַל מַעֲשִׂים בָּזֶה נִמְצָא מַדְרֵגוֹת.

The בֵּית יַעֲקֹב explains more about Moshe Rabbeinu by contrasting him with Yehoshua. The Midrash (*Sifrei Zos Ha-Bracha* 353) equates the quality of Moshe with *hod* and Yehoshua with *hadar*. *Hod* means internal. Deep inside, all of Israel are pure and refined. *Hadar* means on the outside, where there are things that still must be worked out, so that the beauty on the inside can emerge at the surface. Once again, Moshe Rabbeinu's trait is one of unity with Hashem, as opposed to the perspective of Yehoshua, who seeks to narrow the gap between different perspectives.

וְזֶה דְּאִיתָא בַּגְּמָרָא (ב"ב י"ב ב'). תֵּדַע דְּאָמַר גַּבְרָא רַבָּה מִילְתָא. וּמִתְאַמְּרָה הֲלָכָה לְמֹשֶׁה מִסִּינַי כַּוָּותֵיהּ.

The Gemara (*Bava Basra* 12b) explains that sometimes a great man will say something, without realizing that his words are in consonance with a *halachah* from Moshe at Sinai. The implication of the Gemara is that there are times that even we don't know the depths of what we are saying. By extension, we don't know the depths of who we are.

וכמו דאיתא בזה"ק (בראשית כ"א ב'). יעקב מית וגופיה אעלו ליה בארעא קדישא. יוסף מית גופיה לא אתקבר בארעא קדישא אלא גרמוי. משה לא האי ולא האי. כי יעקב אבינו שהיה שלם בכל צד אף לעיני בני אדם. לכן נכנס כל גופו לקבורה בארץ ישראל. ומשה רבינו מפני שלקח אשה כושית. היינו שכל מעשיו לא היו כפי דעת אנוש לכן נקבר כלו בחוצה לארץ. והוא שבירר כי כל המעשים הם טובים. ובכל מקום נמצא קדושה. והנה אף שבאמת כי בכל מקום נמצא קדושה. אכן השי"ת רצה שנקודת הקטרת יהיה דרך שמן:

The בית יעקב cites one more example to explain the nature of Moshe Rabbeinu. The *Zohar* (*Bereishis* 21b) observes that Yaakov died and was brought to the Holy Land. Yosef died and was not buried there but was brought back to Eretz Yisrael later. Moshe died outside of Israel and was not brought in at all. Why is that? Yaakov's life was basically straightforward. Hence, he entered into the Land. However, Moshe Rabbeinu's actions are difficult to understand; for example, he took a woman from Cush. Hence he was buried outside of the land. Throughout the life of Yaakov Avinu, every episode is resolved. This is not the case with the life of Moshe Rabbeinu. The בית יעקב equates the relationship between people being buried in Eretz Yisrael and whether or not their actions can be understood. When a person's life ends in burial in Eretz Yisrael, it demonstrates that his life has taken a predictable course and culminated in his reaching Eretz Yisrael. Moshe Rabbeinu's life culminates in being buried outside of Eretz Yisrael. One would think that Moshe Rabbeinu's life should have also ended in Eretz Yisorel. However, this burial spot demonstrates to us his ability to find *kedushah* anywhere—even if we wouldn't have thought so.

The Izhbitzer Tradition

See מי השלוח, who discusses the concept of the measurements of the Aron in greater detail.

Practical Advice

We are waiting for the point of Hadar, (whose grammatical root means both "beauty" and "to turn around or return") where we can see that the inherent beauty is emerging, that focal point, where retroactively everything will make sense due to our new perspective.

פרשת כי תשא

from Beis Yaakov ha-Kollel

וַיְדַבֵּר ה' אֶל מֹשֶׁה לֵּאמֹר. כִּי תִשָּׂא אֶת רֹאשׁ בְּנֵי יִשְׂרָאֵל לִפְקֻדֵיהֶם (שמות
ל' י"א-י"ב). הנה נשיאות ראש לא יהיה רק מהשי"ת לבדו. כמו שכתוב ואתה
מרום לעולם ה' (תהלים צ"ב ט'). לכן המהלך בקומה זקופה אפילו ארבע אמות
כאילו דוחק רגלי שכינה (ברכות מ"ג ב').

Hashem wanted to lift us up and therefore elevated us through
divrei Torah. Through them a person can reach the truest
pleasure in life. In fact, any elevation in the life of a Jew comes
through the words of Torah. This is the meaning of the word
of David Ha-Melech (*Tehillim* 92:9): "Raise up your heads
and open the gates, let in the King of glory." The gates we are
speaking of are the gates to the soul; when we can open them,
we receive Hashem's light. When the soul's gates open, all of
Israel will be lifted up as a result.

כי מה שנתכנה השי"ת כאן מלך הכבוד הוא. כי ענין כבוד הוא שלא יצרך לזולתו.
לכן נקרא השי"ת מלך הכבוד שכל הכבוד שלו. ויוכל להנחילו גם לבריותיו. ועל
זה מברכין על חכמי ישראל ברוך שחלק מחכמתו (ברכות נ"ח א').

What does it mean Hashem is "the King of Glory"? It means He doesn't need anyone or anything else. He alone owns everything, including all of the glory. He can give it to whomever He chooses, hence the blessing on a great sage of Israel (*Brachos* 58a): "who has imparted a portion of His wisdom."

כי ענין חלק הוא חלק גמור בטובת עין. וכמו דאיתא בגמרא (פסחים ח' א'). למה צדיקים דומין בפני שכינה כנר בפני האבוקה. ולא קאמר כנר בפני השמש. דשרגא בטיהרא מאי אהני (חולין ס' ב'). אך כנר בפני האבוקה כי נר הוא חלק מאבוקה. והוא כי האדם לא יוכל ליתן טובה לחברו בטובת עין. כי מאחר שגם לו נמדד ונחלק טובה בגבול. ולכן מה שנותן לחברו מחסר מחלקו. מה שאין כן השי"ת מאחר שהמקור היא שלו לכן נותן בטובת עין. ולכן הרואה חכמי אומות העולם מברך ברוך שנתן מחכמתו. כי להם נותן כמבתר כתפוי.

What is the meaning of "gave a portion"? It means to be made a partner, and this portion was given generously. For example, the Gemara (*Pesachim* 8a) asks, "Why are the righteous compared to the Shechinah as a candle is compared to a torch?" The fire of the candle is a portion of the fire of the torch. A person can't normally give to his friend with complete generosity because he's still always measuring what he has. He assumes that whatever he gives, he will have less remaining. Hashem, on the other hand, is the source of everything, and therefore gives freely, as He'll never run out.

והנה בזו הסדרה מראה הקב"ה נשיאות ראשם של ישראל. כי נשיאות ראש לא יוכל לבא רק על ידי כשלון. כי אף שצדיקים נקראו כל ישראל. אך התנשאות הוא ממקום שבעלי תשובה עומדין. וכמו שנתבאר בספר מי השלוח (חלק שני על ברכות ל"ד ב'). על מאמר הגמרא כל הנביאים כולן לא נתנבאו אלא לבעלי תשובה. ולזה צריך להיות על ידי כשלון להראות שנפשו גדול מאד. וכמו שנתבאר שם.

126

In this *parsha*, we see how Hashem "lifts up the head of Israel." The only time you need to "lift" is when something has fallen. A person grows when there has been failure and he is then lifted up. Even righteous people, who are also called "all of Israel," grow through failure. How are we lifted up? The strength comes from what Gemara calls "where *baalei teshuvah* can stand," the reservoir of energy that allows someone far away from Torah to return to it. Similarly, the מי השלוח explains the Gemara that the prophets could only prophecy to *baalei teshuvah*, to mean that when a person has failed, then, we see the true greatness of his soul.

ועל זה מורים הקרני הוד שנתנו למשה שהוא על ענינים כאלה. שלא היה יכול להאמר בפירוש התנשאותם כמבואר. כי כל התנשאות אינו אלא על ידי כשלון ונסיון. ודבר זה אינו יכול להאמר מפורש. כי בענין כזה נסתר דעת המפורשת מהאדם וזה ענין גדול יותר מדבר הברור.

Similarly, we see the concept of growth catalyzed by failure in the rays of light that came from Moshe's face. The *pasuk* says that "He didn't know about them." The image of light emanating from someone who is unaware of them parallels a person whose spiritual growth is taking place, although he is unaware of what is taking place. These moments of growth from failure cannot be spoken about at the time they occur; elevation only comes through stumbling and trials. These moments happen when we aren't cognizant of them. At those moments, man's knowledge is hidden from him; they can be described as "he didn't know."

כי בפרשת משפטים (כ"ג י"ז) נאמר. אל פני האדון ה'. וכאן נאמר את פני ה' אלהיך. והוא כמו שנתבאר בספר מי השלוח (חלק שני). על פסוק יאר

פניו אתנו סלה. וזה שבקש משה רבינו אחר החטא כשנאמר לו ושלחתי לפניך
מלאך. ומלאך מורה על יראה. כי בפרשת משפטים (כ"ג כ') כשנאמר לו. הנה
אנכי שלח מלאך לפניך. הסכים משה רבינו עליו השלום. כי שם היה קודם
החטא ואז הסכים להתנהג ביראה מפני השי"ת. אכן אחר החטא כשנאמר
ושלחתי לפניך מלאך. התפלל משה ואמר ראה אתה אמר אלי העל את העם הזה
ואתה לא הידעתני את אשר תשלח עמי כי אחר החטא לא נסתפק במה שהשי"ת
ינהגם מעתה ולהבא ביראה. רק שיראה אהבתו כי גם בשעת החטא היו דבוקים
ברצונו. וזה שאמר וראה כי עמך הגוי הזה. נגד שאמר לו הקב"ה ראיתי את
העם הזה. והוא שיראה אהבתו מעומק איך הוא. ונגד זה רומזין הקרני הוד.

In *Parshas Mishpatim*, the *pasuk* says, "you will go to the face
of the Master, Hashem," but in our *parsha*, it says, "the face of
Hashem, your G-d." The מי השלוח explains that when Moshe
Rabbeinu pleaded with Hashem after the sin of the Golden
Calf, Hashem said, "I'll send a *malach* before you." *Malach*
implies awe and distance, and to that, Moshe agreed. Before the
sin, Moshe had agreed that the way to guide Israel was through
awe before Hashem. But after the sin, Moshe said, "You said to
me, 'Bring out this nation,' and now I don't know what I should
do." Before the sin, Moshe felt that awe would not be enough for
Israel to connect to Hashem. It would only be through feeling
His love. Even during the sin, could they feel connected to His
will. Moshe said, "See this nation," and Hashem responded,
"I saw the nation," demonstrating how deep His love is. The
demonstration of love came from the rays of light that came
from Moshe's face, of which he was unaware.

דאיתא במדרש תנחומא (כי תשא ס' ל"ז) ארבעה טעמים עליהם. כמו שנתבאר
שם מנין זכה משה לקרני ההוד. אמרו ז"ל מן המערה שנאמר והיה בעבר כבדי
ושמתיך בנקראת הצור. נתן הקב"ה כף ידו עליו. ומשם זכה לקרני ההוד. והוא

128

שגם ממה שהשי"ת מסתיר הדעת מן האדם .זה עצמו יאר לו בעומק כי אז רצון השי"ת לנשאו. ויש אומרים שבשעה שהיה הקב"ה מלמדו תורה. מנצוצות שיצאו מפי השכינה נטל קרני ההוד. כי מהדברים שאין ביכולת לפרשם נגד דעת האדם ועוד נשאר רצון אצל הקב"ה. וזה האיר בתוך לבו ובא לו תקיפות וקרני הוד.

The Midrash (*Tanchuma Ki Tissa* 37) explains that there were four reasons why he received the beams of light. When Moshe pleaded with Hashem to save Israel, He asked Hashem "to show me Your face." Hashem responded to Moshe that he should stay in a cave as He passed by, and He would cover His hand over Moshe. Moshe was hidden in the cave, and when he emerged, he had rays of light coming from him. This means when Hashem hid something from his understanding, he emerged with greater understanding.

When Hashem taught Moshe the Torah, the sparks of the Shechinah made the rays. This refers to things that you can't properly express, that we can't understand. That which Moshe understood entered his heart, but those things he could not encircled his head as rays of light.

ורבי שמואל בר נחמן אמר. הלוחות ארכן ששה טפחים. ורחבן ג' טפחים. והיה משה מחזיק בב' טפחים. והקב"ה בב' טפחים וטפחים ריוח באמצע. משם נטל משה קרני ההוד. הוא לפי שבשעת שהיה משה לומד מפי הקב"ה. אז בשעת מעשה היה דעתו אחוז בדעת השי"ת . אף כי אח"כ לא נשאר בו בלתי כפי דעתו. אבל בשעת למודו היה חבור לדעתו עם דעת הקב"ה. ומזה בא לו קרני ההוד. והוא שהאיר לו כי לעולם לא יעזוב הקב"ה את ישראל.

Rav Shmuel ben Nachman said that the *luchos* were six *tefachim* long by three *tefachim* wide. Hashem held two *tefachim*, Moshe held two *tefachim*, and there were two *tefachim* left in the middle, from which the rays of light were formed. Moshe Rabbeinu's grasp, literally and figuratively, was not of the entire Torah. There were three parts to the *luchos* described in the Midrash, the part Moshe was holding, the part Hashem was holding, and the part in the middle. The process of Hashem teaching Moshe the Torah was described as being "given" the *luchos*. He was "connected" to Hashem through the *luchos*, but he grasped only part of it. This demonstrates that he didn't comprehend everything he had learned, but he did have a connection with Hashem. The part of the *luchos* that he did not grasp formed the rays of light, showing the connection between Hashem and Israel.

רב שמואל אמר עד שמשה כותב את התורה. נשתייר בקולמוס קמעא והעבירו על ראשו וממנו נעשו לו קרני ההוד. מורה גם כן שאין יוכל להאמר מפורש. אך כח הרצון גבר ממה שיוכל להאמר מפורש וזה שאמר משה וראה כי עמך הגוי הזה. וכי יעלה על הדעת שחס ושלום הקב"ה אינו רואה.

Rav Shmuel said that when Moshe wrote the Torah, there was some ink left on the quill, as it was passed over his head. These leftovers gave him the rays of light. This is an effort to describe something that can't be expressed in words, try as we may. Hence, Moshe said, "Look that this nation is Yours." He didn't mean to sound as if Hashem couldn't see. Moshe couldn't express what he had wanted to say.

אלא כי השי"ת מתנהג עם ישראל במדת עתיק יומין. והוא כמי שגדול מדבר והקטן אינו מבין. ויש מדה הנקראת זעיר אפין והוא כמו אחד שמדבר עם חברו. והקטן עומד מצדם והם מקטינים דבורם שגם הקטן יבין. ואף כי למעלה אין בלתי אחד. אך מדבור השי"ת יעשה בריה מיוחדת שרצון הקב"ה מופיע עליו.

וממדת זעיר אפין יתחייב שגם פרטי נפשות יבינו. וזהו וראה שגם אנחנו נבין
עומק העמוק. וזהו עיקר נשיאות ראש שאינו מצד האדם רק מה׳. וזהו כי תשא
את ראש בני ישראל לפקדיהם.

Hashem knows that Israel is His Nation. But Hashem interacts with Israel in two ways. One is the way an adult speaks to a child who doesn't understand. Then there are times when Hashem interacts with Israel the way a person speaks with their friend and a child is with them. So they speak in a way that even the child understands. However, neither way actually describes Hashem; it is merely what Hashem wants to express at that time.

What was taking place at that moment was Hashem interacting with them as children. Moshe was asking Hashem to interact with Israel as an adult speaking in front of a child in a way that they all understand. In the aftermath of the Egel Ha-Zahav, Moshe wanted Hashem to reveal the deeper perspective, that failures are opportunities for Israel to grow. Hence the *parsha* begins with the concept of "lifting of the head," in which Hashem opens our eyes to this empowering fact.

The Izhbitzer Tradition

See מי השלוח חלק שני יאר פניו אתנו, which discusses the facets of love and awe. See מי השלוח חלק שני ברכות לד which examines the connection of the prophets to teshuvah.

Practical Advice

In this parsha, Hashem teaches us how he desired to lift us up from the failures, and from our smallness in life. We can't fathom what *is being worked out when we are not paying attention, when we are so focused on how something is not going our way. In trying moments, try to pause to reflect on the fact that so much more is happening, and much like Moshe Rabbeinu, you are not aware of the light shining from your face and in your life.*

פרשת ויקהל

from Beis Yaakov ha-Kollel

וַיַּקְהֵל מֹשֶׁה (שמות ל"ה א'). כי כה אמר ה' לסריסים אשר ישמרו את שבתותי ובחרו באשר חפצתי ומחזיקים בבריתי. ונתתי להם בביתי יד ושם טוב מבנים ומבנות (ישעיה נ"ו). ענין סריס הוא שאינו יכול להוציא דבר מפורש לפועל.

Moshe assembled the children of Israel" (*Shemos* 35:1). The בית יעקב explains this beginning of the *parsha* that starts with the commandment to keep Shabbos. It continues with the building of the Mishkan, with a promise that Hashem makes through his prophet *Yeshaya* (56) to those who are *sarisim*, if they keep Shabbos, do what Hashem asks, and keep Hashem's *bris*. What is the connection? Let's understand. A *saris* is someone who is incapable of having children. To be a *saris* literally means to be unable to bring something into reality.

וכן הוא גם בתפלה אשר לא תפעול מפורש לעיני האדם. ומכל מקום כוונה טובה לא תאבד חס ושלום. אכן ממעשים כאלו יעשה בית תפלה אשר הבית הזה יתפלל מעצמו תמיד.

This *saris* experience comes also in the form of *tefillos* that seem unanswered. A person who prays invests his hopes and dreams into his *tefillos*. When these don't materialize, they have a *saris* quality to them. It is from these unanswered hopes and failed attempts to bring something into the world, which Hashem used to create the Beis Ha-Mikdash, a place in which prayer never ceases. (Hence Yeshaya says afterwards, that that all of the *sarisim* have a place in His House, and they will come to His House, which is the central place of all prayer.)

וכן היה אחר חטא העגל שהיה בלבם צעקה.

Let's understand the connection to our *parsha*. Since this *parsha* follows *Ki Tissa*, which deals with the sin of the Golden Calf, it is about the aftermath of the sin, the ultimate failure. In this post-Golden Calf world, there remains a feeling of guilt and emptiness and, as a result, an unexpressed cry in the heart of every Jew that remains forever.

כי זה נקרא בחרו ולא קרבו שלדעת האדם לא נתקרב. מזה יצא בנין המשכן. וכמו שנתבאר פרשת אחרי מות.

A person has within him a desire to be close to Hashem that can never materialize. The initial desire of the Jewish people to be close to Hashem was created by Matan Torah and the giving of the *luchos*. The ability to achieve this closeness was lost with the sin of the Golden Calf and subsequent destruction of the *luchos*. However, this desire for closeness remained in the hearts of all of Israel; because of the Golden Calf, the seeds for Mishkan were planted in their collective heart.

וזה ענין שומר שבת כי בשבת אין כח האדם פועל. וזהו שישבות מחמת רצון ה'. וכל זה אחר כשלון שיעבור על האדם.

Here is one reason we are commanded to stop doing creative work on Shabbos. We rest because Hashem commanded us to stop trying to achieve, for we are living in the aftermath of our collective failure.

וכמו שמצינו בדוד המלך עליו השלום. אחר כי מה' היה שימנה את ישראל. כדי שאחר כך יצא לפועל בנין הבית.

The same concept is evident when David Ha-Melech counted the Jewish people and a plague ensued. Hashem wanted the people to be counted, in order to create the circumstances that would produce the Beis Ha-Mikdash. The only way that that construction could begin was to awaken the desire for closeness as a result of David Ha-Melech's failure.

וזה דאיתא בגמרא (שבת קי"ח ב'). כל המשמר שבת כהלכתה אפילו עובד ע"ז כדור אנוש מוחלין לו. שנאמר אשרי אנוש יעשה זאת וגו' מחללו.אל תקרא מחללו אלא מחול לו. כי ענין החטא הוא שידמה לאדם שיש לו איזה רכוש בפני עצמו מבלעדי ה'. וזה ענין מחלל שבת. כי בחול שולט השי"ת במדת זעיר אפין. והוא שכל העולמות ישפילו לקבל כחם מעולם הזה.

Let's understand the relationship between failure and Shabbos. The Gemara (*Shabbos* 118b) teaches that those who keep Shabbos, even if they serve idols like the generation of Enosh, will be forgiven. The Gemara cites a *pasuk*, "Happy is Enosh [also translated as 'the man'] who does this, who keeps from violating Shabbos." The Gemara says, "Don't read violation (מחללו), read it מחול לו. What is sin really about? The deepest part of any sin is the assumption that you can own something outside of Hashem.

Violating Shabbos means the belief that your efforts will give birth directly to results. During the week, Hashem runs the world by making certain that all of creation must lower itself to its sustenance.

וכמו כן תמיד כל קבלות האדם מדומם ומצומח ומחי. שהאדם ישפיל כחו לקבל והדברים האלה יגביהו כהם. ואם לא ימתין האדם עד שהדבר תגביה אליו. אז נקרא שאוכל עפר כמו שהוא. וזהו ונחש עפר לחמו (ישעיה ס"ה כ"ה).

This is why we receive our nutrition from vegetation and living beings. They are lower life forms than man, and man must lower himself to receive the nutrients from these things and take energy out from them. However, there are things that are too far away for us to derive sustenance from it.

וכמו כן האוכל מאכלות אסורות והוא שאינם נמסרים לאדם. רק הם מושכים האדם לתכונותיהם. זה נקרא מחלליה. כי אינו ממתין עד שיתמלא החלל אשר בינו ובין הדבר שרוצה לקבלה. רק דולג החלל וההפסק שבינו לבינה. אכן כל זה הוא למעשה אשר לא יוכל האדם לפעול ביום השבת. אבל הראיה היא מפורשת בימי השבת יותר מבימי החול. ויכול לתקן בשבת שיהיה מחול לו הכל.

Forbidden foods, because their lower spiritual status, cause man to descend spiritually. Eating these types of food is called a "desecration" (*mechallelehah* comes from the root *chalal*, which means "hole," or "gap"). This is because the person does not wait until the gap is closed between himself and the thing he wants to receive. If he waits, there will be some way to access the life energy from those things. Instead of waiting, however, the person jumps over the gap; therefore, the violation is called a *chillul*, emphasizing the inappropriateness of the person's partaking in the pleasure before he should. This is part of the mystery of non-action on Shabbos. Through our inaction, we clear our mind. Our vision is clearer on Shabbos than during the week; our goals become clearer to us. Once we are exposed to this clarity, we can repair everything that has gone wrong. This is why someone who keeps Shabbos will be forgiven for all of his sins.

The Izhbitzer Tradition

The Izhbitzer Rebbes often speak about what happens when you aren't active. See ספר הזמנים הגדה של פסח, which describes the benefits of inactivity.

Practical Advice

Sometimes we are driven by the furious feeling that we need to do "something" to react to a situation. Shabbos teaches us that doing something isn't always the correct course of action.

פרשת פקודי

from Beis Yaakov ha-Kollel

אֵלֶּה פְקוּדֵי הַמִּשְׁכָּן מִשְׁכַּן הָעֵדֻת (שמות ל"ח כ"א). ענין שנמנה כל
הצטרכות המשכן. והוא להראות כי יקר בעיני השי"ת ממונן של ישראל וחס
עליו. ואף כי עוד יכול להתוסף יופי עד אין שיעור. מכל מקום כשנתבררו
ישראל שנמצא בהם נדבות לב. אז מה שנשאר להם היה יקר בעיני השי"ת
יותר מאלו היה במשכן. וזה שנאמר משכן העדת שרומז אף במקום שהעדות
היינו הבירור. הוא רק בעומק שוכן ואינה מבורר לפי ראות עין. כמו עתה
שכמה שישראל מוציא מברר השי"ת שהכל היה להרבות כבוד שמים. כמו
שכתוב ונגשיך צדקה (ישעיה ס' י"ז). כל זה יתברר לעתיד.

The בית יעקב explains the phrase "the account of the Mishkan
of testimony" (*Shemos* 38:21), which begins this week's *parsha*.
What is it testifying to? While all of the expenditures that the
Jewish people made are dear to Hashem, most important thing
was that they displayed a strong willingness to give. This feeling
was even more pleasing to Hashem than the Mishkan itself. It
is called the Mishkan of testimony, a place where this testimony
has been realized. The process of giving to the Mishkan brought
to light the fact that each person has a deep desire to give.
Through this experience, they all learned about perfecting the
way of giving. Each person's act of giving was revealed as a way
of increasing the honor of Hashem.

וממילא כשיתברר אז יהיה זה גדול מאד. יותר ממה שהיו ישראל נותנים במקום
שהיו יודעים ברור שהוא רצון השי״ת. ועל זה יקבל שכר כפול. כי בשעה
שמבורר לפני אדם שנותן לכבוד שמים אז נותן בשמחה. ואם אינו מבורר אז
נותן בעצבות ולכן יקבל שכר יותר.

In the future, we will understand the greatness of every action
that we have performed. Hashem has his greatest joy from us
(and consequently gives us the greatest reward) when we figure
out what He wants, even though it may not be obvious. This
is part of the greatness of the act of giving engendered by the
Mishkan. If Israel knew exactly what they were giving for, then
they would give in happiness. On the other hand, when they
didn't really know what they were giving for, there was a feeling
of loss (as they looked at the loss of their money); their giving
was accompanied with a feeling of sadness, and because it was
difficult for them, they would be rewarded even more.

וכן אריכת הגלות כשלא נגלה הקץ קשה יותר מאלו היה נגלה. כמו גליות
הראשונים ולכן לעתיד יהיה לזה שכר גדול.

Similarly, the Midrash explains that this last exile, the exile
of Rome, seems to have no end—unlike the previous exiles.
Therefore it is harder to live with than an exile whose end we
know is coming, even if we don't know when. As a result, our
reward will be greater as well.

והנה בהקמת חצר המשכן לא נאמר כאשר צוה ה' את משה. והוא על ענין כמו
שנתבאר בספר מי השלוח (חלק א' פקודי). כי כאשר צוה ה' מורה שבכל מה
שעשה היה מאמר השי״ת מפורש נגד עיניו. וכיון שהקים המשכן נפסלה כל
המדבר לדבור (תנחומא בא ס' ה').

139

The בית יעקב quotes מי השלוח, who poses the question: Why doesn't the Torah say "as Hashem commanded" when the courtyard of the Mishkan was assembled He answers that when the Torah says "as Hashem commanded," it was immensely clear that B'nei Yisrael were performing Hashem's will. However, once the Mishkan was set up, one could no longer hear Hashem's voice outside of the Mishkan—despite the fact that inside the Mishkan, it could be heard. When you could hear Hashem, His commandments were compelling and clear, but once you left the Mishkan, it was no longer so clear.

והענין בזה כי בבגדי כהונה נאמר שבע פעמים כאשר צוה ה'. כי לשון צוה ה' מורה שהיה מבורר מראש ועד סוף. ולכן בבגדי כהונה היה יכול להאמר כאשר צוה ה'. כי תכף בשעת עשיה היה ניכר איזה בית ידור. ואיזה מלבוש ילבש. ולכן היה ניכר הקדושה מהם מפורש.

We see the same thing regarding the clothing of the *kohanim*, about which the Torah says, "as Hashem commanded" seven times. There we could understand very clearly what Hashem wanted from the beginning to the end: what to put on and where things would be placed. Therefore, it was appropriate to say, "as Hashem commanded."

וכן בהקמת המשכן אז נתברר איזה קרש יעמוד בקדשי הקדשים ואיזה בחוץ וכן השלחן באיזה צד יעמוד לצפון ובאיזה לדרום. ולכן באלו השנים נאמר כאשר צוה ה'. כי היה ניכר כח תשוקות ישראל. ומילוי הקדושה איך תמלא תשוקתם. אבל בשעת עשייתם לא נאמר. לפי שאז לא היה מבורר איזה קרש יעמוד בצפון ואיזה בדרום וכן כלם. ולא היה ניכר כח הקבלה וכח ההשפעה איך יתאחדו. ולכן גם בשעה גמר ההקמה שאז נתמלא כל כלי הקבול. וכמו בשעתא דזווגא לית ניכר בין המשפיע והמקבל. לפי שאז נתמלא כלי הקבלה. לכן לא נאמר כאשר צוה.

When the Mishkan was assembled, it was made clear which planks would go on the inside of the Kodesh Kodashim, and which would go on the outer wall; or which side of the *shulchan* would go north and south. Therefore the Torah said, "as Hashem commanded" with regards to these items. The power of the Jewish people's desire for Hashem was certainly evident. They wanted to know what He wants, and as a result He fulfilled their heart's desire and revealed to them where to put each one of the boards and the *shulchan*. However, when the *shulchan* and boards were made, it wasn't clear where they went. This is because the people of Israel were confused regarding the act of giving. Hence, it didn't say, "as Hashem commanded." It wasn't clear what Hashem wanted from them with these Mishkan pieces, until the end of the process of giving and building the Mishkan. However, after the Mishkan was assembled, the *pasuk* no longer uses the words "as Hashem commanded." This means that once the Mishkan was completed, we could no longer hear the command of Hashem.

The Izhbitzer Tradition

See פרשת פקודי (חלק א) מי השלוח, which is cited above, and בית יעקב שמות פקודי (נו), which discusses the ideas in greater detail.

Practical Advice

As the pieces fall into place, it becomes clear what we have to do, and we see what Hashem wants. Then the walls are assembled, *and we feel as if we're on the outside of the Mishkan and can't feel Hashem's presence; we don't know what we're doing. As the parsha and Sefer ends, we know we must look for Him in the wide world, the avodas ha-korbanos.*

פרשת ויקרא

from Beis Yaakov ha-Kollel

וַיִּקְרָא אֶל מֹשֶׁה (ויקרא א' א'). קריאה הוא ענין תשוקה. כמו שכתוב והיה טרם יקראו (ישעיה ס"ה כ"ד). ומשה היה הכלי המוכנת להקריאה הזאת. כי לא היה נמצא בו שום תשוקה לעניני עולם הזה. כי שמו מורה עליו כי מן המים משיתהו (שמות ב' י').

"Hashem called to Moshe" (*Vayikra* 1:1). This call to Moshe means that Hashem desired Moshe and Israel. Just as the *pasuk* says, "Even before you call, I will answer." There is such love between Hashem and the Jewish people that He is attentive to the needs of the people even before they call. Moshe was the vessel that was predisposed for this job of listening to the call of Hashem.

He was removed from desire for things of this world, as is evidenced by his name, which means withdrawn from the water, meaning physicality.

והנה בהסדרה הזאת נוסף להתורה ענין הקרבונות. כי עד זאת הסדרה היה עניני תורה. ועתה נוסף לאדם כי תפלתו תוכל להסתעף על מעשים ופעולות שיעזרו לתפלתו. כי קרבן הוא ענין תפלה. כי באמת בכל מעשה המצוה יש כוונה עמוקה שאין בכח האדם להשיגה.

In this *parsha* we are introduced to the idea of *korbanos*. Until this point the Torah spoke about instruction and wisdom. From this point on, the Torah will help us to uplift our *tefillos* through the understanding of the *korbanos*. Each *korban* contains an idea of *tefillah* within it.

כי באם היה בכח האדם להשיג עומק הכוונה היה די לו הכוונה לבדה. כי במעשה לא יסכון גבר לה'. כמו שכתוב האוכל בשר אבירים ודם עתודים אשתה (תהלים נ' י"ג). אך כי האדם לא יוכל להשיג עד תכליתה של הכוונה. לכן יצרך מעשים ופעולות שיעזרוהו להכניס כח עבודה בקביעות גם בהגוף. והנה לאשר יש באדם נפש החיוני והשכלי. ובאם יחטיא האדם את המטרה בשכלו לבד. נגד זה מועיל תפלה ולא יצרך לפעולות. אך לאשר נמצא באדם כח הבהמיות בהסתרה ושכחה. שיוכל לשכוח ולומר אני הוא וכחי ועוצם ידי עשה לי את כל. וזה הכח מההסתר והשכחה יוכל להסתעף על המעשה. נגד זה נתן הקב"ה עבודה גם כן בכח פעולות הגוף. וכמו שמבאר הרמב"ם הקדוש ז"ל בספר המורה (ח"ג פמ"ה מ"ו). שלפי שהיו מורגל להקטיר לע"ז לזה ניתן להם מצות קרבנות. ירצה בזה כי באם לא היה ביכולת האדם להסתעף מחשבותיו נגד השי"ת. היינו שלא יוכלו לבא עד על הפעולה.

In every mitzvah there is a deep *kavanah*, an intent that is impossible for man to fathom. If a person could understand the importance of each mitzvah, then its intrinsic idea would be sufficient. He would not need to do anything more. However, a person does not understand, and he therefore needs actions to help him bring *avodah* to the body. We know that a person has an animating soul and an intellectual soul. Should a person sin with his mind alone, *tefillah* could repair the problem, without any need for action. But a person's animal soul has strength in the physical world, but with this influence can also come darkness and loss of memory. It can give a person the ability to act, but it can also cause a person to forget and say, "I have achieved by myself, without Hashem." Therefore, Hashem requires that we use our physical power and the physical world to act in our service of Him. It is for this reason, the Rambam explains, that people used to sacrifice animals, wine, and grain to idols, which is why we have the mitzvah of *korbanos*, which looks like the same activity. The same faculty can be used for Hashem, or against Him.

אז לא היה מהצורך לעבוד את ה' רק במחשבה ובתפלה. אבל מכוון שיכול לעשות דבר נגד השי"ת במעשה פועלת. אז צריך לעבוד את ה' גם כן במעשים ופעולות. וכעניין שנאמר ולא צויתים ביום הוציא אותם מארץ מצרים על דברי עולה וזבח (ירמיה ז' כ"ב). ואף כי באמת נצטוו על הקרבנות אך כי מצד השי"ת לא יתחייב לאדם שום פעולה רק מצד האדם.

There would be no need to serve Hashem except in thought and prayer. But because people can act against Hashem, so we need to serve him with our actions also. This is the meaning of Yirmiyahu's complaint (7:22), "I never commanded you to bring *korbanos* in your ascent from Egypt." Even though we were commanded to bring *korbanos*, they aren't for Hashem; they are for us, to give us actions to correct our corruption of action.

והנה התחילה התורה לסדר דברי תורה על מעשים ופעולות. וכמו שבפרשת יתרו נאמרו דברי תורה בכלל. ואח"כ יצא פרשת משפטים פרטיים. וכמו שנתבאר שם. כן אחר זה הסדרה יצא פרשת צו. והוא נגד עשרת הדברות. ונגד דיבור אנכי נאמר תורת העולה:

The Torah begins to teach us about the *korbanos* in the same order that we learn about the Aseres Ha-Dibros—the Ten Commandments. In *Parshas Yisro* we learn the *klalim*, principles, but in *Parshas Mishpatim* we learn the details. In this *parsha*, we begin to learn the principles of *korbanos*, and in subsequent *parshios* we'll learn the details. In the same vein, the first principle of Torah we learn is *Anochi*, the all-encompassing statement of understanding and belief. This week the first principle of *korbanos* that we learn about is the *olah*, which is also an all-encompassing statement; how all our are involved in serving Hashem.

The Izhbitzer Tradition

See (יא) בית יעקב ויקרא, where he discusses similar themes.

Practical Advice

In this week's parsha, we learn how Hashem called to us to begin our avodah in the physical world. When you say the korbanos before davenning, or are learning sefer Vayikra, try to remember how each korban is a story of avodas Hashem.

פרשת צו

from Beis Yaakov ha-Kollel

וַיְדַבֵּר ה' אֶל מֹשֶׁה לֵּאמֹר. צַו אֶת אַהֲרֹן וְאֶת בָּנָיו לֵאמֹר זֹאת תּוֹרַת הָעֹלָה
(ויקרא ו' א'-ב'). טעמו וראו כי טוב ה' (תהלים ל"ד ט'). הענין הוא כי בעולם
הזה המטעים את חברו יטעימו מגוף הטובה. אבל המראה את חברו מראהו רק
הגוון. אבל השי"ת לפי שעיקר הטובה הוא כשהאדם רואה כי רק לה' הכל. לכן
גם בהטעם אין לאדם רק ראיה.

Hashem spoke to Moshe, "Speak to Aharon and his sons, saying
this is the Torah of the *olah*" (*Vayikra* 6:1-2). The *parsha* speaks
of the *olah*, but then it discusses the *terumas ha-deshen*, the
collection and burning of the leftovers the night following the
offering of the *korban*.

The בית יעקב explains the opening of this week's *parsha* with
the *pasuk* in *Tehillim* (34:9): "Taste and see that Hashem is good."
When a person wants to give someone a taste of something, it
comes from the very body of the object. But when Hashem
wants to show them something, it is just the outside appearance.

וזהו פרשת צו שנאמרה אחר פרשת ויקרא כדוגמת לילה ויום. שבלילה נחתם
כל מה שעשה האדם ביום יקבע בלילה בלא דעתו. באפיסת כח בחירתו יקבע
יחד שלא תמוט.

Parshas Tzav, which comes after *Vayikra*, is like night following day. We learn about the *terumas ha-deshen*, which follows the *olah*. This relationship describes how to concretize the dreams and aspirations of *Parshas Vayikra*. What happens during the day is ingrained into the person, made permanent, without his knowledge. When a person exerts himself in order to accomplish something, that is what transforms an idea into a conscious choice. Night is a time when the waking mind is not functioning. This is the time when inspiration is processed and made a part of the persona.

וכן בזו הסדרה נקבע קדושת הקרבנות בלבות ישראל. כי פרשת ויקרא מורה על תשוקה. וזאת הסדרה מורה על קביעות בלב כל התשוקות שהאדם משתוקק ומקבל טובה ונקבע בו. כי בזמן שבית המקדש קיים מזבח מכפר על אדם. עכשיו שלחנו של אדם מכפר עליו (חגיגה כ"ז א'). כי שלחן הוא שהאדם מקבל טובה ומעלה אותה שמדומם יכנס לצורת אדם.

This *parsha* deals with concretizing the concepts of the *korbanos* into the hearts of the Jewish people. *Parshas Vayikra* showed us the desire; this *parsha* instills it into the heart. This *parsha* explains how the things that a person desires and receives can become a part of him.

The Gemara teaches that during the time when the Beis Ha-Mikdash stood, the *mizbeach* was *mechaper* for each person. Nowadays, a person's table is *mechaper* for him. What does the word *mechaper* mean? Here it means to be able to receive the things you've wanted and make them a part of your life. "Nowadays, a person's table is *mechaper*" means that it is where we place the food that we want prior to eating it.

וכן על המזבח היה מעלה הקרבן שיכלל באש שלמעלה. אלא שבשלחנו של
אדם יש לאדם ירידה בשעת קבלת הטובה שנמשך אחר הטובה. אלא שאח"כ
תתעלה עם האדם יחד.

The בית יעקב contrasts the *mizbeach* and the table. On the
mizbeach the *korban* was consumed by the fire and ascended,
but on a person's table, the food is received and person descends,
eating like any other animal. But afterwards the food and person
ascend together.

ובמזבח לא היה שום ירידה לאדם בהקרבת קרבנותיו. וכאשר יראו הברואים
שבבואם לתוך האדם יתעלו. יעוררו חשק בלב האדם לקבלם. וכן הוא עניני
קרבן שהאדם מבין שבבא קרבנותיו למזבח יתעלו. אז יחפוץ להתקרב אל ה'
ולקבוע קדושת השי"ת בתוכו יתד שלא תמוט.

When the *korbanos* are offered on the *mizbeach*, that is the vehicle
to return that which is physical to the realm of the spiritual.
Similarly it becomes apparent that the entire physical world
can be uplifted and brought back to spirituality through man's
partaking of it. As a result of the *korban*, man is inspired to uplift
the world. Through his *korban*, he wants to be uplifted, never to
slide backward into the uninspired way of life he led before.

ועל זה מורה תרומת הדשן. ולכן כל הלילה כשרה לתרומת הדשן (יומא כ' ב').
ולקצירת העומר (מגילה כ' ב').

Therefore, the *terumas ha-deshen* takes place at night. This idea
of the night following the day is a *din* unique to *korbanos*, as
we know in *halachah* the day usually follows the night. But the
terumas ha-deshen is the collection and burning of the day's

leftovers. The Gemara (*Yoma* 20b, *Megillah* 20b) tells us the entire night is appropriate for the *terumas ha-deshen* and the cutting of the *omer*-barley. Why?

תרומת הדשן מורה לקבוע הקדושה שתעמוד לעולם. וקצירת העומר מורה שזה הקביעות מעורר בפנימית האדם רצון להתחלת הוספות טובה. ואלו השנים יעשו באדם בלתי ידיעתו. ועל זה מורה שעבודתם בלילה היינו ההתחלה והסוף. אלא בין אלו השתים יש מקום גם לאדם לטעום ולראות כי טוב ה':

As the *terumas ha-deshen* of the *mizbeach* was to clean out the ashes of the day's *korbanos*, it means to concretize that inspiration, the *korban olah*, which burned brightly earlier on that day. Hence it is introduced with the phrase, "This is *toras ha-olah*," the internalization of the passion of the *olah*.

Since the cutting of the *omer* shares the same time period, the fact that the Gemara mentions these two *mitzvos* together is revealing to us and important idea.

The *omer* is cut at night. Why at night? As we have learned, in the world of *korbanos*, the day follows the night. It is the opportunity to concretize the passion of the day. The *omer* offering is the beginning of the mitzvah of counting the *omer*. It demonstrates a materialization of the inspiration of the holiday of Pesach, and then to awakens the man's deep desire, the impulse to add, counting one more each day. Since the *korban* is brought at night when most people are asleep, it occurs almost subconsciously. This is why the night is appropriate for both *avodos*. Nighttime is both an end of a process (*terumas ha-deshen*) and a beginning of day (*ketziras ha-omer*). Through both dimensions it is possible "to taste and see how Hashem is good." A person "sees," glimpsing the end goal (*ketziras ha-omer*) of his dreams and desires, and a person "tastes" by concretizing (*terumas ha-deshen*). Hashem gives us a little taste of our goals and dreams to inspire us, but then he inspired to achieve our goals.

The Izhbitzer Tradition

See (בית יעקב ויקרא צו (יג, which explores the concepts in greater detail.

Practical Advice

We are engaged in a constant struggle to bring the brachos down into our lives. Sometimes we try too hard, and that's the problem. There are times that we need to take a step back, and when we least expect it, we can reprocess the brachos coming into our lives.

פרשת שמיני

from Beis Yaakov ha-Kollel

וַיְהִי בַּיּוֹם הַשְּׁמִינִי קָרָא מֹשֶׁה (ויקרא ט' א'). מזמור שיר ליום השבת. טוב
להדות לה' ולזמר לשמך עליון (תהלים צ"ב). הנה משם הויה יוצא כל מיני
הוייה. אך עוד צריך האדם להטות לבו למקום שהשי"ת נקרא עליון. והוא כי
יבין שאף שהכל ממנו יתברך. מכל מקום יש מקומות שצריך לצמצם עצמו
ומזה יצמח לו טובה לעתיד. והנה על זה רומז זה המזמור. כי שבת הוא כולל כל
מיני טובות. ונמצא בו התפשטות וגם צמצום. וזה רומז מזמור שיר. כי מזמור
היינו צמצום ושיר הוא התפשטות.

"And it was on the eighth day..." (*Vayikra* 9:1). The בית יעקב
explains this *parsha*'s opening *pasuk* of the "eighth day" with the
pesukim in *Tehillim* (92); "A song for Shabbos, it is good to thank
Hashem, and to sing to His name, Most High." We understand
that Hashem's name, which means "to be," is the source of all
realities and possibilities. Everything is from Hashem, but
there are situations when Hashem does conceal His Presence.
His concealment is for the benefit of the world, allowing good
to blossom there in the future. By not displaying His presence
so openly, Hashem empowers man to choose for himself, as
opposed to overwhelming mankind with His presence. This
Song for the Shabbos describes both ways in which Hashem

rules the world. It speaks of Hashem's Presence, bestowing good to the world, and His concealment, which also causes blessings in the world. Hence, the two words which explain the song of Shabbos, *Mizmor Shir*, also depict revelation and concealment. *Shir* means a "line," depicting Hashem's constant presence. *Mizmor* means "prune or cut," depicting His concealment.

והנה השי"ת ברא דברים שהאדם יכיר מהם את גדולתו יתברך. כי על ידי שיצמצם עצמו יכיר כי השי"ת גדול ממנו כמו שאל טורנוסרופוס לרבי עקיבא למה השי"ת מוריד גשמים בשבת. והשיב לו שנים הדרין בחצר אחד כו' (מדרש תנחומא תשא ס' ל"ג). והוא כי עיקר ענין שבת הוא שדעת האדם ישבות מטירדא. ובאם יטלטל לחצר שאינו שלו אז הדעת בטירדא. אבל אצל הש"ית לא נמצא טירדא בשום פנים. ומזה שהאדם שובת יוכר רוממותו יתברך.

Hashem created things so that man can perceive His greatness, and through His concealment, recognize Hashem is greater than him as well. We see this in the Midrash (*Tanchuma Ki Tissa* 33) where Turnus Rufus asked Rabbi Akiva, "Why does Hashem make it rain on Shabbos. Isn't it moving something from one domain to another?" Rabbi Akiva answered him, "When two people live in one courtyard, they can put up an *eruv* and carry from one to another. However, one person who enters another's property can carry wherever he wants because it is all one area." Hashem encompasses everything and is everywhere, and therefore can "carry" wherever he wants. The בית יעקב explains that the concept of Shabbos is to allow a person to stop all mental distraction. If a person goes to a place which is not his, he is busy thinking about the exertion. Hashem is never occupied or busy. When a person rests, he recognizes that Hashem never does, and how Hashem is great.

וכמו כן במאכלות אסורות שברא הקב"ה. כי אצלו יתברך אין הפרש בין בריה לחברתה. כי כלם מודים לשמו. אך מצד האדם יש הפרש. והשי"ת בראם במכוון כדי שהאדם יכיר שעל זה נאסר לו הנאסרים. כי באם יכניסם האדם לתוכו יוטרד דעתו ויטומטם לבו. וכן כל איסורים אינם רק שמהם יבח הסתרה בלב האדם שישכח בהשי"ת. כי בעת שהאדם שובת ודעתו מיושבת אז זוכר כי ה' הוא הנותן. וכדאיתא בירושלמי דמאי (פ"ד ה"א). עם הארץ אימת שבת עליו. כי כשינוח מטירדות אז יזכור את בוראו.

We see a similar idea with regard to the forbidden foods, which is present in this week's *parsha* as well. To Hashem, there is no difference between cows and pigs. But to man, there is great difference. Hashem created them in order to teach man the nature of things that are prohibited. Were a person to ingest them, he would become confused about the world, his spiritual sensitivities blunted. In fact, all of the prohibitions cause concealment in the heart of man, making him forget Hashem's Presence in the world and in his life. When man rests and his mind is cleared, then he knows that Hashem is the giver. The *Yerushalmi* (*Demai* 4:1) says that when a person who is ignorant rests, then his confusion about the world and its purpose is diminished, and he remembers his Creator.

והנה טבע כל הברואים שחפצים להטריד דעתם ולהשבית מאתם יראת השי"ת. וכן היה בהתחלת הבריאה מצד העולם בחרו בהסתרה. עד שהקב"ה הגביה מדותיו ובא מבול עליהם. כמו שנתבאר בפרשת נח ובפרשת מקץ. עד שקמו אבותינו והראשון היה אברהם אבינו שהתחיל לצמצם את הבריאה. עד שניתן לו מצות מילה והסיר ממנו כל מיני חמדות ובטלם משרשם. עד שהיה לבו מזוכך שהיה מסכים להקריב את בנו לכבוד שמים.

All of creation, by its very nature, want to busy itself in order to forget the awe of Hashem, and through it be able to expand. When one is confronted by Hashem's overwhelming presence, it is paralyzing, and the only way to grow is through a person's forgetfulness. We see this from the beginning of the creation, the world chose the darkness and concealment, forgetting and ignoring Hashem, through that, the world grew and increased. Then Hashem reasserted His presence, literally, and figuratively flooded the world. The world continued to forget Hashem until Avraham Avinu. Avraham began to cause the world to contract by reintroducing the Creator. When Hashem gave the mitzvah of *milah*, to remove the *orlah*, the covering, it was to remove this desire to conceal Hashem and expand against Hashem's will from the core of man.

והנה אחרי העקדה נשא את עיניו לראות מה נתפעל ממעשה הזאת בעולם. ואז הראהו הקב"ה והנה איל אחר נאחז בסבך בקרניו (וירא כ"ב י"ג). והוא כי העולם לא היה עוד כ"כ משוקע בחמדות. רק התחילו להסתבך ולא ישרו עוד בעיני האדם כ"כ והבחירה התחילה להתגבר. וזה נרמז באיל כי בו נגמרה הבריאה כי נברא בין השמשות (אבות פ"ה מ"ו). ואח"כ כשנתצרף ונזדכך אז בא תעוררות בלב כל הברואים המותרים וחפצו להתדבק בו . אז היה מותר להתפשט ולקבל הכל כפי רצון ה'.

We see this idea in the *parsha* of the *Akeidah*, when Avraham lifted his eyes and had a new perspective on life. He saw a ram, caught by its horns in the bushes. The ram represented the world and the bushes, the physicality in which the world was submerged. Since Avraham noticed this ram and extricated it, he demonstrated the power of free choice to remove mankind from a world of confusion. This ram alludes to fact that creation was almost complete. The Mishnah in *Avos* explains that the ram was created right before sunset on the last day, showing this event's relevance in the world's march towards completion. After the *Akeidah*, the world was purified and inspired to reconnect with Hashem. They gained the awareness to peel back the concealment of creation and perceive how everything fits in according to the will of Hashem.

וזה דאיתא בזה"ק (שמיני ל"ח א'). ואיל לעלה תמימם תמימם תמים מבעי ליה. אי תימא דעל איל ועגל קאמר לאו הכי. דהא תרוייהו לא סלקין לעולה. דהא כתיב לעלה תמימם ועגל לחטאת סלקא. מהו תמימם וכתיב איל. אלא אילו דיצחק לקרבא לגבי פרה דאדכר תרי זימני בקרא. חד דכתיב וישא אברהם את עיניו וירא והנה איל הא חד .וחד וילך אברהם ויקח את האיל הא תרי. ויעלהו לעלה. ועל דא ואיל לעלה תמימם .תרי איל דאיהו תרי. ועל דא גבורות תנינן. כי איל הראשון היה צמצום שבא בחירה והיה יכול לצמצם עצמו. ואיל השני היינו אחר שנתברר היו חוזרים אליו כל דברים המותרים ורצו להתקרב אליו ולהתדבק בו.

The *parsha* describes the inaugural *korbanos*, the purpose of which was to bring in Hashem's presence into the Mishkan and the world. The word *millui* means both "inaugurate" and "fill." The *pasuk* says that the ram should be *temimim*, using the plural. The *Zohar* (*Shmini* 38b) says it should be *tamim*, in the singular. One would think that the word *temimim* must be referring to the ram and the cow. But both of them are not part of an *olah* offering. The *olah* is only a ram, and therefore should be singular, *tamim*. But the ram's adjective of *temimim* is plural. Rather, the *Zohar* says, *temimim* refers to the effect that the ram had in the inaugural offering. It is evocative of the ram that was offered in the place of Yitzchak. This ram, the *Zohar* says, lessened the power of *din*, judgment, which is called "*parah.*" The ram is mentioned twice in the *pasuk*, "Avraham saw a ram, took the ram and offered it as an *olah.*" This is why it referred to as an *olah* (singular) *temimim* (plural). It is an *olah* with double power, to lessen the power of *din*. The double effect is that, first, a person restrains himself; second, as a result of that restraint, it becomes clear to the person that he can connect to the entirety of creation.

וזה דאיתא בזה"ק ועל דא גבורות תנינן. כי בעולם הזה נקרא גבורות צמצום. אבל כשיתברר יבא לגבורה האמיתית.

When the *Zohar* refers to the power of *din*, it often speaks about *gevuros* in the plural, similar to what we discussed above. In this world, *gevuros* means contraction, but when we reach a place of clarity, we reach the true *gevurah*…

וגם שבת מורה על זה שקרבנותיו כפולים (מדרש תהלים מזמור צ"ב). שעל ידי הצמצום נזכה לכל טוב הצפון בו .

Shabbos displays this as concept as well, for on it, the *korbanos* are doubled. Therefore, there is a double effect on the day. The *korban* alludes to the fact that due to the contraction (a person not working on Shabbos), a person will be able to see things in a new way, whereby he can perceive all of the good that is hidden within the world.

וזה דאיתא בבראשית רבה (י"א ס' ב'). ברכו במן וקדשו במן. ברכו במן שכל ימות השבת היה יורד עומר ובערב שבת שני עומרים. וקדשו במן שלא ירד בו כל עיקר . והוא כי נמצא בו ברכה צפונה. ובעולם הזה צריך לצמצם עצמו.

The Midrash (*Bereishis Rabbah* 11:2) explains that Shabbos was both blessed by the *man* (manna bread) and sanctified by the *man*. What does it mean "blessed by the *man*"? The *man* fell every *erev* Shabbos in double portions, two *omer*. How was it "sanctified by the *man*"? By the fact that it didn't fall on Shabbos. We see the concept of the hidden *bracha*, which is accessible by restraining one's self.

והנה כמו שחקק השי"ת שבע מדות מפורשים. בהם צריך האדם להתברר ולאחוז בעולם הזה רק בהצמצום היוצא מהם. כי כן הוא בעולם הזה עשיר האמתי זהו השמח בחלקו. וגבור הכובש את יצרו (אבות פ"ד מ"א). וכן הכל. אבל בשלשה מדות הנסתרים בהם לא נמצא צמצום. כי כשיגיע האדם אליהם יתברר לו כי כל היה לטוב לפניו. ועל זה רומז ויהי ביום השמיני. כי למעלה מהיקף השבעה אז יתברר כי הכל טוב הוא.

Despite the fact that Hashem used such great light in creation, man can only grasp a small portion of it. All of a person's *middos* are receptacles for Hashem's blessings, but man's grasp is limited by his perceptions. As a result, the blessings descend to the world in a constricted fashion. As the Mishnah (*Avos* 4:1) tells us, a truly happy person in this world is someone who is happy with what he has. A strong person conquers his inclination. However, this is only regarding the seven revealed *middos* of the the heart. (They are *Chesed, Gevurah, Tiferes, Netzach, Hod Yesod*, and *Malchus*.) The three hidden *middos* (*Chochmah, Binah, Daas*) transcend the concealment and constriction. When a person reaches that level, all of Hashem's goodness becomes clear, while the concealment and constriction disappear.

This is the significance of starting the *parsha* off "on the eighth day." In the world above that is contained by the seven *middos*, everything becomes clear, that all is good.

The Izhbitzer Tradition

See (א) בית יעקב ויקרא שמיני, where the בית יעקב explains the same idea, with more emphasis on contraction and concealment. See (א) בית יעקב בראשית וירא where he explains free choice, the beginning of the world, the Akeidah, and the ram.

Practical Advice

What is the sweetness of holding back? Is there any progress made by not doing? Rav Hutner writes that one can taste the sweetness of the positive commandments in the prohibitions of Shabbos. The restraint that we display propels us into the world of the "eighth day," which is the middah above the normal midos of our life. This is the case with all of the Torah's prohibitions. By avoiding things that are forbidden, we might think it limits our horizons. However, it actually allows us to access a higher perspective.

פרשת תזריע

from Beis Yaakov ha-Kollel

וַיְדַבֵּר ה' אֶל מֹשֶׁה לֵּאמֹר. דַּבֵּר אֶל בְּנֵי יִשְׂרָאֵל לֵאמֹר אִשָּׁה כִּי תַזְרִיעַ וְיָלְדָה
זָכָר **(ויקרא י"ב א'-ב')** . אשרי אדם לא יחשב ה' לו עון ואין ברוחו רמיה
(תהלים ל"ב ב). לא יחשב ה' לו עון הוא שהשי"ת לא יחשוב לו שום דבר
שנראה חס ושלום שהיה הפך מרצונו. לא יחשוב לו ה' שהיה במזיד. והוא
מפני שאין ברוחו רמיה שהוא מבורר בדעתו שאינו רוצה רק בכבוד שמים. וזה
דאיתא בגמרא (ברכות ס"א ב). לידע איש בנפשיה אם צדיק גמור הוא. ובאם
האדם יודע שבמעמקי לב הוא טהור. אז בטח גם על כל מעשיו הפרטיים יעיד
השי"ת שהם טובים.

"Hashem spoke to Moshe saying, speak to the children of
Israel and tell them that a woman who becomes pregnant and
gives birth to a boy..." (*Vayikra* 12:1-2). The בית יעקב explains
this *pasuk* with one from *Tehillim* (32:2): "Happy is the man
whose wrongdoings Hashem does not consider, and there
is no deception in his soul." The בית יעקב explains the clause,
"...whose wrongdoings Hashem does not consider...," that he
does not do anything against Hashem's will and think that it is
right. This is because there is no deception in his spirit. He has
worked through his thoughts and feelings to make it clear in
his heart that his sole motivation is for Hashem's honor. This is
what the Gemara (*Brachos* 61b) refers to when it says, "A person

will know himself whether he is completely righteous." When a person knows in the depths of his heart that he is pure, then Hashem will testify that all of their individual actions are good.

והנה פרשת ויקרא ופרשת צו הם מעניני קרבנות והוא עניני תפלות כמו שנתבאר שם. ופרשת שמיני היא איך יקבע בלב הקדושה היוצאות מהתפלות. כי ענין שנאסרו הבהמות והחיות והעופות הטמאים הוא לפי שמטמטמין את הלב (יומא ל"ח א'). ומסתיר דעת האדם לבלי יוכל להסתכל לבוראו. כי באם דעת האדם מיושבת עליו אז זוכר את ה' כי הוא הנותן לו כל. כדאיתא בירושלמי דמאי (פ"ד ה"א). שבשבת אף עם הארץ נאמן לפי שאימת שבת עליו.

What does it mean to know your heart is pure? Thematically, this clarity is appropriate to *Sefer Vayikra*. Both *Parshios Vayikra* and *Tzav* speak about the *korbanos* and *tefillos*. *Shemini* deals with how to instill the holiness that results from the *tefillos*. The reason for the prohibition of non-kosher animals is because they make the heart impure and conceal Hashem from man. If man is calm and his thoughts clear, then he remembers Hashem is the giver of everything. It for this reason that the Yerushalmi says that on Shabbos, even the ignorant do not lie because of the clarity that Shabbos brings to the world, so that even the most ignorant person cannot ignore it.

וענין הטמאים היא עקשות בדבר אחד אף שנראה כמדה טובה. כגון חסידה שנאמר עליה בגמרא (חולין ס"ג א'). שעושה חסידות עם חברותיה. מכל מקום לפי שאינה יכולה להתיישב ולהתהפך ממדה הזאת ברצון השי"ת. על זה נאמר כל המרחם על אכזרי סופו שנעשה אכזר על הרחמני (קהלת רבה פ"ז פט"ז). וענין הטהורים הם בהפך שנקבע בהם מדות טובות. ועיקר הוא ישוב הדעת ובחירה ובאכול האדם את הטמאים יוכל להקבע בו מדתם. אבל כשאוכל הטהורים אז נקבע בו מדות טובות ותפלות. כי כל הנבראים מתפללים לה'.

What does the word *tamei'im* mean? Here it means stubbornness, an unwillingness to do something different, even if it would be a good thing. An example of this is the bird called *chasidah* (*Chullin* 63a), which Chazal prohibit its consumption, as it only does good for fellow *chasidos*, but not to its own brood. These birds are unwilling to change their behavior and will continue in that way. The Midrash speaks of a character distortion in which a person who is not sensitive in this way will have mercy on the cruel people and will come to be cruel to merciful people. We are what we eat. An animal that acts in such a *tamei* way will affect a person's behavior and world view. The *tahor* animals are the opposite; they are receptive and serene to the messages how to adapt their behavior and repair themselves. Man is commanded to eat *tahor* foods in order to have the serenity to have the animal's good attributes implanted within one's self.

וסדרה הזאת תדבר בהשפעת האדם איך יחל להתפשט ולהשפיע ולהוליד מאשר נקבע בו.

Let's return to our *parsha* and ask about giving birth. The *parsha* speaks of the ability of man to spread his influence and give birth to what is within him.

ועל זה נפסק הענין בכתוב וביום השמיני ימול בשר ערלתו. שמורה כי בכל עניני עולם הזה צריך האדם לצמצם עצמו.

But we are commanded on the eighth day to circumcise one's son. "Circumcise" means to decrease or keep one's self away from certain things, to have the serenity to choose only good actions.

כדאיתא בזה"ק (תזריע מ"ג ב'). דעד שבעה הוא תחת זוהמא דאימיה. ואח"כ ביום השמיני שמורה על לעתיד אחר צמצום בשבע המדות.

The *Zohar* (*Tazria* 43b) says that as long as the baby is seven days old, it is still with the birth-*tumah* of its mother, because on the eighth day, which refers to the future, one has the capacity to choose.

כמו שנתבאר בפרשת שמיני. אז מותר להתפשט כי אז נקבע באדם קדושה בקביעות. ועל זה רומז מצות מילה שהיא בשמיני. כי מצות מילה היא גם כן בקביעות שאין ביד האדם להסירה מעליו. ואף בלי כל הלבושים נקבע בו קדושה. וזה דאיתא במדרש תנחומא (תזריע ס' ה'). מעשה ששאל טורנוסרופוס הרשע את רבי עקיבא. איזו מעשים נאים של הקב"ה או של בשר ודם. אמר לו של בשר והם נאים וכו'. הביא לו רבי עקיבא שבלים וגלוסקאות. אמר לו אלו מעשה הקב"ה ואלו מעשה יד אדם. אמר לו אין אלו נאים יותר מן השבלים כו'. ולפיכך לא ברא השי"ת את האדם מהול לפי שבכל דבר צריך האדם לתקן.

Once we have reached the world of the eighth day, then a person can let *kedushah* grow from the place where it is implanted. The mitzvah of *milah* imparts *kedushah* in a way that cannot be removed, as it is impressed into his body. The Midrash (*Tanchuma Tazria* 5) records a discussion between Turnus Rufus and Rebbe Akiva. Turnus Rufus asked Rebbe Akiva whether Hashem's actions are better or are man's actions better. His intent was to ask about the mitzvah of *milah*. Rebbe Akiva said the actions of man are better and took out bread and stalks of wheat. Rebbe Akiva asked Turnus Rufus which is better, bread or wheat. Rebbe Akiva said, "Hashem desired man to be circumcised because everything needs to be repaired."

והוא כי בעולם הזה אין לך נאה מן הצמצום. כי כן יסד השי״ת שתתברר כל
הבריאה על ידי צמצומים. אבל לעתיד יהיה מעשה הקב״ה נאים. כי עתידה
ארץ ישראל שתוציא גלוסקאות (שבת ל׳ ב׳). לפי שאז יהיה מותר להתפשט
על פי רצון השי״ת.

Hashem desires concealment and constriction, because even
though He initially made the world with unbridled good and
blessing, it needed to be contained. In the future, the world's
unfettered good will become apparent. This is what the Gemara
means when it states that in the future, the land of Israel will
sprout loaves of breads. Then it will be possible to spread out in
accordance with Hashem's will.

והנה מה ששאל אותו רק על המילה. ולא על הגלוסקאות עצמן מפני מה לא
נבראו שלמים. כי זאת ידע בברור כי בעולם הזה אין להביט לשום טובה רק על
ידי צמצום. כי הקב״ה בורא כל הפירות ושומר להם. ועל ידי זה נקרא המוץ
שומר לפרי. כי על יד הצמצום יכול לקבל הטובה ותשתמר. אבל על אדם שאלו
למה לא ברא אותו הקב״ה בשמירה. שמאליו לא ישאף לשום דבר רק ברצון
השי״ת. וממילא יוכל לקבל כל הטובות בלי צמצום.

But Turnus Rufus only asked Rebbe Akiva about *bris milah*,
but not about bread, as that isn't created in a completed state.
This tells us that this world is not a place where one can see the
good directly. Therefore, there must be something intervening.
Similar to a shell that protects the fruit, stopping it from being
eaten, soiled, or spoiled. Hashem sets up something concealing
the unadulterated good in the world in order to assure that
people do not misuse the *brachos* that Hashem has given. Only
by getting through this shell can a person reach the hidden
good. In the story of Rebbe Akiva, no one was arguing why

fruit needs to be protected. The question that was being asked is why doesn't man naturally have that kind of protection? Why doesn't man only desire what Hashem wants, so he will not make mistakes in using the world? He would, therefore, receive the all of the good without the need for concealment.

ועל זה השיב לו ולמה שוררו יוצא עמו והוא תלוי בבטנו ואמו חותכו. והוא באם יהיה נברא האדם שלם אז לא יבין שנמצא גדול ממנו. אבל כשנברא בחסרון שלא יוכל לקבל טובה בשלמות. מזה יבין כי בשורשו נמצא חסרון. וזה שנרמז בשוררו. כמו שנתבאר בספר מי השלוח (חלק א' לקוטים מכתובים משלי). על פסוק רפאות תהי לשרך. ועל ידי זה יכיר זה את בוראו:

This is why Rebbe Akiva answered him, "Why would he think he could rule over anything? He is dependent on his mother who then cuts the umbilical cord." This means if man were created whole, he'd never understand that there is anything greater than him. Now that he was created with something missing, that he cannot receive good in its entirety. He understands that there is something missing, which must be repaired. The מי השלוח explains a similar idea in *Mishlei*: "through his healing he becomes your servant." When Hashem heals what ails man, then man recognizes Hashem as his Creator.

The Izhbitzer Tradition

See מי השלוח חלק א משלי discusses the concept of Hashem's healing the ills of man and the blessing of recognition. See also בית יעקב הכולל לך לך.

Practical Advice

Man's dynamism, his constant state of change, is evidence that Hashem has a plan for man to be in a constant state of self-improvement and progression.

פרשת מצורע

from Beis Yaakov ha-Kollel

וַיְדַבֵּר ה' אֶל מֹשֶׁה וְאֶל אַהֲרֹן לֵאמֹר. כִּי תָבֹאוּ אֶל אֶרֶץ כְּנַעַן אֲשֶׁר אֲנִי נֹתֵן
לָכֶם לַאֲחֻזָּה וְנָתַתִּי נֶגַע צָרַעַת בְּבֵית אֶרֶץ אֲחֻזַּתְכֶם (ויקרא י"ד ל"ג-ל"ד).
ענין שנאמר תחלה טומאת נגעי אדם. ואח"כ נגעי בגדים. ואח"כ טהרת בגדים.
ואח"כ טהרת אדם. ואח"כ נגעי בתים וטהרתן.

The בית יעקב asks why the *parsha* first deals with the *tumah* that results in having discolorations on the body, then on clothing, then the process of being *metaher* from the *tumah* of the clothing, and then the discolorations on the body. Finally, the *parsha* deals with the *tumah* from the discolorations on a person's house and then the *taharah* process.

כי ענין נגעי בגדים הוא כשהאדם יתחיל לעבוד את השי"ת והשי"ת רוצה
לבררו. אז ישלח לו מחשבות הסותרים כל מעשיו ופעולותיו כי אינם נחשבים
למאומה.

According to the Torah, the discolorations, come when we begin to serve Hashem, and He wants us to progress in our personal growth. Hashem wants to motivate us further toward greatness and sends us thoughts that our actions are not worth anything. Hence they are נגעים on the garments. In Chassidus, "garments" refer to actions. as the non-physical soul "wears" them to interact with this physical world. Through the *negaim* on clothing, we are jarred into starting to see the imperfections of our actions.

ואח"כ כשיתחיל להתקרב יותר להן אז יבררו במדותיו הטבועים בו. והנה באם ירצה האדם לברר את עצמו במעשיו. על זה נאמר אין חקר לתבונתו (ישעיה מ' כ"ח). שלהתפשטותו של השי"ת אין קץ ולא יוכל האדם לבא לידי סוף הבירור כל ימי חייו. אך במדות יוכל האדם לברר עצמו. ובאם יתברר במדות אז יתרפא על נגעי בגדים. כי בירור המדות מכונה לנגעי אדם והתורה מדברת מעניני הבירורים. ותחלת הבירור צריך להיות בנגעי אדם. כי במעשיו אין קץ לבירורים כי הם רבים ותמידיים. ואח"כ כשיתחיל להתברר בנגעי אדם אז כתיב נגעי בגדים וטהרתן. כי אז יטהר מנגעי בגדים.

When we see the blemishes caused by our actions, we are horrified, and we are compelled to seek the source of these imperfections. We realize that it would take forever to repair all of our actions, as there are so many of them. Rather, what must be repaired is the character traits that underlie these actions. So we seek to repair the character traits which are the basis for our actions. Hence, the first process of *taharah*, of purification and repair, that we learn about is the *negei adam* (blemishes on the person) and only then *negei begadim* (blemishes on the clothes). First, the *oved Hashem* sees what is going wrong in his actions. Then he sees that the root is deeper, that the problem is that something is going wrong with himself. So he begins to correct his character traits. Once he has committed himself to begin to repair the character traits (corresponding to *negei adam*), the *negei begadim* can be repaired as well.

ואח"כ לעת זקנת האדם כשיתברר במדות גם כן. אז ישלח לו השי"ת בירורים
חדשים. והיא שיבוא לו מחשבות פן הוא חס ושלום אינו נקי ביסודו שאינו חס
ושלום מזרע אבות.

When a person reaches an old age and has completed repairing
his *middos*, Hashem sends new things to repair. This comes in
the form of thoughts that maybe do not come from the Avos.
This means that the person is tested in ways that cut to the very
core of his Judaism, namely his *emunah*.

וזה דאיתא בגמרא (ערכין ח' ב'). צדקתך כהררי אל אלו נגעי אדם. משפטיך
תהום רבה אלו נגעי בתים. והוא אף כי בנגעי אדם ובגדים קרובים הנגעים יותר
לאדם. אכן לבית נמשל היסוד מהאדם. ואם יבא מחשבה כזאת לאדם בנערותו
מאלו הבירורים ביסודותיו. אז היה נופל מכל יסודו ואפסו בו כל תשוקותיו.

The Gemara (*Erechin* 8b) explained that the *pasuk*, "Your
righteousness reaches the tops of mountains, and Your
judgments reach to the deepest pits" refers to *negei adam* (Your
righteousness) and the *negei batim* (Your judgments). Only
because a person has traversed the heights of the mountains,
does he know that Hashem can sustain him through the pits.
The בית יעקב explains that only after someone has passed the test
of *negei adam*, is he equipped to deal with *negei batim*. While
the *negaim* on the person or his clothes are within man's reach,
the house itself is the foundation, the *emunah*. To consider that
there is something wrong there would be devastating for the
person who has not worked on those things which are more in
his control.

אכן ה' ברוב רחמיו מבררו בזה לבסוף כשהוא נשלם בכל ענייניו. וכמו דאיתא
במסכת (ברכות ה' ב'). על נגעים אם הם יסורין של אהבה. ומתרץ הא לן והא
להו. דבארץ ישראל שהדר שם דומה כמי שיש לו אלוה (כתובות ק"י ב'). שם
עיקר הנסיון בנגעי בתים :

Therefore, Hashem tests him with these *negaim* of the house only
after he has gone through many other tests. These *negaim* are a
test that is so debilitating that if they were the first test a person
would encounter, he would be unable to keep serving Hashem.
The Gemara in *Brachos* (5b) asks if *negaim* are suffering of love.
The Gemara answers that outside of Eretz Yisrael they are. The
Gemara in *Kesubos* (110b) says that in Eretz Yisrael, anyone who
lives there, it is "as if" he has a G-d. What does it mean "as if"
you have a G-d? "As if" refers to person's preconceived notion
of Hashem and the way He runs the world. These *negaim* of the
house show that Hashem is testing the person's house; the very
foundation of a person's life and belief system.

The Izhbitzer Tradition

*The concept of "What you thought you knew" is found a lot in
the Izhbitzer teachings. When Hashem revealed Himself, He said,
"Don't think that now that you have received this revelation, you
understand Me or My Will entirely."*

Practical Advice

*Rav Freifeld would say, "Life is an evolution, not a revolution."
Our lives are a work in progress. Every step of the way, we are
challenged, and Hashem gives us the gift of self-recognition,*

rather than allow us to grope in the dark. When presented with a challenge—the detection of one of your flaws—despite the embarrassment, thank Hashem for the gift of recognition, the ability to make it right.

פרשת אחרי מות

from Naos Deshe

וַיְדַבֵּר ה' אֶל מֹשֶׁה לֵּאמֹר. דַּבֵּר אֶל בְּנֵי יִשְׂרָאֵל וְאָמַרְתָּ אֲלֵהֶם אֲנִי ה' אֱלֹהֵיכֶם.
כְּמַעֲשֵׂה אֶרֶץ מִצְרַיִם אֲשֶׁר יְשַׁבְתֶּם בָּהּ לֹא תַעֲשׂוּ וּכְמַעֲשֵׂה אֶרֶץ כְּנַעַן אֲשֶׁר
אֲנִי מֵבִיא אֶתְכֶם שָׁמָּה לֹא תַעֲשׂוּ וּבְחֻקֹּתֵיהֶם לֹא תֵלֵכוּ. אֶת מִשְׁפָּטַי תַּעֲשׂוּ
וְאֶת חֻקֹּתַי תִּשְׁמְרוּ (ויקרא י"ח א'-ד').

This week's *parsha* includes the following section, "Hashem
spoke with Moshe saying, speak to the Jewish people and tell
them I am Hashem, your G-d. Don't commit acts like those
of Egypt, from where you dwelled, or those of the land that I
am bringing you. Do not follow their laws. Do My *mishpatim*
and keep My *chukim* to follow them. I am Hashem, Your G-d"
(*Vayikra* 18:1-4).

פירוש רש"י משפט דברים הכתובין בתורה בדין שאילו לא נאמרו היו כדאי
לאמרן וחוקה דברים שיצר הרע ואומות העולם משיבין עליהן ומסיים רש"י
ז"ל ליתן שמירה ועשייה לחוקים ושמירה ועשייה למשפטים ומסיים אשר
יעשה אותם האדם וחי בהם. ויש להבין כל זה כי דבר שחיי האדם תלוי
בו ככתוב צריך להבין הדבר כדי שיוכל לקיימו. וגם מה העניין התחלה דבר
ואמרת אני ה' אלקיכם מה שאין כן בכל התורה. וגם פרוש רש"י ז"ל כמעשה
ארץ מצרים מלמד שמעשה מצרים וארץ כנען מקולקלים מכל האומות. ויש

להבין למה הביא הש"י את בני ישראל לארצות מקולקלות מכל האומות. וגם מה ענין שנתן הקב"ה לישראל משפטים וחוקים.

The נאות דשא quotes Rashi, who explains that a *mishpat* means a commandment that we would still do even if it weren't written, whereas a *chok* is a commandment whose logic or validity the *yetzer hara* and nations of the world question. Then Rashi continues to explain that we must do and guard both *mishpatim* and *chukim*. He concludes that a person must do them in order to live. The נאות דשא is puzzled: Why all of this is indeed necessary to tell us we will keep the *mitzvos*? Additionally, why does this section begin with the statement, "I am Hashem, Your G-d." When isn't Hashem our G-d? Additionally, Rashi comments that acts of Egypt or Canaan are the most depraved in the world. The נאות דשא asks why then is Hashem sending us to all of these disgusting places?

אך הענין היא רומז לנפש האדם שיש באדם ב' חסרונות. חסרון אחד מתולדתו כמה שכתוב כי יצר לב האדם רע נעוריו (בראשית ח' כא') משננער לצאת ממעי אמו וזה נקרא מעשה ארץ מצרים אשר ישבתם בה. והחסרון הב' מה שאדם לקח מעצמו מדעת ובתאוה וזה תלוי בזה שאם היה נולד נקי ממעי אמו לא היה לוקח החסרונות של העולם הזה. למשל מי שהוא בריא בשלמות לא יזיק לא לו שום אכילה ואף לפעמים שאוכל אכילה גסה או דברים אשר לא טובים במעט חמין אשר ישתה יחזיר לבריאותו. אבל מי שאינו בבריאות בשלמות אזי צריך תמיד להיות נזהר ונשמר מאכילה גסה ודברים אשר לא טובים כי בקל יכול להזיק עצמו. כמו כן נפש האדם מחמת שיש לו חסרון בתולדה אזי עלול הוא לקבל טומאה. חסרון הב' מה שאדם מקבל מחמת שאינו מבורר אם ירצה לעזוב דרך הרע באמת אזי יכול לעזוב אותו. אבל החסרון שיש לאדם מתולדתו הוא קשה מאוד לעזוב אותו וצריך להקיא החלב שיניק משדי אמו.

173

The prohibition of committing acts of Egypt and Canaan is actually reflective of two different types of problems in the life and soul of a Jew. There are two problems which people often encounter. The first is a predisposition with which a person is born. The Torah explains this by saying that a person's heart is evil from its inception. This is reflected in the prohibition to commit Egyptian acts, which refers to the specific predispositions which we all have. Just as the Jews have Egypt in their national past, each Jew has his own personal problems in his personal past. Each person has challenges which they are born with, to act on them, which are Egyptian acts. The second type of problem is the kind of bad choices that people make for themselves. These problems are ones of their own making. These are therefore referred to as Canaanite acts. These are not problems of where we came from, but of where we are going to. However, the past problems can set the stage for future problems. The נאות דשא explains that just as a person who is healthy can eat whatever he wants, and if he overeats, he can have a little hot water and be fine. But a person who is sick to begin with has to be very careful lest he damage his constitution by eating. In the same way, a person who has "Egypt" in his past has to be careful, as he knows there is a predisposition to do the wrong thing. To get away from the Canaanite problem is relatively easy; just recognize that you are not doing the right thing, and decide to fix it. When a person is not committed to making things better, then he will stay with his Canaanite acts. However, it is a lot harder to deal with the demons of the past, the Egyptian acts which come as predisposed characteristics.

ולזה נתן הקב"ה עצה לאדם אשר יעשה אותם האדם וחי בהם ונתן להם חוקים
ומשפטים מרפאים את האדם מחסרון השני מה שלקה הוא בעצמו מדעת ולזה
ניתן המשפטים שאילו לא נכתבו היו כדאי לאמרן. וכנגד החסרון הראשון
שהם מתולדה נתן לו חוקים שהם בלא טעם שיצר הרע ואומות העולם משיבין
עליהם ואם האדם שומר החוקים אף שאינו יודע טעם הדבר כמו כן נתרפא לו
החסרון מתולדה שהיא גם כן כמו חוקה בלא טעם למה נולדתי בזה החסרון.
וזה שפירש"י ז"ל מלמד שמעשה ארץ מצרים וארץ כנען מקולקלים מכל
האומות כי כל הגדול מחביריו יצרו גדול הימנו ונתן עשיה למשפטים ושמירה
לחוקים כי למשפט שייך עשיה כי היא דבר הנתקבל לשכל האדם ושמירה
לחוקים כי דבר שאינו יודע טעמו של דבר שייך שמירה ואם מקיים הדבר הזה
אזי הוסיף הכתוב שמירה למשפטים ועשיה לחוקים פירושו כי יש במשפט גם
כן שמירה היינו חוקים ובחוקים יש גם כן עשיה היינו משפט.

Therefore, this section includes the declaration and "You'll live with them," in which Hashem gave us *chukim* and *mishpatim* to heal us. Hashem gave us *mishpatim* to cure the problem of Canaanite acts. These are *mitzvos* whose truth is so apparent, it will allow us to reorder our priorities, to make the right choices. This will allow us to leave the Canaanite choices behind us. The *chukim* are there to repair the defects that came about without our choices and thought process, called "Egyptian acts." Therefore, they are given to us without a reason as to exactly why we must perform them. It is for this reason that Hashem brings us to the most damaged of places, (Egypt and Canaan) because greatness lies in the places of temptation and brokenness. As the Gemara says, the one who is the greatest also has the greatest temptation towards evil. Why are we told to <u>do</u> *mishpatim* and <u>guard</u> the *chukim*? A *mishpat* is something that lies in the realm of action; it makes sense; we do it. *Chukim*, however, we are told to guard. We need to guard them, because we don't understand them truly. When we do this adequately, the *pasuk* guarantees that we will as well guard the *mishpatim* and do the *chukim* as there is something unknown about *mishpatim* and a logical understandable side to the *chukim*.

להבין דבר זה כמו שאמר דוד המלך ע"ה וישב ה' לי כצידקי (תהילים י"ח
כא') ופרש"י ז"ל בכרתי כנף מעיל של שאול המלך ולא הרגתיו ודבר זה הוא
כנגד המשפט כי לפי דברי תורה היה מצוה להרגו כי רודף הוא. וזה שאמר
דוד המלך ע"ה כי כל משפטיו לנגדי (שם פסוק כג) המשפט מתנגד לי כי על
פי המשפט מצוה להרגו כי רודף הוא רק דוד המלך היה לו בינה בלב שהקב"ה
אינו רוצה שיהרוג את שאול וזה שכתוב וישסע דוד אנשיו (שמואל א כ"ד
ז') כי אבישי רצה להרגו כד"ת ולא היה לדוד המלך [לומר] בפה מלא שאסור
להרוג אותו רק דחה אותו וזהו וזהו וחוקותיו לא אסיר מני שהבין החוקים שיש
במשפטים וזה נקרא שמירה למשפטים ואם האדם הוא מבורר אז יש לו בינה
שיעשה חוקים שיש במשפטים כמו דוד המלך שלא רצה להרוג את שאול.
וישב ה' לי כצדקי היינו שניתן לו עשיה לחוקים היינו כל רז לא אנס לך לך
אני מגלה טעם פרה.

נאות דשא explains another application of this concept. David Ha-Melech (*Tehillim* 18:21) said, "Hashem repaid me for my righteousness." Rashi explains that David Ha-Melech's righteousness was that he cut the corner of Shaul's cloak instead of killing him (*Shmuel* I 24:7). This was against the *mishpat*, the logic of the law. David should have killed Shaul because he was a *rodef*, a person pursuing someone with murderous intent, whom the Torah commands us to kill before they kill you. However, David Ha-Melech also said, "All of His *mishpat* is against me; I will not remove his *chukim* from me." Despite the fact that David did not follow the *mishpat* that Shaul was a *rodef*, to the extent that even his own men were arguing with him about whether or not to kill Shaul; and he did not answer them that it was forbidden. David Ha-Melech understood there was something more about the situation that was not understandable, something with *chok* properties. We see, therefore, that David Ha-Melech perceived *chok* in *mishpat*.

וזה אשר יעשה אותם האדם וחי בהם וכפי הנראה דבר זה הוא קשה עד מאוד לכן התחיל אני ה' אלקיכם שאני מסייע לך כי הבא לטהר מסייעין אותו וזה דבר ואמרת כי כל התחלות קשות.

As a result, Hashem repaid this righteousness by giving him understanding (*mishpat*), into the mystery of *parah adumah*, which is called <u>the</u> *chok*. Finally, the *parsha* concludes by saying *ve-chai bahem*, "you'll live with them (commandments)." This is the Torah's assurance that we will be able to withstand the challenges of trying to work on the Egyptian problems, as well as those of the Canaanites. As Chazal have told us, when people come to purify themselves, Hashem will help them.

The Izhbitzer Tradition

The Izhbitzer seforim discuss the notion of deep rooted problems in ourselves that are the cause of aveiros. See בית יעקב הכולל מצורע *and the* ספר הזמנים הגדה של פסח, *which deals with* בדיקת חמץ.

Practical Advice

Especially in these pre-Pesach days, we are looking for our spiritual chametz. There are two types of chametz. There is the kind that you can reach and remove, and the kind that you can't reach and must nullify. Based on what we've learned, the "Canaanite" is the obvious chametz in your life, which must be removed. The "Egyptian" is the chametz that we have to be nullify. It is in the past, and the only thing we can do is nullify it in our minds.

פרשת קדושים

from Beis Yaakov ha-Kollel

וְלֹא תִשָּׁבְעוּ בִשְׁמִי לַשָּׁקֶר וְחִלַּלְתָּ אֶת שֵׁם אֱלֹהֶיךָ אֲנִי ה' (ויקרא י"ט י"ב). עניין השינויים שלפעמים נאמר אני ה' ולפעמים אני ה' אלהיכם. כי אני ה' אלהיכם מורה שאל יפול לב האדם מדבר שידמה לו שלא יוכל לקיים. ואני ה' מורה שאל יהרהר אדם אחר מדותיו של הקב"ה. וכמו שנתבאר כל העניין בספר מי השלוח (חלק ראשון קדשים). והנה כאן נאמר בשבועת שקר וחללת את שם אלהיך אני ה'.

In this week's *parsha*, we are commanded "not to swear by My name falsely, for you will profane the name of Elokeicha (your G-d); I am Hashem" (*Vayikra* 19:12). The בית יעקב explains the usage of "I am Hashem" and "I am Hashem, Elokeicha" as a beginning or ending to the *mitzvos* in this week's *parsha*, and what swearing falsely means by profaning the name Elokeicha. He quotes a teaching from his father (מי השלוח) that the phrase "I am Hashem Elokeichem" means that a person shouldn't be depressed when it appears to him that he cannot do something that Hashem is asking him to, as He has not abandoned us. We see this as the Torah uses the possessive "Your G-d," that I am Your G-d, and I have not abandoned you, even if you think the contrary. The phrase "I am Hashem" tells us that you shouldn't try to second-guess the way Hashem runs the world. By only using the name Hashem, we are stressing that He in His essence is above our understanding.

וגבי עושק שכר שכיר ולא תעמד על דם רעך ולא תקם ולא תטר נאמר באלו הארבעה אני ה' .והענין הוא דנכתב באלו הארבעה אני ה'. מפני שיוכל האדם להרהר חס ושלום על מדותיו של הקב"ה באלו הארבעה. וחללת את שם אלהיך אני ה' מורה ששם ה' לא יתחלל ודבריו חיים וקיימים לנצח. ואף שלפי ראות עיני האדם יוכלל דמות חס ושלום שכמה הבטחות הבטיח ה' ולא נתקיימו .

The בית יעקב applies this teaching to our *parsha*. Regarding the four *mitvzos* of not withholding a day laborer's wages, not standing idly by when one's fellow's blood is being spilled, not taking revenge, and not bearing a grudge, each conclude with the phrase "I am Hashem," because each of these *mitzvos* could cause a person to have questions regarding how Hashem runs the world, as they seem to be contradictory. If Hashem wants us to act in a certain way, why does it appear that He acts in the very way He told us not to?

Therefore the name "Hashem" is used to tell us, "Don't try to second-guess the way Hashem runs the world." Just as we can't pronounce the name, we can't fully understand how He runs the world. Similarly, the prohibition of profaning the name Elokeicha, the *pasuk* says, "I am Hashem," teaches us that Hashem's name will not be profaned. This means that His promises will not be found empty. His words are alive and true, forever, even though it looks that many of Hashem's promises haven't come true.

וכמו שנתבאר בספר תהלים (פ"ט כ'). אז דברת בחזון לחסידיך ותאמר שויתי עזר. על גבור הרימותי בחור מעם .מצאתי דוד עבדי וגו'. לעולם אשמור לו

חסדי ובריתי נאמנת לו ושמתי לעד זרעו וכסאו כימי שמים. אם יעזבו בניו
תורתי ובמשפטי לא ילכון וגו'. ופקדתי בשבט פשעם ובנגעים עונם. וחסדי לא
אפיר מעמו ולא אשקר באמינתי. לא אחלל בריתי ומוצא שפתי לא אשנה וגו'.
ואתה זנחת ותמאס התעברת עם משיחך. נארתה ברית עבדך חללת לארץ נזרו.
ונראה כי חס ושלום חלל בריתו על זה נאמר אני ה'. כי אך מפני האדם נסתר
אבל השי"ת אינו מחלל דבריו והם חיים וקיימים.

In *Sefer Tehillim* (89:20-21, 29-35, 39-40), David Ha-Melech
speaks about his feeling that Hashem has promised to have a
relationship with him, yet he feels abandoned, that Hashem has
not kept to His promise. It is in response to these feelings and
many similar ones, that Hashem ends each of the paragraphs
with exclamation "I am Hashem!" This means that His words are
true and He will keep His promises, even when it is not apparent!

והנה בעושק שכר שכיר שהקב"ה הזהיר ביומו תתן שכרו (כי תצא כ"ד ט"ו).
ולנו צוה לעבור אותו. ונאמר היום לעשותם (ואתחנן ז' י"א). ודרשינן היום
לעשותם למחר לקבל שכרם (עירובין כ"ב א'). וכתיב אל תאמר לרעיך לך
ושוב ומחר אתן (משלי ג' כ"ח). על זה נאמר אני ה'. כי דברי השי"ת כמשמרות
נטועים וקבועים לעד. ואף האדם לא ישיגם. ועל לא תעמד על דם רעך כתיב
קול דמי אחיך צעקים אלי מן האדמה (בראשית ד' י'). והנה אחרי שביד השי"ת
כל העולם איך ינוח להיעשות כזאת. על זה נאמר אני ה' כי הוא למעלה מגבול
שכל האדם.

Therefore, we can now understand why those four *mitzvos* end
with the statement "I am Hashem!" In the case of a day worker,
we are commanded to pay him his wages at the end of the day.
At the same time, we are commanded to serve Hashem, and He
will pay us at a later time. But we couldn't do that to a worker!
Therefore, this mitzvah concludes with the exclamation "I am

Hashem," meaning: Don't ask Me why I am running this world in a way that you don't understand, even if your understanding is based on the Torah! Hashem's laws are deep, and His promises forever, but man does not understand them. Furthermore, there is a commandment not to stand idly by when a person is being murdered, and yet in *Bereishis* (4:10), the *pasuk* says, "Your brother's blood cries out to me from the ground." Since the world is in Hashem's hands, how did he allow murder to take place. If we are commanded to stop murder, why didn't He? Again the *pasuk* says, "I am Hashem," meaning: This is above the understanding of man."

וגבי לא תקם ולא תטר מצינו שנאמר פקד עון אבות על בנים ועל בני בנים (כי תשא ל"ד ז'). ואף שאיתא בגמרא (ברכות ז' א'). שהוא רק כשאוחזין מעשה אבותיהם בידיהם. אכן מה שנאמר ביאשיהו מלך יהודה אשר עשה הישר בעיני ה'. וכמהו לא היה לפניו מלך אשר שב אל ה' בכל לבבו ובכל נפשו ובכל מאדו ככל תורה משה ואחריו לא קם כמהו. אך לא שב ה' מחרון אפו הגדול אשר חרה אפו ביהודה על כל הכעסים אשר הכעיסו מנשה (מלכים ב' כ"ג). ונדמה כי הקב"ה חס ושלום נוקם ונוטר. על זה נאמר שלא ירעים אדם אחרי מדותיו של הקב"ה. כי באמת הקב"ה מקיים דבריו רק מפני האדם נעלם. אבל נמצא בזה טובה יותר מכפי שכל אדם. וכן לא תעשק את רעך. וכתיב ושבתי אני וראה את כל העשקים (קהלת ד' א'). וכי מה יוכל לעשות הממזר הנולד ונאסר לבא בקהל. בכל אלה נאמר אני ה' שיש לו עומק עמוק יותר משכלך והכל לטובתך.

Regarding the commandment about bearing a grudge and taking revenge, we see that Hashem says (*Shemos* 34:7) that He punishes to the third and fourth generations, even though the Gemara says this is only when they continue in the evil ways of their ancestors. One might raise a question regarding

Yoshiayhu, the son of Menashe, who caused the entire people to return to Hashem in *teshuvah*. The Navi (Melachim II Chapter 23) says there was no one like him in terms of his *teshuvah*. Yet ultimately he was killed because of Menashe's sins. This seems as if Hashem does take revenge and holds a grudge. Therefore, we are told, "I am Hashem." It is beyond your comprehension; don't ask Me about this contradiction. The בית יעקב says, in fact Hashem keeps to all of these things. It's beyond our understanding how and what Hashem does; how it will benefit us has repercussions that are far beyond our understanding.

Similarly, are the commandments not to defraud or deal with each other crookedly or unfairly, but what did a *mamzer* do to be prohibited from entering the Jewish people? With all of these apparent injustices, we are only seeing a small part of the picture, and therefore He declares after each one "I am Hashem!" Hashem is working everything out in a way that will be so great for us; it is above our understanding.

והנה נאמר כאן כל ענין שנאמר בו אני ה' אלהיכם נאמר נגדו ענין שנאמר בו אני ה'. וכמבואר במי השלוח (פרשת קדשים). ענין אני ה' אלהיכם ואני ה'. נגד קדשים תהיו שמורה על שמחה של מצוה. ועיקר שמחה האמתית הוא שהאדם רואה ומשיג השגה גדולה מהשי"ת. ובזה נאמר אני ה' אלהיכם. שהאדם הרוצה לברר עצמו בזה. רואה כי זה הוא הפך מחיי עולם הזה ויכול לבא התרשלות בדעתו. לכן נאמר בו אני ה' אלהיכם שרומז לבטחון שלא יעזבו ה'.

When the *pasuk* speaks about a mitzvah, it concludes, "I am Hashem Elokeichem (Your G-d)," to balance out the *mitzvos* of "I am Hashem." It is for this reason that the *parsha* opens up (*Vayikra* 19:1-2) with the statement of be *kadosh*, because I am Hashem, Elokeichem. It is to give a person joy in serving

Hashem, because the greatest joy is in the ability of a person to recognize Hashem's greatness. The fact that Hashem calls Himself "Your G-d" means that He is giving you the ability to grasp a little bit. This is why the phrase "I am Hashem Elokeichem," appears. A person wants to meet Hashem, but he sees this is impossible in this world, and therefore becomes depressed. Therefore, when Hashem says "be *kadosh*, recognize My greatness," a person thinks, "but how?" Then Hashem responds, "I am Hashem, Elokeichem; I won't set up a situation where you can't achieve it. Look, I am saying I am your G-d!"

אכן כאשר יחטיא אדם בענין הזה וידמה לו שיש לו איזה רכוש מכחו ועוצם ידו שהשיג. אז נקרא גנב שנוטל בלא רשות בעלים. ונגד זה נאמר לא תגנבו. וכאשר ירצה לנדק משפטו בשקר נגד זה נאמר ולא תכחשו. כי עיקר הוא שלא יכחש האדם בדעתו נגד השי״ת. וכאשר השקר גובר אצלו להעיז פניו נקרא משקר. ולזה נאמר ולא תשקרו. ויש יותר העזת פנים הנקרא נשבע לשקר. גם על זה מורה לא תגנבו שלא יעלים אדם דברי תורה. כי האדם הרואה שהכל מה׳ הוא. יש לו טובת עין לגלות לחברו כל מה שלבו יודע. כי אינו מנושא בזה.

The בית יעקב continues based on this idea to explain the *pesukim* that come before the commandments of not swearing falsely (*Vayikra* 19:11-12), stealing, giving contradictory testimony, lying, and swearing falsely. A person can twist the concept of Hashem's giving a person the ability to achieve and corrupting it into thinking that he "owns" his strength. This is called being a thief, as he takes something which belongs to another owner (Hashem) and keeps it for himself. The *pasuk* goes on to say that when this person wants to try to justify his theft, he becomes a contradicting witness. When this falsehood gains strength within him, he is called a liar and the person's life itself is defined by falsehood. Therefore the *pasuk* says that a person profanes the name Elokeicha. Hashem gave us the ability to achieve and understand, which is symbolized by the name Elokeicha. Someone can take this opportunity and twist it to create his own reality, until he swears that his version is the true one.

Additionally, within this concept of not stealing is that a person shouldn't withhold *divrei Torah*. When a person sees that it is all from Hashem, he is generous in revealing what he knows to his fellows and is does not become conceited because of it. This could be considered stealing because what Hashem gave the person to understand does not come from the learner at all. A person could make the mistake of believing that he is the one who achieved by himself, and as a result, withholds Torah from other people. This is stealing Hashem's glory for himself, for the Torah belongs to Hashem and no one has the right to act in such a way.

וזה דאיתא במסכת פסחים (נ' א'). סבר רבא למדרשה בפירקא. אמר ליה ההוא סבא לעלם כתיב. כי אם היה מגלה סוד שם המפורש. לא היה נשאר לו שום דבר התנשאות בידיעת התורה על חבריו כי בזה נכלל הכל. והיה לו טובת עין לגלותו לכל תלמידיו. עד שאמר לו ההוא סבא כי אין זה כבוד השי"ת:

There was a story in *Pesachim* (50b) in which Rava wanted to expound upon the meaning of Hashem's name. An old man (Eliyahu Ha-Navi) stopped him by saying that this should be hidden. The בית יעקב explains that Rava did not see a problem disclosing the secrets of the name of Hashem to everybody. It was Torah that Hashem had given to him; therefore he must share it. The old man (Eliyahu Ha-Navi) told him that even though he was correct that it is all Hashem's Torah, by the same virtue this specific area, of Hashem's name should not be revealed. This is a similar concept about profaning the name Elokeicha. Although Hashem gives us the ability to understand, it could lead to His name being profaned. In this Gemara we can understand the *pasuk* being read, "Don't steal" by holding back Torah, but don't profane the name Elokeicha by revealing things that are not for public consumption, such as the name Hashem."

The Izhbitzer Tradition

In many Izhbitzer teachings, we are often faced with navigating among many concepts that are true and trying to learn what is within our human ability to make sense of the contradictions of life.

Practical Advice

When we are caught between two truths that seem contradictory, Hashem tells us, don't try to understand the way that I work. But then we can become depressed. If that is the case, that we are all walking around in the dark and we really don't understand anything, that so much is outside of our abilities, then what's the point of doing anything? Hashem says, I am giving you the ability to achieve and to understand. Don't give up, but don't make the mistake of using these abilities to create an independent artificial reality or to withhold Torah.

During these days of Sefirah, where we are touched by the deaths of Rebbe Akiva's talmidim, who died for not sharing Torah with each other, we are called to share what we know and not to hold back Torah from others.

פרשת אמור

from Mei ha-Shiloach

בהסדרה הזאת יש ה' פרשיות עד פרשות המועדות והם נגד ה' מיני תרעומות שיוכל להמצא בלב האדם על מדותיו של הקב"ה.

Emor has five *parshios*, each one contains a complaint that a person can have against how Hashem runs the world. These complaints form in a person's mind, due to his perception of the "unfairness" of a situation created resulting from the *halachah*.

הפרשה הראשונה הוא מנפשות מת הוא נגד תרעומות שיש בלב האדם על המיתה וההעדר המצוי בעולם.

The first *parsha* talks about death, and the complaints that a person has against Hashem are that death exists and that the world is constantly moving toward decay.

ופרשה השנית היא מבעל מום שיוכל להמצא בלבו תרעומות על מדותיו של הקב"ה אחר אשר התנטע בגזע אהרן והיה ראוי להקריב לה' ולעבוד אותו. למה ברא בו מום שימנע אותו מזה הקדושה. כי קדושת כהן העובד אין לשער. כמו שנראה שצוה לנו הש"י אכילת מצות כמה קדושה יש בזה האכילה. וכל שכן אכילת קדשי שמים, כמו שמצינו בגמ' (פסחים נ"ז א') שצווחה העזרה

יכנס וימלא כריסו מקדשי שמים. נראה מזה איך יקר הוא בעיני ה' אכילת
קדשים. וכ"ש הכהן העובד כמה קדושה ימצא בו בעבודתו לה'. ולזה כאשר
ימצא מום בכהן יוכל להמצא בו תרעומות. כי אחרי גם אכילת קדשים הותרה
לו. אך מעבודת הש"י הוא מרוחק.

The second *parsha* deals with the concept of a defect that
disqualifies a *kohen* from serving in the Mikdash. Even though
he is from the family of Aharon, he cannot serve there, due to
this defect. The *kohen* could say, "Hashem, what is the point,
why did you do this to me? To make me a *kohen* but not allow
me to serve You?" We cannot fathom what the honor of being
able to serve there means. Despite the fact that they can eat
kodshim, which is also a great honor, it still pales in comparison
to being able to serve Hashem through the *avodah*.

ופרשה השלישית היא מכהן שנטמא. כי בטח הכהן שהיה מוכן לעבוד את
ה' היה משמר עצמו קודם לכן וזיכך את לבו כפי יכולתו שלא יארע לו שום
תקלה אף במחשבתו. וכ"ש מטומאת הגוף. ואח"כ אירע לו דבר שירוחק על
ידה מעבודת הש"י ומאכילת קדשים וגדלה צעקתו מדוע לא עזר לו הש"י שלא
יהיה מרוחק מעבודתו.

The third *parsha* is that of a *kohen* who had the opportunity
to serve Hashem, but somehow or another he becomes *tamei*.
We can be certain that he was watching himself and preparing
himself to make sure that nothing inappropriate transpired,
whether in action or even in thought. However, something did,
and he can neither serve in the Mikdash nor eat *kodshim*. His
heart is broken and cries out to Hashem, "Why didn't you help
to stop me from being distanced from your service?"

ופרשה הרביעית הוא ממומי קרבן שיש צעקה בלב בעליו מדוע ינחיל לו הש"י
טוב ורכוש כזה שלא יוכל להקריבו אליו.

The fourth *parsha* is a *korban* that has a defect, and the person asks Hashem, "Why did you have to give me things that are lacking and cannot be brought close to You?"

ופרשה החמישית הוא מזבח תודה שנאמר בה ביום ההוא יאכל. היינו שהאדם
מחויב לתת הודאה על לשעבר ולצעוק על להבא שלא יבטח על יום מחר רק
שיהיה תמיד בתפלה וביראה. ועל ידי זה נאסר להותיר ממנו ליום שני וימצא
צעקה בלבבות בני האדם. מדוע לא יתן להם הש"י מבטח עוז שיוכלו לעשות
כל דבריהם בבטחון שהש"י יעזרם.

The fifth *parsha* and the fifth complaint is regarding the *korban todah*, which can only be eaten on the day that it is brought. Its purpose is to thank Hashem for the kindness of the past, but it also has another effect. People doesn't know what will be tomorrow, and as a result they are scared, spending their time in tefilah and fear. They will complain, "Why couldn't Hashem give us a future that we can rely upon."

וע"ז אמר דוד המלך ע"ה (תהלים צ"ב) במזמור שיר ליום השבת היינו (תמיד
ל"ג ב') לעתיד ליום שכלו שבת טוב להודות לה'. היינו שהקב"ה יורה בינה
לישראל ויבינם כי כל הדברים לא היו רק למען יוטב לאדם. וע"ז נאמר ולזמר
לשמך עליון כי במקום שהש"י ינהג למעלה משכל האדם אז יקרא עליון.

The next *parsha* speaks about Shabbos and is an answer to all of these questions. David Ha-Melech spoke about in the chapter of *Tehillim* called "*Mizmor Shir Le-Yom Ha-Shabbos.*" It speaks of the how Hashem will teach us how to understand the world, so that we will see that everything is for our own good. This perspective is called *shimcha elyon*, Your Highest Name, which enables us to see the world from a higher perspective.

ונגד החמשה פרשיות נתן להם לישראל חמשה פרשיות מועדות והם תקופות לאדם והרחבות דעתו לבל ימצא בו שום תרעומות.

Corresponding to these *parshios* are these five of the holidays, times that give strength to the person and help to widen his perspective so he can clarify the complaints that he has with Hashem.

וניתן להם נגד פרשה ראשונה פרשת פסח. כי פסח הוא התחלת הארה שהש"י הוא הנותן חיים לישראל.

Pesach corresponds to the first *parsha* of the dead, as it is a Yom Tov that has been an infusion of life into the Jewish people, time and time again, since the beginning of our life as a nation. It could be for this reason that we read the *haftarah* of *Techiyas Ha-Meisim* on Shabbos Chol Hamoed.

ושבועות הוא נגד פרשת בעל מום כי במתן תורה נתרפאו כל בעלי מומין ושבועות יורה כי הש"י ירפא הכל שיהיה לטוב.

Shavuos corresponds to the *parsha* of the *kohen* with a defect, as during Matan Torah/Shavuos time, all of the defects of the Jews were healed. The complaint is essentially that the *kohen* was unable to serve Hashem, just to eat *kodshim*. In the same way, up until Matan Torah, the Jews could not serve Hashem; we could only partake in the good that He gives to the world.

Once we have the Torah, we have the ability to serve Him, and not be freeloaders.

וראש השנה הוא נגד פרשת טמא. כי טמא הוא עצבות כמבואר [לעיל ד"ה אמור ב'] וע"ז הוא בר"ה מצות תקיעות שופר שלא יבא לאדם שמועה שיגיע לו ממנה עצבות.

Rosh Hashanah is the third *parsha*, corresponding to the *parsha* of the *kohen* who became impure and couldn't serve Hashem. *Tumah* represents sadness, and the *shofar* is used to make a loud sound so that we can't hear anything that is sad. On Rosh Hashanah, there is only one thought and one theme to the day, "Ha-Melech," the King. There is no mention of sin, as we are simply filled with the awareness of Hashem's Kingdom. It's for this reason the *shofar* cannot have gold in it or be from the horn of a cow, both corresponding to the sin of the Egel Ha-Zahav. There is no *tumah*, no sadness, only being in His Presence.

ויום הכפורים הוא נגד מומי הקרבן כי בעת שישראל עוזבים כל טובות והנאות עוה"ז כדי לקיים רצון הש"י. אז יבא כח וחיזוק לכל הטובות והרכוש שלהם.

Yom Kippur corresponds to finding a defect in the *korban*. When the Jews leave behind all of the pleasures of this world in order to serve Hashem, then they find strength and inspiration from all of the things that they posses. People complain about their lives and everything they have, and in truth, the entire world. We say, "Hashem, You've given me a life that's a mess; if it were different, then I could serve You." So we're given Yom Kippur to teach us that when you step outside of the world for a day and then you return, you'll realize what you can do with a day and with your life.

191

ונגד תודה היינו שהאדם צריך להיות תמיד בiraה. נגד זה ניתן להם מצות סוכה היינו שהש"י יגין על האדם ויקיף אותו. וחג הסוכות נקרא זמן שמחתנו היינו שהש"י יתן שמחה להאדם בהבטחתו שלא יעזוב אותו.

Corresponding to the *korban todah*, which tells us that a person must be fearful of the future, is Sukkos, which tells us that Hashem protects us and surrounds us. This is why Sukkos is called the time of our rejoicing, because Hashem gives us the assurance that He'll never abandon us. The *sukkah* is called *tzeila de-meimenusa*, "the shade of *emunah*," which combats the ever present fear of the world falling apart, and that we do reside in Hashem's Presence; He loves us and will not abandon us. Even though sometimes life is tough, we are not tossed to the random forces of the world.

The Izhbitzer Tradition

Many Izhbitzer teachings help us deal with the fallacies that a thinking oved Hashem can encounter and teach us how to get through them. See בית יעקב הכולל פרשת קדושים ד"ה לא תשבע *. See* בית *יעקב בכולל פרשת שמני ד"ה ויהי ביום השמיני, which also discusses the notion of Shimcha Elyon.*

Practical Advice

Hashem gives us the answers to the complaints and questions in our hearts through the Torah. When we have a problem with the way it seems that Hashem rules the world, look into the Torah for the question and the answer. Use the Yamim Tovim to gain the perspective that will see us through life's challenges. The

Gemara teaches us there is no greater simcha then the answering of our sfeikos, our fundamental questions in emunah. Now, that's simchas yom tov!

פרשת בהר

from Beis Yaakov ha-Kollel

וְשָׁבְתָה הָאָרֶץ (ויקרא כ"ה ב'). קרוב ה' לכל קוראיו לכל אשר יקראהו
באמת (תהילים קמ"ה י"ח). באמת היינו בסדר שסדר השי"ת. כי השי"ת סידר
כי על ידי מצוה שמטה יזכה האדם לקדושת יובל. כי שמטה הוא צמצום ועל
ידי זה יזכה לקדושה הקביעה.

The בית יעקב explains the mitzvah of *shmitah*, that the land will
"rest" (*Vayikra* 25:2), by quoting the *pasuk*, "Hashem is close
to all those who call to him in truth." What does it mean, "call
to him in truth"? "Truth" means that Hashem set up a system.
Despite His apparent distance, anyone can draw close to Him
by going through the system. Only through the mitzvah of
shmitah, by counting seven *shmitos*, forty-nine years, can a
person can touch the holiness of the world of *yovel*, the fiftieth
year. *Shmitah* is just a little bit of the world of *yovel*. Every
shmitah there is a certain level of freedom from the curse of
"You shall eat bread only by the sweat of your brow." However,
the curse returns with the passage of the *shmitah* year, whereas
the effects of *yovel*, such as the freedom for slaves, and return of
land to the correct inheritors, lasts forever.

194

כי כמו שבעולם הזה כשהאדם מקבל טובה מהארץ אשר הכל היה ממנה. אינו
מקבל רק אם הארץ תגביה נגדו ותחל תת כחה בצמיחתה כל פרי אוכל. כן
האדם כנגדה ישפיל דעתו וחשקו לעומתה. עד שיפגש חשק האדם אשר ירד
את חיל הארץ אשר עלה נגדו ואז יקבל האדם. זה הסדר האמתי. ואז מברך
האדם את ה' הנותן לו בסדר הזה אבל כשהאדם אינו ממתין שהארץ תעלה
כחה נגדו ואוכל העפר עצמה. אז תזיק לגופו כי צריך האדם והארץ להפגש בל
יישאר שום חלל. ובאם האדם מדלג החלל אז נקרא ונחש עפר לחמו (ישעיה
ס"ה כ"ה). וכמו שנתבאר בפרשת אמר.

We can see, using farming as an example, the value of having
a process to reach a goal. When a person wants to be able to
draw sustenance from the land, there is a system of how to do
it. Plants grow up from the ground, and man lowers himself
spiritually to take from those plants. Then, man thanks Hashem
for this process. When man does not wait for the process to play
out, he eats dirt, which damages his body. Both sides must come
together so that there is no distance between the two. When
man jumps over the gap, then he is just like the snake who "eats
dirt." By skipping the process to get to the product, the product
becomes dangerous.

וכן הוא הסדר בקדושה גם כן. ולכן בשמטה נאסר לעבוד השדה. כי אז יורד
השפעה גדולה שאין בכח האדם לקבלה. ובאם ירד האדם אז לקבל טובה. אז
לא תוכל הטובה להתכלל באדם ולעלות עמו למעלתו רק הוא יישאר בשפלות
כי יתמשך אחריה. כי יש בהטובה אז יותר כח ממה שיש בהאדם.

Just as this relationship exists in the natural order, it exists in
the world of holiness as well. Therefore, during *shmitah*, it is
forbidden to work the fields. During the *shmitah* year, such
unbelievable blessing enters the world, more than a man could

fathom. Normally, good things lift a person up, but when man does not have the ability to receive them, he will remain at his present low level.

וכמו כן נאסר בשבת לעבוד. כן תיקן השי"ת שעל ידי השמטה נגיע ליובל.

How then can we access this *kedushah*? By waiting through those forty-nine years of seven *shmitos*, we can reach it on the fiftieth year of *yovel*. In order to receive the *kedushah* of *yovel*, we must go through the cycle of *shmitah*.

כי יובל הוא התגלות האמתי בלי אמצעות דבר. כי ענין עבד הנרצע שיוצא ביובל מורה על זה. דענין הנמכר בגנבתו מבואר בפרשת משפטים כי הוא רק לטובתו. שאין בכחו לעמוד ולהתפלל להשי"ת שישפיע לו כי יבוש לעמוד נגד ה'. ולכן העצה לפניו שימכר ויקבל השפעה על ידי בעליו. אבל ביובל יראה השי"ת לכל אחד ואחד איך לא סר השגחתו מאתו. והוא משפיע לכל אחד לא על ידי אמצעות.

This *kedushah* of *yovel* is the revelation that there is nothing that stands in between Hashem and the world. Let's understand this concept further. During *yovel*, a Hebrew slave goes free, even though his ear was pierced, and the Torah says he should be a slave forever. The Torah dictates that the slave is to be sold because of his theft; therefore, his sale must be for his own good. The slave's underlying problem is not just that he stole. The slave feels he is unable to stand before Hashem and have a relationship with Him. The slave feels embarrassed to speak to Hashem Himself for his needs, and consequently tries to get things from other people. Therefore he is sold, and for this reason, does not receive anything directly; rather, he gets it through his master, trading the Master for a human master. But in *yovel*, Hashem shows each and every person that He never left him, and how He wants to give to each person without anyone in between. Therefore every slave goes free and everyone goes back to his ancestral land, where his soul has its roots.

וכן לכלל ישראל יראה כי כל אחד מקבל השפעה בפני עצמו לא על ידי מלך וכהן. ולזה הקדושה יכול האדם לבא אחרי שיספור וישמור שבע שמטות.

Shmitah shows the entire Jewish people that everyone receives their brachos only from Hashem, not through anyone else, even a king or a *kohen*. But you only can reach this level of understanding by counting the seven *shmitos* which lead up to *yovel*.

כי ענין שמטה הוא נגד מדה שלי שלך ויובל הוא שלך שלך. כמו שנתבאר במי השלוח (חלק א' בהר) והוא שנקבע קדושה בהאדם שלא מדעתו ולא יצרך להשתמש בדעת. וכן הוא המדה שעל ידי שמטה יגיע ליובל.

Shmitah can be likened to the attribute in *Pirkei Avos*, "What's yours is yours and what's mine is yours." A person understands that everything is Hashem's, even the things that he believes he has accomplished. Similarly, the מי השלוח explains that *shmitah* plants *kedushah* into a person without his input. It is through this willful inaction, listening to the "It's all Hashem," that we can reach *yovel*.

והנה המקלל רצה לפתוח מדת היובל לא על ידי עבודה. כי מאחר שלעתיד יראה השי"ת כי מעשה הנעשית בלי פעולת שכל האדם. גדולה ממה שהאדם עושה בשכל. כמו שכתוב נקבה תסובב גבר (ירמיה ל"א כ"א). והנה לעתיד יראה השי"ת כי הנוקבא תקיף. והוא מפני שהיתה אמו מישראל. לכן רצה

197

לפתוח שזה העיקר. וכל מעשי הזכר שנקראים פעולות שכל האדם יפלו. כי
על ידי זה נשים פטורות ממצות עשה שהזמן גרמא (קדושין כ"ט א'). כי היא
נקבעת בקדושה למעלה מהזמן ולא תפול תחת שנוי הזמן והעת. כי רק הזכר
מצדו צריך להוסיף קדושה לפי הזמן. כמו שכתוב ואני תמיד איחל והוספתי על
כל תהלתך (תהלים ע"א י"ד). אבל מצד הנקבה אין צריך להוסיף.

We read in last week's *parsha* about the *mekallel*, the person
who cursed Hashem and was killed. What was he thinking? He
wanted to access the world of *yovel* without the "access point"
of *shmitah*. He wanted to jump into the future, where a person's
plans and calculations pale in comparison to things that happen
without man's input. The Navi Yirmiyahu explains this future as
"the male is encircled by the female." In the future, the feminine
power will be more prominent than that of the masculine.
What are feminine powers and masculine powers? The male
power refers to those capabilities that must act to add *kedushah*,
as opposed to the female which does not. In the future the
masculine powers (which are bound to space and time) take
a back seat to those of female, (which are transcendent). The
mekallel felt that he should be able to camp with the tribe of
Dan, his mother's tribe (his father was an Egyptian), touching
the world of *yovel*, the future, in which the female's contribution
will be the determinant.

ולכן נאמר בטענת בני יוסף נגד בנות צלפחד. ואם יהיה היובל לבני ישראל
ונוספה נחלתן (מסעי ל"ו ד'). כי בדרך העולם הציב השי"ת גבולים שהזכר
יורש. ובאם תלך הירושה לנקבה נקרא העברה. אבל באם יהיה היובל שהשי"ת
יראה כי מעשה הנעשה שלא על פי שכל האדם זה גדול מאד כי מה יחשב
האדם בשכלו. ובמקום שלא הגיע שכל האדם שם השי"ת שולט.

Similarly, the children of Yosef complained that the daughters of Tzlofchad would inherit their father and then marry out of the tribe, causing the land to be lost to the tribe. They would marry a man from another tribe, and then when the *yovel* would come, the land would not go back to the children of Yosef. Through *yovel*, Hashem shows us that when He guides the world in a way that is counterintuitive, it is greater than when He guides it in a way that makes sense to us. When Hashem guides the world in a way that is hard to understand, it is readily apparent that Hashem is the guiding force.

ומזה פחדו שיתוסף חלקם על המטות. והשי"ת יחתום את שמו כי לא היתה זאת במקרה רק ידו היתה בזה וזהו יובל. והנה השי"ת העמיד שלא נגיע ליובל רק על ידי שמטה. וזהו הסדר לכל אשר יקראהו באמת. והמקלל רצה לפתוח לא על ידי שמטה. לכן נדחה משתי קומות. כמו שנתבאר בפרשת אמר. והשי"ת בנה שינתן לישראל אחר מעשה המקלל פרשת שמטה ויובל.

The tribe of Yosef feared most that they would lose their land to whomever the Bnos Tzlofchad would happen to marry. Hashem showed that nothing occurs by chance. Those moments that seem to be without rules and that go against a person's understanding are moments where we see Hashem's plan unfolding. But Hashem set up the world such that you can only reach *yovel* through *shmitah*. This is how "A person calls to Hashem in truth." The *mekallel* wanted to bring the days of *yovel* without *shmitah*; therefore he was thrown out in this world and the next. However Hashem taught the Jewish people that there is some truth to the claim, through *shmitah* and then *yovel*. Hence, we learn the *parsha* of *yovel* and *shmitah* after the *mekallel*.

והנה ענין יובל הוא הערה על לעתיד. כי לעתיד ילך השפעת השי"ת לכל אחד
בשוה. כי בעולם הזה צריך לקבל השפעה על ידי מלך וכהן. ולעתיד תהיה
השפעה מפורשת לכל אחד. אך בעולם הזה צריך עוד לבירורים. ועל זה מורה
ענין יובל שישוב איש לאחוזתו. וכן גם העבד נרצע מאחר דאינו נרצע רק
לטובתו. כי ענין עבד הנמכר בגנבתו מבואר בפרשת משפטים כי הוא לטובתו.
כי הוא לא יוכל לעמוד נגד ה' להתפלל אליו. ויוכרח לקבל על יד אמצעי.
וביובל יראה לו השי"ת כי גם לו ישופע מהשי"ת לבדו:

Yovel is a glimpse into the future when each person will meet
Hashem equally. In this world, we need to receive our sustenance
through various ways and means, In the future, everyone will
receive what they need directly from Hashem, as opposed to.
this world in which we still require a process. This is why during
yovel everyone returns to his ancestral land. We have seen this
concept with regards to a person who sells himself into slavery
and decided to continue in this condition after the seven-year
period is up. There is a reason why the Torah permits such an
institution to continue. The basis of the slave's problem is that
he does not perceive Hashem to be the sustainer of his needs, to
whom he should be davening. Therefore, he acquires "a master,"
a middle man, to provide his needs. During yovel, even such an
entrenched personality goes free, as he is returned to his land,
with proper understanding of Hashem as the true Master and
Sustainer.

The Izhbitzer Tradition

See מי השלוח חלק א בהר who discusses the kedushah of shmitah.
Also see בית יעקב הכולל פרשת משפטים which discusses the slave and
his theft.

Practical Advice

There are many experiences in the world that require us to ease into them, rather than jump into them all at once. When waiting for things leaves us frustrated, understand that in order to enter into kedushah we have to be patient. There are two extremes that the בֵּית יַעֲקֹב is warning us against. On one hand, a person needs to feel that he can approach Hashem; on the other hand, he can't rush into kedushah too quickly, lest it be dangerous for him.

פרשת בחוקתי

from Beis Yaakov ha-Kollel

אִם בְּחֻקֹּתַי תֵּלֵכוּ (ויקרא כ"ו ג') .ענין שלא נאמר וידבר ה' אל משה. כי אלו העניינים מורים על דברים שהם למעלה משכל ותפיסת האדם.

The *parsha* this week opens with the words, "If you will follow my *chukim*-laws…" (*Vayikra* 26:3). The בית יעקב asks why this *parsha* doesn't start with the preamble, "Hashem spoke to Moshe saying…." He explains that this *parsha* deals with matters that are outside of man's understanding. Hence the word *chok* is used, referring to a law whose meaning is above the understanding of man.

והנה בעניינים אלו נמצא דברים שאין כח עבודת האדם מגיע לתקנם. כי כשיחטא אדם חס ושלום רק כנגד השי"ת אז יכופר לו תכף כשישיב. כי השי"ת הוא רב חסד. אך כי יש הרבה עניינים שהם נוגעים בין אדם לחברו .ומהם יתחייבו כל מיני יראות.

There are things such as these that man is not able to repair with his actions. When a person sins against Hashem, he is forgiven as soon as he does *teshuvah*, because Hashem is full of kindness. But when the sin is against another person who must do the forgiving, the sinner is understandably afraid.

202

כי כל היראות בעולם הזה יבואו מהתנשאות האדם פן עבר גבולו ועלה לגבול
שאינו שלו. ועל זה נאמר כי טוב אמר לך עלה הנה מהשפילך לפני נדיב אשר
ראו עיניך (משלי כ"ה ז').

These fears are the result of one person having influence over
another and there is the possibility of one person overstepping
his boundaries into someone else's territory. Shlomo Ha-Melech
(*Mishlei* 25:7) reflects on this reality by commenting "that it
is better to sit in a place of lowness, and let them tell you to
rise, rather than sit in a place of greatness and they tell you to
descend, as you are in someone else's place."

ובזה אין יד האדם משיג לברר את עצמו. אך באם האדם מברר את עצמו קודם
לכן עד הוד שבהוד. אז מכאן ואילך יעיד עליו השי"ת.

This reality is something that is not in any one person's capacity
to fix. However, a person can work on what he has the ability
to repair. The בית יעקב explains that the day of *hod shebe-hod* in
Sefiras Ha-Omer (which is Lag Ba'Omer) signifies that, once
a person has done everything he can to make things better,
Hashem will testify that he has done so and will assist him,
going forward.

כי ברור כוונתו. וענין הוד שבהוד הוא. כי הוד מורה על בירור. והוד שבהוד
הוא כשהאדם עושה מעשה בלי דעת.

Hod shebe-hod means that a person is trying to do all that he
can do, and, as a result, Hashem is blessing his actions with
further success, which would not have occurred if the person
had been left to his own devices. Each of the seven *middos* of

the heart (that we work on throughout the year, but especially during *Sefiras Ha-Omer*) is useful in repairing something in our personality. Each of these *middos* is a world unto itself, requiring us to deal with the details of the application of that *middah*. *Hod* means "clarification," the demonstration of what really was going on, and the admission that a person is not in control. By doubling the *middah, hod she-behod* means not only admission that a person is not in control, but even when a person thinks he know what he is doing, he doesn't truly comprehend the extent of his limitations.

כגון כשהאדם אובד מעות ואח"כ יושיעו השי"ת שימצא אותם אדם כשר. וזה בירור שהאדם זך בפעלים. ובאם זה המוצאם ילך ויעשה בזו האבדה דבר מצוה. זה נקרא הוד שבהוד. כי בכל עניני עולם הזה יש בירורים כאלה.

(For example a person loses money and then Hashem makes it happen that a kosher person finds it and uses the money to be able to do mitzvah. The person had no control over what happened, and didn't intend to empower someone else when he lost the money. But we see that great things came out of this action without intending it. In running the world this way, Hashem makes it happen that people do what they can and great things happen that were not intended. This is *hod shebe-hod*.)

באם האדם עושה מעשה בחשבון. כגון שנותן לקופה של צדקה דממני עליה גבאי הגון ובזה נמצא דעת. אך למי יתנה הגבאי בזה אין דעת האדם הולך. רק תפלת האדם גם שם נמצאת שמתפלל שיזמין לו השי"ת עני כשר. אבל שילך העני בזה הכח ויעשה מצוה לזאת גם אין כח תפלה מגיע כל כך.

Let's take an example. A person does an action with a specific intent, like giving money to a certain charitable institution that has a supervisor appointed over it to make sure that the money is given out properly. Nonetheless, a person can't control to whom the supervisor of the charity gives the money. The only thing that the donor can do is pray that Hashem send a poor person who is righteous who needs the money. But even our *tefillah* cannot make certain that the poor person uses the money in the right way.

רק הערת צעקה בלב. ובאם עד מקום שיד האדם מגעת מברר עצמו בעבודה ותפלה. אז השי"ת יגמור בעדו שיעיד עליו ויגמור לטוב.

A person could become frustrated and say, "If it were within my reach, I would do everything I could. Whether it be davening, learning, or serving Hashem, I'd try my best. But now it seems as if what is being asked of me is out of my reach." In such a situation, Hashem completes it for him.

ולכן זאת הסדרה תדבר מעניינים כאלה שנקראים חקים. וגם היא סדרה הל"ג שהיא הוד שבהוד כפי ספירות הגלויים. ונמצא בה ל"ג ברכות. ול"ג פסוקים מתוכחה. וכנגד זה ניתן ל"ג פסוקים פרשת ערכין חוץ פסוק אלה המצות שאינו מעניין הערכין. שהוא פדיון על כל. וכמבואר במי השלוח (חלק א' בחקתי).

Therefore, this *parsha*, *Bechukosai*, speaks about things that are *chukim*, things which are beyond our understanding or ability to influence. This *parsha* is the 33rd in the cycle, which corresponds to the *middah* of *hod*. Here, Hashem teaches that when we do everything that we can, He will help them to finish the rest—as signified by the number 33. It is appropriate that in the *parsha*, there are 33 blessings and 33 curses. Similarly, there are 33 *pesukim* of *Erechin*, dealing with the worth of things when sanctified to the Beis Ha-Mikdash, and how much it would

205

explains that these *pesukim* בית יעקב cost to redeem them. They contain within them the ability to transform everything in the world to *kedushah*. This means that even the things which it seems impossible to sanctify, such as things which are not normally used in the Beis Ha-Mikdash, can also be redeemed. This teaches us that when a person wishes to do something good, and tries to, but apparently hits a roadblock, this desire to do so does not go unheeded. Hashem teach us the 33 *pesukim* of *Erechin* to show when a person wants *kedushah*, and tries his hardest, Hashem will create solutions which go above the realm of the understandable to empower them.

The Izhbitzer Tradition

See (א) מי השלוח, which explains Erechin as a redemption for everything, and ספר זמנים הגדה in the section on חמץ which deals with the realms that we have the ability to effect.

Practical Advice

When frustration sets in, and you feel like a failure due to your inability to achieve, consider that Hashem runs the world in mysterious ways. When you've tried your hardest, and there is nothing more you can do, remember it is in His hands. You cannot control everything, nor are you expected to be able to. Sometimes, we must "Daven for the ability to change what we can, accept what we cannot, and have the sechel to understand the difference." The middah of hod shebe-hod and with it, the 33rd of anything, always means you've done what you can, now only Hashem can take over.

פרשת במדבר

from Beis Yaakov ha-Kollel

וַיְדַבֵּר ה' אֶל מֹשֶׁה בְּמִדְבַּר סִינַי בְּאֹהֶל מוֹעֵד בְּאֶחָד לַחֹדֶשׁ הַשֵּׁנִי בַּשָּׁנָה הַשֵּׁנִית לְצֵאתָם מֵאֶרֶץ מִצְרַיִם לֵאמֹר. שְׂאוּ אֶת רֹאשׁ כָּל עֲדַת בְּנֵי יִשְׂרָאֵל (**במדבר א' א'-ב'**). הענין שצוה הקב"ה למנות את ישראל אף שהכל גלוי לפניו. אכן בהמנין נתחזק מצב ישראל. כי כמו שניתנה התורה לישראל אף כי כל העולם נברא בדברי תורה. כמו דאיתא בזה"ק (ויקרא י"א ב'). עשרה עשרה הכף בשקל הקדש כו'. עשרה מאמרות במעשה בראשית ועשרה מאמרות במתן תורה. אך כי בעת שניתן התורה נתקרבו דברי תורה יותר לדעת האדם. וכמו שאחר מתן תורה נצטוו שיעשו משכן. היינו קביעות לקדושתם שקבלו שיהיה יתד בל תמוט. וכאן נעמדו על מקומם כל אחד במקום הראוי לו. ועל ידי זה נתחזק כחם .

Why did Hashem command that the Jews be counted? He knew the number already; He knows everything. The בית יעקב explains that the Jews were counted to strengthen and encourage them. Let's understand what that means. The בית יעקב asks a fundamental question: Why was the Torah given? The entire world is based on the Torah. He cites the *Zohar* (*Vayikra* 11b) to make a point. It says that the *pasuk* (*Bamidbar* 7:86) contains "ten" twice, referring to the Ten Commandments and the Ten Statements with which the world was created. These tens are

207

the same, the only difference is that, once the Torah was given, the *divrei Torah* became closer to us. There are many times that Torah needs to be brought closer to us, so that *kedushah* has a base in the world. It is for this reason that the Mishkan was built after the Torah was given. Once the Jews were counted, they were told "where to stand," and they felt as if they were in their proper place. When people feel like strangers, they cannot use their talents and abilities properly.

כי כל עניני היראה שמרפפת דעת האדם הוא. פן הוא חס ושלום במצב מקום יותר מהראוי לו. וכמו שכתוב מהשפילך לפני נדיב (משלי כ"ה ז'). ומזה נתחייבו כל האיסורים שנאסרו ישראל מלקבל איזה דבר. כי גם בשרפי מעלה נמצא יראה על ענינים כאלו. ולכן נאמר וקרא זה אל זה (ישעיה ו' ג'). שמקבלים רשות שלא יעלה אחד למדרגה שאינה שייכת לו .

Conversely, a person could try to become someone different from who he really is. We are obligated to observe the negative commandments in order that we learn not to be anything else other than ourselves. Even the *malachim* ask each other permission before acting to assure that they are at the spiritual level which is relevant to them, and not anyone else.

כי כמו שיש בעולם דומם צומח חי מדבר. וכל מה שלמעלה במדרגה נמצא בו בחירה יתירה. עד כי לגדול שבמדברים הוא המלך לו הותרה לפרוץ גדר (ב"ב ק' ב'). לפי שהוא יותר בדעת מיושבת לכן לא יחפוץ רק בטובת הכלל. ואף שנראה כעושה מעשה חימה .

The בית יעקב explains the levels of choice that exist. We know that traditionally there are four different levels of creation: nonliving matter, vegetation, animals, and speaking creatures, i.e., humans. Each successive level brings with it a greater ability to choose. Among the "speakers," the one with the most unencumbered choice is the king, who the Gemara (*Bava Basra* 100b) notes has no constraints on his choice at all. For the king there are no boundaries or limits to his authority, as he acts with eminent domain. This is granted to him as he is acting for the greater good of the nation, even though you might think has other motives.

ועל זה מורה הסדר שבהדגלים. הראשון היה נחשון בן עמינדב מורה אף
שעושה מעשה שנראית כעקשות. מכל מקום הוא מלא נדיבות. כמו דאיתא
בזה"ק (שמיני מ' ב'). הא דוד מלכא איש תרומה הוה. ומשמע שמורם מכל.
ומכל מקום הוא מלא רחמנות.

This is the reason for the arrangement of the camp. The first one is that of Nachshon ben Aminadav. Nachshon is part of the lineage of Moshiach, the Jewish royalty, and therefore, the Midrash tells us, he leapt into the water first before it had split, showing how he broke through all of the constraints around him. In addition to his strength of character and forcefulness, he is also "ben Aminadav," benevolent and giving to his people. He is both in lineage and in attitude the precursor to the kingdom that would be established centuries later. Similarly, the *Zohar* notes that David Ha-Melech was a person of *terumah*, which means both "uplifted" (jumping over the boundaries) and "giving."

והאחרון היה אחירע בן עינן מורה שהולך לבסוף וכח הפעולה נקטן בו. מכל
מקום עינו זך מאד שנהנה מראיתו. כי יש שמותר לו לקבל טובה ויש שאין לו
רק ראיה. ולו היה ראיה מפורשת מאד.

On the other end of the spectrum, the last of the camps is Achira ben Einan, who walks at the end. His actions are small and don't amount to much. While Nachshon seems to be able to do anything, Achira appears not to be able to do anything, merely to watch things unfold.

והנה כמו שהציב השי"ת שעל ידי דברי עולם הזה יוכל האדם להפסיד כל חייו חס ושלום. כן העמיד השי"ת עבודה ומעשים בעולם הזה שיוכל האדם לקנות חיי עולם. וזה הכח ניתן בהאדם. ועל זה יסד הקב"ה באופן הזה כדי שכל השכר יקרא על שם האדם שהוא יגיע כפיו.

However, despite the difference in each camp, within each person's *avodas Hashem*, meaning the seeming difference of efficacy of his choices, we know that Hashem created the world in a way that a person can lose his spiritual stature. At the same time, Hashem created *avodah* and good deeds by which a person can earn the world to come. Hashem gave these awesome potentials to each person, so that he may serve Hashem and be rewarded in accordance with his exertion.

וזה שנאמר וצבאו ופקדיו צבאו הוא הכח שעל ידו יוכל האדם לקנות חיי עולם. ופקדיו הוא החסרון שנטבע באדם מתולדתו. כי פקדיו הוא לשון חסרון. כמו ויפקד מקום דוד (שמואל א' כ' כ"ה).

The בית יעקב explains two words used in the *parsha* to describe a person's *avodas Hashem*. *Tzeva'o* means the power make spiritual acquisitions, such as the world to come. However, the word *pekudah*, means to fill in something which is missing. We see this from the *pasuk* in Shmuel, using the word *va-yifkod*, denoting that Shaul noticed David was missing.

ומשה רבינו עליו השלום הוא היה המאחד לב ישראל והוציא כחם אל הפועל. הן כח הטוב לסגל מעשים טובים והן לתקן כח ההפסד מהחסרון הנמצא

210

בהאדם. כי מקום משה רבינו עליו השלום היה במזרח מקום זריחת השמש
ודעתו נתקרבה לה'. כי בלוים נתן הבחירה היותר גדולה. וליותר במשה רבינו
עליו השלום. ובזה היה משה רבינו מדוגל מאד.

Moshe Rabbeinu is the person who brings the heart of the
Jewish people together and brings their potential into reality, it
is the ability of the Jews to bring about good deeds and repair
what is missing within them. The בית יעקב explains more of the
relevance of the positioning in the camp. Moshe's camped in
the east. Just as the sun rises in the east and fills the world with
light, Moshe fills the world with knowledge; therefore Moshe
placed his tent in the east.

כמו האדם המדוגל על כל בעלי החיים אף כי האדם מאוחר לכל מעשה בראשית.
וכמו שנתבאר בפרשת בא. כי נמצא בברואים כחות גדולים. כמו שכתוב מלפנו
מבהמות ארץ ומעוף השמים יחכמנו (איוב ל"ה י"א). וכמו דאיתא בגמרא
(סנהדרין ל"ח א') אומר לו יתוש קדמך במעשה בראשית. אבל בזה האדם
מדוגל כי יש לו בחירה בדעת. ובזה היה מקום המקדש מדוגל. וכמו כן גם כאן
אף כי השכינה במערב (ב"ב כ"ה א'). שנקרא אויר יה. מכל מקום בזה מדוגל
צד המזרחית. כי שם פתיחת האור והבחירה שם בהתגברות:

People are of a higher spiritual quality than all other creatures,
even though man was created last. Each level of creation has
its own strength and ability, but man remains greater due to
his knowledge and ability to choose, which sets him above
everything else. The בית יעקב explains that the Mikdash is in
the east as well, as it teaches us of the power of our choices, and
empowers us to choose.

The Izhbitzer Tradtion

See נאות דשא אחרי מות who discusses a person's potential and their lacking.

Practical Advice

The Jews were counted to teach them that each one of us despite the perceived efficacy of our choices, or inefficacy of our choices, still have the ability to serve Hashem, to acquire and repair that which is broken, and each one of us has a place. Moshe came to teach us how to use our choices and serve Hashem in our specific life situations. Whenever we feel as if we are "stuck" and our choices are not effective, we need to sit and think whether or not this is truly our avodah, or maybe it's someone else's, which is why it isn't working for us.

פרשת נשא

from Beis Yaakov ha-Kollel

וַיְדַבֵּר ה' אֶל מֹשֶׁה לֵּאמֹר. דַּבֵּר אֶל בְּנֵי יִשְׂרָאֵל וְאָמַרְתָּ אֲלֵהֶם אִישׁ אוֹ אִשָּׁה
כִּי יַפְלִא לִנְדֹּר נֶדֶר נָזִיר לְהַזִּיר לַה'. מִיַּיִן וְשֵׁכָר יַזִּיר (במדבר ו' א'-ג'). איתא
בזה"ק (נשא קכ"ז א'). הכא אית לאסתכלא כיון דאסור ליה חמרא ענבים למה.
דהא בכהני כתיב יין ושכר אל תשת וגו'. יכול ענבים נמי. לא. בענבים שרי.
הכא לנזיר מאי טעמא אסר ליה ענבים. אלא עובדא דא ומלה דא רזא עלאה הוא
לאתפרשא מן דינא בכלא כו'. ואי תימא דהאי נזיר שביק ממהימנותא עלאה.
לאו הכי אלא לא אתחזי ביה עובדא מסטר שמאלא כלום.

This week's *parsha* discusses the restrictions of a *nazir*. We know
that he is prohibited from wine or any grape products, and he
is commanded not to cut his hair. The בית יעקב cites the *Zohar*
which expresses astonishment why the *nazir* is prohibited from
eating grapes, while a *kohen* is only forbidden to be drunk.
(The *Zohar Naso* 127a explains that the *nazir* must stay away
from any of the grapes as they manifest the power of judgment,
concealed blessings. The *Zohar* asks in astonishment, "A *nazir*
is separating himself from the higher levels of *emunah*? Rather
the *nazir* has to separate himself from the left side entirely.")

והענין בזה דהנה יש באדם נפש רוח ונשמה. והנפש הוא הקטן שבכלם כי היא
משותפת עם הגוף. אבל מצד האדם הנפש הוא גדול. כי בגבוהות אין לו תפיסה.

213

ועל ידי הנפש יזכה למדרגות לטעום מפרי מעשיו בעולם הזה. וכל מה שיצמצם
עצמו יזכה להתנשא על ידו.

In order to understand what this selection from the *Zohar* is
saying to people like us, the בית יעקב begins with an introduction.
A person has a *nefesh*, a *ruach*, and a *neshamah*, three different
levels to the soul. While the *nefesh* is the lowest level, it is
working within the body, and compared to the body, it is the
greatest, as the body does not understand the greatness of the
soul at all. Through its connection with the *nefesh* soul, the body
can taste a little bit of the result of its actions in this world. As
much as people restrain themselves, they rise in spiritual status
in relation to that.

והנה מצד התורה נאמר סוטה קודם לנזיר. כי באמת טומאה ותגלחת והיוצא מן
הגפן הם נגד כועס ואינו משתכר ומעביר על מדותיו. ותלמיד חכם מותר
בכל אלה. כמבואר במי השלוח (חלק א' פרשת נח).

In *Chumash*, the *pesukim* that deal with the *sotah* (the married
woman who has been acting inappropriately, but does not admit
to having been intimate with a man who is not her husband)
comes before the *pesukim* that discuss the *nazir*.

The בית יעקב explains that the three things a *nazir* is forbidden
to partake in are impurity, shaving, and that which comes from
the vine, which are parallel to the attributes of not getting angry,
drunk, and going against one's nature. While these self-imposed
limitations are all good in and of themselves, they are regulated
by the Torah and do not necessarily have a connection with the
sotah. Moreover, the uniqueness of the *sotah* is that we are not
certain if she was intimate with another man.

214

אבל חכמינו ז״ל סדרו בש״ס נזיר קודם לסוטה (סוטה ב' א'). שהאדם יגדור
עצמו אף בדבר המותר לו. לבלי יצרך לראות סוטה בקלקולה. וכמבואר במי
השלוח (חלק א' פרשת נשא).

But Chazal put the Mishnah and Gemara of Maseches *Nazir*
before that of *Sotah*, and the Midrash comments on their
juxtaposition, that whatever was wrong with the *sotah*, the
nazir is a preemptive measure against. Avoiding impurity,
shaving, and that which comes from the vine, are equivalent
to the attributes of not getting angry, not getting drunk, and
one's obligation to go against one's nature. All of them share the
fact that, despite that they are not prohibited by the Torah, they
must be avoided, in order to make oneself holy, even in areas
that are not forbidden, so as not to fall into the same trap as the
sotah did, of falling into this gray area.

והנה שלשה אלה. יין שכר וענבים הם נגד בינה גבורה ומלכות. וכדאיתא
בזה״ק (נשא קכ״ז א'). יין לעילא הוא בינה. שכר לשמאלא. הוא גבורה. ענבים
דכניש כלהו לגבה. וזהו מלכות.

There are three types of grape products: wine, aged wine, and
grapes. Each one of these corresponds to a different way in which
Hashem describes how He runs the world and His expectation
of how we should act in it. These descriptions are called *sefiros*.
All of these grape products demonstrate to us that Hashem runs
the world in a nuanced way, whereby is difficult to see the entire
picture at once. The *sefirah* that is associated with wine is *Binah*,
the need to work through a concept and understand it, as wine is
intoxicating and its taste is complex. Aged wine, whose alcohol
level is higher, corresponds to *Gevurah*, which requires a person

to use his emotional strength and fortitude to persevere and act with strength in differing situations. Finally, grapes correspond to *Malchus*. While the potential for both types of wine is within the grape, it in itself has no alcoholic properties.

והנה הכהן שהוא רומז לתלמיד חכם נאסר רק ביין ושכר. למען תהיה דעתו בישוב. ונזיר מורה שהוא מצמצם עצמו אף במותר לו נאסר אף בענבים. כי ענבים רומזים לנפש. והוא שימסור הכל לה' ולא יגיע לו אף טובת הנאה. כי בהשתלשלות העולמות כל אחד מראה גדולתו להנמוך ממנו. וכן הנפש היא הנמוך לכן תראה גדולתה ותתפאר נגד הגוף. כי הנפש חיים והגוף דומם. ובנזיר גם זה נאסר.

A *kohen*'s prohibition of wine is based on that of a Torah scholar, as both are required to have clarity to issue rulings and the exactitude of the service in the Beis Ha-Mikdash. Only the non-intoxicating grape, therefore, is permitted to them. However, the *nazir* is a person who restricts himself so that even grapes are forbidden. This is because the grapes allude to the *nefesh*, that you are willing to give everything for Hashem, and want to avoid all pleasures. It is the way of the world for everything that is great to display its greatness to things smaller than itself. As the *nefesh* soul is alive and the body by itself would be inanimate, the soul's greatness is astonishing to the body. Hence, a *nazir* is forbidden to have this type of pleasure, to show off the *nefesh*'s greatness over the physicality of the body.

וכמו שנתבאר בפרשת ראה על פסוק כל הבכור. ועל זה מסיים הזהר ואי תימא דהאי נזיר שביק ממהימנותא עלאה. כי באמת ביין נאמר בגמרא (ברכות נ"ז א'). תלמיד חכם לעולם טוב לו. ולא נאמר כי אינו מקבל הקדושה הנמצאת ביין ואינו אוכל פירות ממנו. לאו הכי אלא לא אתחזי ביה עובדא מסטר שמאלא כלום.

Now, we will return to the *Zohar*'s question, "Is the *nazir* walking away from *emunah*?" Is the *nazir* leaving the concept of *bracha*, which a person must work through to receive? The Gemara explains that wine is good for a *talmid chacham*. The *nazir* does not deny its *kedushah*, or that it is the way that Hashem runs the world and requires that we act in that way. It's simply that the *nazir* must avoid all of the grape products that correspond to the "left sided sefiros," namely *Binah*, *Gevurah*, and *Malchus*.

והוא כי השערות נראים ככעס. כי כל מקום שהאדם משפיע יכתר סביבו
בשערות. ולפעמים שהאדם משפיע וירצה להבין לחברו דבר שהוא גדול
משכל חברו. אז נראה ככועס עליו ואף שהוא מלא טובה. אבל בנזיר עיקר
קדושה בשערא תליא. כדאיתא בזה״ק (נשא קכ״ז ב'). אך כי תחלה לא היה
רשאי להראות זאת כלל. וזהו קדש יהיה גדל פרע. שיקדש עצמו בשערו מבלי
להראות מהם דבר הנראה ככעס.

The *Zohar* continues that it's because of the requirement that the *nazir* grow out his hair. The *Zohar* makes a startling statement that long hair can seem angry, as the growing out of hair means an extension of the attribute of judgment. In order to understand this, we'll need to understand what the *Zohar* means when referring to hair, and what it means in in context to the *nazir*. The *Zohar* explains that this hair means the overflow of giving. What does that mean? Sometimes a person wants to share something with his friend, but that friend is not ready to receive it. So the person who wants to give "looks angry" that the recipient isn't ready. This isn't the case. The truth is that he's really just filled with the desire to give. Therefore, the real key to understand the *nazir* is his hair, which the *Zohar* says means his overwhelming desire to give. This is why the *Zohar* explains that the *nazir*'s holiness is dependent on his hair and desire to give. But in the beginning, he couldn't demonstrate it at all, hence the hair is *kadosh*, off limits, and it is forbidden to cut it. The *nazir* undergoes a process that takes himself away from all things that seem like anger, whether it be on the giving side—the overabundance of giving (his hair is forbidden)—or the receiving (grape products), which would place him on the recipient side, as they both contain hidden blessings, which a person is not always ready to receive.

ואח״כ יבא לו הנאה משערות האלו כי יתנם תחת הדוד של השלמים. המורים לטובה מפורשת. שהם שלום למזבח ולכהנים ולבעלים (ספרא ויקרא פ״ג פ״א). שלום מכל צד. ועל ידי השערות יתבשלו השלמים ויגיע לו מהם הנאה. ויטעום מפרי מעשיו במה שצצמם עצמו מזה יבא לו טובה מפורשת. וזה שנאמר ואחר ישתה הנזיר יין. כי מהשערות יגיע לו שלמים. שלום לה׳ ולבעלים לבלי יצרך עוד לבירורים. וכל זה יגיע לו ממה שהיה נראה לו עד עתה כמותרות:

At the conclusion of the *nazir*'s journey, he can give to everyone. The *nazir*'s hair is used to cook the *shlamim* meat—the *korban* that everyone can benefit from. The *nazir* can safely give to everyone and brings peace to everyone. The *nazir* then is allowed to partake in the grapes, the fruits of his labor and restraint. The Torah says, "Then he will drink wine." The Torah uses the future tense to show that he is now able to receive the hidden blessings. Through his hair, he can now obtain benefits for himself and benefit others.

The Izhbitzer Tradition

See נשא יוסף תפראת which discusses the gray areas in life. מי השלוח
תורה discusses how בית יעקב הכולל ואתחנן and נשא, נאות דשא דברים
שבעל פה teaches how man can perfect himself.

Practical Advice

There are times when we want to give, but it comes out the wrong way. Even giving, one of the most intrinsic human desire can be damaging when done in the wrong way. The nazir teaches us that before we try to give or influence others there must be a preparatory process that we must undertake.

פרשת בהעלותך

from Naos Deshe

בְּהַעֲלֹתְךָ אֶת הַנֵּרֹת (במדבר ח' ב'). איתא במדרש כמה פעמים הזהיר הקב"ה
על הנרות שלא תאמר לאורך אני צריך עיין שם באריכות. ומביא ראיה מבית
המקדש שהיו החלונות צרים מפנים ורחבות מבחוץ כדי שיהא האור יוצא
מבית המקדש להאיר לעולם. ומביא שם עוד כמה ראיות שאין הקב"ה צריך
לנר של בשר ודם ומביא ראיה מן העין של אדם שיש בו שחור ולבן ואין אתה
רואה מן הלבן רק מן השחור הקב"ה שהוא כולו אורה על אחת כמה וכמה.

The נאות דשא quotes the *pasuk* that begins our *parsha* about the
lighting of the Menorah in the Beis Ha-Mikdash (*Bamidbar*
8:2), and then cites the Midrash (*Bamidbar Rabbah* 15:7) that
Hashem tells the Jews several times: I don't need you to light
anything for Me.

The Midrash illustrates its point by explaining that the
windows in the Beis Ha-Mikdash were thin on the inside
and wide on the outside to show that there was more than
enough light in the Beis Ha-Mikdash to light up the world.
The Midrash also demonstrates its point, that Hashem and the
Beis Ha-Mikdash are full of light, by comparing man's vision
to Hashem's. There is white and black in the human eye, but
people only see through the black, and not the white. Hashem
is entirely light, and he does not need our light.

220

ויש לדקדק למה הוצרך להביא כל כך ראיות שאין הקב"ה צריך לנר של בשר
ודם הלא לפי הנראה הוא דבר פשוט. וגם מה שמביא ראיה מן העין של אדם
שרואה מתוך השחור ולא מן הלבן קשה להבין.

The נאות דשא asks: Why does the Midrash need to bring proofs
for a concept that is pretty straight forward, what is the Midrash
talking about regarding eyes, what is the comparison being
made, and what is its point?

אך הענין הוא כי מה נקרא האור של בשר ודם הוא התעוררתא של אדם לעבודת
השי"ת כי נר אלקים נשמת אדם לכן מודיענו המדרש שאין הקב"ה צריך
להתערותא של אדם כי אף התערותא שיש לאדם היא ג"כ מן הקב"ה.

When the Midrash is talking about "our light," it means our
hisarusa (which means as "awakening"). This concept in
Chassidus refers to the Jews' awakening out of the sleep of
ambivalence, apathy, and inaction to serve Hashem. There is
no better analogy than light for this concept. As light banishes
darkness, this awakening banishes the sleep of ambivalence,
apathy, and inaction. The Midrash exclaims that Hashem
doesn't "need" this awakening, because even that comes from
Hashem Himself!

ומביא מבית המקדש שנבנה מפעולת ישראל ומראה הקב"ה לישראל שאם לא
הייתי מראה לך המקום מהיכן היית יודע היכן לבנות בית המקדש. וזה רחבות
מבחוץ שהארתי לך מקום האור כמו לאברהם וירא את המקום מרחוק.

The Midrash gives the example of the Beis Ha-Midkash, which
the Jewish people built. It would seem that the building of the
Beis Ha-Mikdash is an achievement that truly belongs to the

Jews; they contributed the materials and they did the work. However, the windows in the Beis Ha-Mikdash are described as being small inside and wide outside. This teaches us about the process of the building of the Beis Ha-Mikdash, and what it essentially is. There is a crack of light on the inside which makes for a wide window on the outside. Hashem says to the Jews, "If I wouldn't have shown you the place, you couldn't have built it either." Hashem started the process by opening a crack in creation, the place of the Mikdash, and we widen it through our action. This is similar to the way that Hashem showed Avraham the place for him to perform the *Akeidah*. Despite the fact that the *Akeidah* is considered Avraham's crowning achievement, Hashem took him to the place where it happened. Without that unique setting, the *Akeidah* wouldn't have happened. The נאות דשא demonstrates how it all starts with Hashem.

ומביא ראיה שאין הקב"ה צריך לאור של בשר ודם כי האדם אינו רואה מן הלבן רק מן השחור פירוש האור שלך הוא רק אחר החטא כי אין אדם עומד על דברי תורה אלא אחר הכשלון והאיך תאמר שהקב"ה צריך לאורך כי הוא כולו אור כי חושך לא יחשיך ממך.

The Midrash's other proof that Hashem doesn't need our actions to serve Him, because we only see out of the black of our eyes. What does it mean? The נאות דשא explains explains this concept of the black and the white of one's eyes with a famous Izhbitz teaching (based on the Gemara, *Gittin* 43) that a person only keeps the Torah after he has stumbled. The מי השלוח teaches that real knowledge only comes as a result of a person's failures. Clearly, a person cannot choose his own failures, but it is through them that a person learns. These failures were part of

Hashem's plan to educate each person. We can now understand the Midrash, "despite the white in a person's eyes," to mean that despite the places unaffected by failure, a person only views the world through the knowledge he has gained through defeat. Hashem orchestrates a person's failures, which are the most serious learning experience. Hashem does "need our light," as the Midrash says. He doesn't need our success, as the *pasuk* (*Tehillim* 139:12) says, "the dark does not blind you," it's what makes us grow.

ואמר שם המדרש כי משה היה מתקשה על מעשה המנורה עד שאמר לו הקב"ה השלך ככר לאש והיא נעשית מאליה. ומסיים שם שהיה משה מתקשה על המנורה ואמר לו הקב"ה לך אצל בצלאל והוא יעשה אותה מיד ירד משה אצל בצלאל ועשה אותה. ויש לדקדק וכי בצלאל היה גדול יותר ממשה הלא הקמת המשכן יוכיח. ועוד מתחלה אמר המדרש השלך ככר לאש והיא נעשית מאליה ואחר כך אמר שבצלאל עשה אותה.

Along these same lines, the נאות דשא explains how we can see this approach—of Hashem being involved in all of our actions—in the making of the Menorah itself. The Midrash (*Bamidbar Rabbah* 15:4) recounts that Moshe Rabbeinu didn't understand how to make the Menorah until Hashem explained, "Throw the gold into the fire and it will make itself." The נאות דשא quotes another Midrash (*Tanchuma Behaaloscha* 6) that Moshe didn't understand how to make the Menorah, so Hashem told him to go to Betzalel and he will make it. Moshe immediately went to Betzalel, and he did it. The נאות דשא asks, was Betzalel greater than Moshe? Moshe could put up the Mishkan, and Betzalel couldn't. Furthermore, how was the Menorah made? Was the gold thrown into the fire and it emerged formed, or did Betzalel made it?

אשיבך בקוצר שבצלאל עשה את המנורה מה שלא נקרא אצל משה עשייה
כזו כי עשייה של בצלאל כמו שאמר המדרש למעלה השלך ככר לאש פרוש
שעשה אותה כמו האב שמוליד לבן שבלא פעולת האב לא יולד ואעפ"כ פעולתו
קטנה עד מאוד כי היא נעשית מאליה וד"ל.

The *pesukim* say that Betzalel made the Menorah, but the Midrash says that he was told to throw the gold into the fire. The נאות דשא says this is comparable to a father's contribution to making a child, a small act, which then progresses without any more input on his part.

Moshe couldn't understand how to make the Menorah, and Hashem taught him to make it by abandoning his notion of personal achievement and putting it in Hashem's "hands." In the next Midrash, Moshe did the same thing and not only put it in Hashem's "hands" but also abandoned his *kavod* and goes to Betzalel.

In this way, Betzalel recognized that the desire started with Hashem. His job was to "throw the gold into the fire," meaning to make the efforts in *avodah*, and at the same time to recognize Hashem's role in granting him success in his accomplishments.

Moshe and Betzalel looked through the "black of one's eyes," their failure to be able to create it themselves. They learned how to create it, by realizing Hashem as the source of knowledge and success.

The Menorah itself is the vessel which contains light in this world. The underlying question is how to contain and perpetuate man's light, his desire to serve Hashem. How do you take the desire and make a vessel for it? Hashem told him, just do your little part, and I'll grant you success in your endeavor.

The Izhbitzer Tradition

Hashem orchestrates our failures to teach us lessons, and these failures were part of His plan. אין אדם עומד על דברי תורה אם כן נכשל בהם.

Practical Advice

When we want to light the neros (candles), meaning when we want to serve Hashem, we must appreciate the fact that Hashem opens narrow cracks inside of us. He makes us learn the greatest lessons through our failures. We need to understand that our greatest successes are built on Hashem making beginnings for us, and our greatest failures are based on Hashem teaching us a lesson. Many times we are shaped by our failures, and we must daven for greater vessels of perspective.

פרשת שלח

from Beis Yaakov ha-Kollel

וַיֹּאמֶר מֹשֶׁה אֶל ה' וְשָׁמְעוּ מִצְרַיִם כִּי הֶעֱלִיתָ בְכֹחֲךָ אֶת הָעָם הַזֶּה מִקִּרְבּוֹ (**במדבר י"ד י"ג**). הנה נראה לעיני בשר כי כל תקומת ישראל בעולם הוא רק למען לא יאמרו הגוים. וכמו שהתפלל משה כאן. וכן בשירת האזינו (ל"ב כ"ז) כתיב. לולי כעס אויב אגור.

In this week's *parsha*, Moshe Rabbeinu pleads with Hashem not to destroy the Jews in the aftermath of the spies, who returned with a bad report. Moshe Rabbeinu's argument was, "What will the Mitzrim say if you destroy them?" The בית יעקב asks: Is this the reason for the Jewish people's existence? Of all of the reasons that Moshe Rabbeinu could give to save the Jews, why use this one? To compound matters, Moshe Rabbeinu uses this line of reasoning again in *Haazinu* (*Devarim* 32:27), that if the Jews would be destroyed, their enemies would say that they did it, not Hashem.

אך כי באמת לעתיד ישום ה' מקום לעמו ישראל. כי מעולם כל העולם לא עמד רק עליהם. והנה כשהתפלל משה לפני ה' במעשה העגל ביקש. זכר לאברהם (כי תשא ל"ב י"ג). כי אז היה מאמר השי"ת הרף ממני (עקב ט' י"ד). וכפי פשט המאמר לא היה חס ושלום השארה לישראל.

226

The בית יעקב explains that even though the Jews' present is shaky, their future is assured. When Moshe davened to Hashem after the sin of the Golden Calf (*Shemos* 32:13), he asked Hashem to remember Avraham and Hashem's promise to him. Hashem told him, "Step aside, I'll destroy them." The present did not look good for the Jewish people. Therefore, Moshe Rabbeinu invoked Hashem's promise of the future.

לכן ביקש הלא הבטחת להאבות כי תרבה את זרעם. אבל כאן אמר השי"ת כי בניהם יבאו לארץ וישאר תקותם עד נצח.

Moshe Rabbeinu davened, "Didn't you assure the Avos that you would increase their children?" Moshe Rabbeinu's "strategy" in *tefillah* was to anchor his claim based on Hashem's future promise. But here, Hashem said that their children would come to the land, but not these people. Their hope that Hashem would bring them to their Land of Israel would be fulfilled through their children. This is because they said, "we'll never enter the land and our children will be captives."

וכן דעת האדם גם כן בנייחא. כי רואה תקוה מכל דבריו כי אחוזים ומקושרים מעולם הזה לעולם הבא. כי זהו לשון תקוה. כמו תקות חוט השני (יהושע ב' י"ח). שיש לו אחיזה ושייכת מעבר לעבר.

The בית יעקב explains what the nature of *tikvah*, "hope," is. Hope has the unique quality of being able to set a person's mind at ease. Why is that? When a person has hope, he sees a connection between this world and the next. He sees that the promises that Hashem made will last from when they are expressed into the future, when they will materialize. The word *tikvah* means "hope" but it also means "cord," something that is used to connect two separate things. We see in this week's *haftarah* the crimson cord that Rachav hung out her window was also called a *tikvah*. It represented the promise between the *meraglim* and Rachav to spare her family.

ודור המדבר ראו תקותם מפורש. והנה אחר כך ניתן להם פרשת נסכים וחלה
ופרשת עבודה זרה.

The generation of the desert saw this very clearly expressed, because after this incident Hashem revealed the *parshios* of the wine offerings (*nesachim*), the portions of dough given to the *kohanim*, and the *parsha* of idol worship.

These *parshios* again connect us to the future life of the Jews in Eretz Yisrael. They are the *tikvah*, the hope and the cord between the Jews and the future.

נסכים מורה שהסכימו להיות מנוצחים מאת השי"ת. וזה נקרא שהוא משמח
את השי"ת בזה. כמו דוד המלך עליו השלום שנקרא בדחנא דמלכא (זה"ק
משפטים ק"ז א') והוא שהסכים להיות מנוצח. כמו שכתוב למען תצדק בדברך
(תהלים נ"א ו'). וכמו שמבואר במי השלוח (חלק א' פרשת אמר). במעשה
דמקלל. וזהו שאין עכו"ם מביא נסכים (מנחות ע"ג ב').

The *nesachim* show that Jewish people accept Hashem as the winner. Wine offerings, the בית יעקב says, "make Hashem happy." This is comparable to the *Zohar's* (*Mishpatim* 107a) teaching that David Ha-Melech was Hashem's jester. He brought *simchah* to the Shechinah, because he accepted Hashem's will in difficult situations, despite the fact it was against his own.

The סוד ישרים explains the connection between David Ha-Melech and the *nesachim*. David Ha-Melech created the holes in the *mizbeach* for the *nesachim*, which extended deep into the earth, just as Hashem's plan for the world is sometimes buried deep in circumstances. As a result, the person's acceptance of this higher plain brings *simchah* to Hashem.) The מי השלוח explains the same concept when discussing the *mekallel*, the person who cursed Hashem. Despite the fact that Hashem has made a promise regarding the perfection of the future and how He's going to make it happen, a person must be able to let go of his preconceived notion of how he thinks Hashem will make it happen. The *mekallel* could not let go of how he thought the future was supposed to be, and he was trying to force his vision into reality. David Ha-Melech, according to the *Zohar*, was able to (as was the generation of the desert) accept it. The Gemara states that a non-Jew cannot give wine offerings, and the מי השלח explains from the Gemara that Hashem will respond to the request of the nations of the world at the end of time to give them a mitzvah. Hashem will tell them to sit in a *sukkah*. It will become too hot, and they will leave the *sukkah*, kicking it. The מי השלח explains that the point of failure was their inability to recognize that sometimes you will not succeed in the way that you thought you would.

וחלה מורה כי הם קנו את הארץ בשלמות. כמו שכתוב ראשית ערסתכם
ומפרשינן כדי עיסת המדבר (ערובין פ"ג א').

The message behind *challah* is that the Jews will enter and own the land. However, the amount of dough that must be taken from the *challah* is based on the size of dough from the desert.

The significance of this is in order for the Jews to be able to connect the future entrance into the land with their present desert life.

ופרשת עבודה זרה מורה כי לא יהיה עוד הסתרה ושכחה כזו. רק יעמדו תמיד נגד השי"ת ויראו כוונתו. וראשית מורה שהם הראשונים שקנו את הארץ.

This is followed by the *parsha* of the removal of *avodah zarah* (idol worship), which tells us there will no longer be obscurity or forgetfulness, like the one that precipitated the sin of the spies. Through the *mitzvos* of *challah* and *nesachim*, the Jewish people can maintain their awareness of standing before Hashem forever, so they can see what Hashem intends for the future, even in the present. The first of the dough, the *challah*, is representative of this concept as well, as it connects the Jews with the people who will be the first to acquire the land.

The Izhbitzer Tradition

See שלח תנינא ישרים סוד, where the Radzyner discusses nesachim, the Spies, and David Ha-Melech in depth. See אמור מי השלוח, where he discusses the mekallel's mistaken assumptions.

Practical Advice

We have so many things that tear at our tikvah—our lifeline, our hope, and threaten to blow us off course in our lives. When facing a setback in your goals, keep your destination in mind (challah, tikvah) and remember that Hashem runs the world (nesachim), and often has another route that He wants us to go in reaching our destination.

פרשת קרח

from Tiferes Yosef

וַיִּקַּח קֹרַח בֶּן יִצְהָר בֶּן קְהָת בֶּן לֵוִי וְדָתָן וַאֲבִירָם בְּנֵי אֱלִיאָב וְאוֹן בֶּן פֶּלֶת
וגו' **(במדבר ט"ז א')**. כתיב (איוב ט"ו ט"ו) הן בקדושיו לא יאמין ושמים לא
זכו בעיניו. איתא בזוה"ק (ויגש רז) ה' בחכמה יסד ארץ כונן שמים בתבונה
עלמא עלאה לא אתברי אלא מגו חכמה ועלמא תתאה לא אתברי אלא מגו
חכמה תתאה וכו' כונן שמים בתבונה מאי כונן וכו' בכל יומא אתקין ליה והיינו
רזא ושמים לא זכו בעיניו וכי סלקא דעתך דגריעותא דשמים חשיבותא הוא
וכו' ובגין כך כונן שמים בתבונה מאן שמים דא הוא רזא דאבהן וכו'.

In explaining the complaint of Korach, the תפארת יוסף quotes a
pasuk in *Iyov* (15:15), "He did not believe in holiness and the
skies did not shine in his eyes." What is the meaning of this
pasuk? תפארת יוסף quotes the *Zohar*, (*Vayigash* 207) which
explains that Hashem created the earth with wisdom, prepared
the sky with wisdom, but only with lesser wisdom created the
world. The *Zohar* asks, "How did Hashem fashion the sky?
Every day he does it; what could there be wrong with the sky?
The sky is the secret of the fathers." We know that the *Zohar*
often refers to wisdom as "the father."

231

אמר כבוד אאמו"ר זללה"ה ששמים מרמזים על המאמר יהי רקיע שהציב
השי"ת מסך המבדיל בין מים העליונים למים התחתונים וזה המסך נקרא
שמים וכמו שכתיב (בראשית א' י"ד) ויקרא אלוהים לרקיע שמים.

In explaining this piece from the *Zohar*, the Izhbitzer Rebbe
said that the word for "sky," *shamayim*, carries within it the
statement (*Bereishis* 1:14): "Let there be something in heavens
dividing the higher waters from the lower waters." This divider
is called *shamayim* and hence the *pasuk* says, "Hashem called
the divider *shamayim*."

וענין של זה ההבדל שהציב השי"ת הוא מחמת שהי"ת חפץ להיטיב לבריותיו
ורצה שהעבודה של האדם יהיה נקרא על שם האדם על כן הציב זה המסך
המבדיל שלא יהיה אור ה' מפורש כך לעיני האדם. כי באמת אם יהיה אור ה'
מפורש לעיני האדם לא יהיה שייך שיהיה נקרא העבודה על שם האדם כי יכיר
האדם שאם פורש עצמו רגע אחת מרצונו יתברך פורש מן החיים.

What is the purpose for this division? Hashem set it up to benefit
his creations, that we should not perceive Him. If we could see
Hashem, we would be overwhelmed with His presence, so that
nothing we did would be considered of our own volition, as any
separation from Hashem would be like separating from life.

ויען שהשי"ת רצה שהעובדה של האדם יהיה נקראת על שם האדם לזה הציב
המסך הזה והאדם בעבודה צריך לבקוע את ההסתר ויגיע בחזרה לזה האור
על ידי עבודתו ועל ידי אתערותא דלתתא ואז מכיר האדם שבאמת לאמיתו אין
שום מסך המבדיל כלל ורק כל ענין ההבדל שהציב השי"ת הוא הכל לטובת
האדם כדי שתהיה העבודה נקרא על שם האדם ותהיה נקרא כפר יגיע כפו.

Hashem wanted us to be able to transcend this divider on our
own and reach a unified perception of His Presence. But the

only way that a person can have free will is if the person reaches that realization himself, so it will be his own achievement.

וזה הענין דאיתא בזוה"ק (בראשית יז.) שמזה המאמר יהי רקיע נתהוה מחלוקת בעולם. וזה לשון הזוה"ק יהי רקיע הכא בפרט רזא לאפרשא בין מיין עלאין למיין תתאין ברזא דשמאלא ואתברי הכא מחלוקת ברזא דשמאלא וכו' (עיי"ש היטיב) וכן מסיים (שם) הזוה"ק שמזה נתהוה מחלוקת שמאי והלל. וענין בזה כי אם יכיר האדם אחדות ה' מפורש בזה העולם שיכיר שהכל נכלל באחדותו יתברך אז אין שום מקום לעבודה אך יען שהשי"ת רצה שיהיה מקום לעבודת ישראל לזה הציב השי"ת התחלקות המדות כמו שכתיב (דברי הימים א' כ"ט) לך ה' הגדולה והגבורה וגו' עד לך ה' הממלכה כמו שאיתא בש"ס (ראש השנה ל"א ב') בשני חלק מעשיו ומלך עליהם שזה רומז שהציב השי"ת התחלקות המדות ועל ידי זה יהיה מקום לעבודה וע"ז איתא בזוה"ק (ויקרא ה) גדול ה' ומהלל מאד (תהילים מ"ח) אימת אקרי קוב"ה גדול בזמנא דכנסת ישראל אשתכחת עמיה וכו' ובגין דא תושבחתא דא בשני וכו'.

Hence, the *Zohar* (*Bereishis* 17a) says that the statement "creating *shamayim*" created distance between the higher and lower waters, The *Zohar* also makes the startling assertion that this division is what created the disputes between the great teachers of Israel, Hillel and Shammai!

Let's understand what the word שמים has to do with any of this. If Hashem's unity is so pervasive in the world, then there is no room for a person to be able to serve Hashem. Therefore He created the ability to only perceive part of the way that Hashem runs the world, and how to act accordingly. This enabled David Ha-Melech to proclaim "Hashem, Yours is kindness, *chesed*, strength, *gevurah*… Yours is *Malchus*." This means that Hashem rules, and we can serve him as a result of Him limiting the amount of His power that we can see. On the second day of creation, when this dividing שמים was formed, the Gemara says that Hashem divided his creation and ruled over it. The *Zohar* (*Vayikra* 5) explains that Hashem is "great and praised" (from the song of Monday, the second day) when the Jews are His nation, meaning they do His will and this is made possible by the aftermath of the second day of creation.

שכפי ענין הלא גדול רומז על מדת חסדו יתברך. ולמה אומרים אותו בשני אך לזה מתרץ הזוה"ק (שם) שעיקר גדולת השי"ת מכירים אנו בשני שמזה שאנו רואין שכל כך הגדיל חסדו עד שהצציב השי"ת מדת הגבורה שרומז על צמצום. היינו שמזה שאנו מצמצין עצמינו על ידי זה יכולים אנו להגיע לאורו יתברך מזה ניכר גדולת ה' מאד. ונמצא מכוון מאד מאמר הזוה"ק שהמאמר יהי רקיע שמורה שהשי"ת חפץ בעבודת ישראל והציב מסך בין אורו יתברך ובין הבריאה נסתעף מזה שהציב השי"ת התחלקות המדות בזה העולם ומזה נסתעף מחלוקת כידוע.

We normally refer to Hashem's greatness to mean His kindness. Why then do we speak about it in the song of the second day, which is connected to His *gevurah*, the *middah* of the withdrawal of His Presence? The *Zohar* explains that until Hashem applied this *middah*, we couldn't learn how to limit ourselves to let his light in. and through that we see how great He is. Therefore on the second day, when Hashem made this *shamayim* boundary, that created the ability to serve Him, by allowing us to see different ways of how He runs the world. By creating different ways we can perceive and act, it brings with it the ability for dispute as well. Hence the disputes between Hillel and Shammai were created on Monday.

והנה כל זמן שאדם מכיר שהמדות האלה הציב השי"ת לטובת האדם כדי
שיהיה מקום לעבודת האדם ומכיר שאין שום מקום אצלו שיהיה כל כך נתרחק
מאור ה' שלא יוכל להחזירו להשי"ת ואז נקרא עדיין מחלוקת לשם שמים.

Each *middah* is a demonstration of one of the different ways
that Hashem has runs the world, and the different ways that
we can react to these *middos* for the betterment of man. This
demonstration of a singular *middah* creates possibility for man
to serve Hashem. There is no part of man so far from Hashem's
light that it cannot be returned to Him. This is called a dispute
for the sake of *shamayim*. The only reason why this disparity in
creation exists is due to this separation.

וזה מורה מאמר הזוה"ק ששמים הוא רזא דאבהן והיינו שזה מורה שעוד לא
נתרחקו המדות ממקורם שמכיר האדם שאין שום התנגדות בין המדות אלא
שדבוקים במקורם אבל אם כל כך נתרחקו שכבר יש מקומות שנדמה לאדם
שזה המקום אין ביכולתו להחזירו לאור ה'. ואז נדמה לאדם שהמדות המה
באמת הופכיים ויש התנגדות ביניהם ואז נקרא מחלוקת שלא לשם שמים.

The *Zohar*'s statement, that *shamayim* is the secret of the fathers,
means that all of the *middos* are not so far away from Hashem.
Any time we see a seemingly apparent contradiction between
them, the truth is it is only in perception, because they are all
intrinsically connected. Two brothers may be very different,
yet they come from the same father. This is what the *Zohar* is
referring to as the "secret of the fathers." No matter how distant
a *middah* may seem, ultimately its source is clear. However,
when something is so far that you cannot trace the light back to
Hashem, and the *middos* are truly in conflict, then this is not a
dispute for the sake of *shamayim*; it is not an argument that you
can trace back to Hashem.

זה מורה מה דאיתא בזוה"ק (קרח קעו.) ת"ח קרח אזיל בתר מחלוקת מאי
מחלוקת פלוגתא פלוגתא דלעילא ותתא וכו' מחלוקת פלוגתא דשלום ומאן
דפליג על שלום פליג על שמא קדישא וכו'. והיינו שהשיג שיש הבדל בין
המדות וזה רומז פלוגתא דעלאה ותתאה. ולזה האדם יכול לדמות שיש לו איזה
כח פעולה וזה מורה דפליג על שלום פליג על שמא קדישא וזה נקרא מחלוקת
שלא לשם שמים שכל כך התחלקות נסתעף ממאמר יהי רקיע עד שהוא שלא
לשם שמים.

The *Zohar* explains how all of this relates to Korach. He engaged
in a dispute against peace itself, meaning against Hashem's
name, which is peace. He argued not just that the *middos* are
different ways that Hashem runs the world, but there is actually
a separation and disparity between them, that there is not only
one source. His argument was not for שמים, the cause of the
perceived separations.

והנה איתא במדרש (תנחומא קרח) ויקח קרח מה כתיב למעלה מן הענין ועשו
להם ציצית מה עשה קרח נתעטף בטלית שכולה תכלת הלך אצל משה ואמר
זה חייבת או פטורה אמר ליה חייבת התחיל לשחק עליו אשפר חוט אחד של
תכלת פוטר טלית שכולה תכלת חייבת וכו'.

The Midrash (*Tanchuma Korach*) explains, (based on the fact
that the Torah teaches us about *tzitzis* before the *parsha* of
Korach) that Korach had his followers each put on a *tallis* made
entirely of *techeles* blue wool, and asked Moshe Rabbeinu if they
required a string of blue *techelis* as *tzitzis*.

וענין בזה כמו דאיתא בירושלמי (מעשרות פרק ה) לית רבוע משש ימי
בראשית והיינו שזה רומז שזה שאצל השי"ת עומד כל הבריאה בשוה לפניו ואין
שום מקום שנתרחק מנוקדה האמצעית שזה רומז עיגול. ואצל האדם מורה

PATHWAYS TO THE HEART

שאין שום מקום שיכול לומר עליו שזה המקום נתרחק מאור ה' ולא יוכל
להחזירו להשי"ת פנים בפנים. וזה הוא מצד השי"ת אבל מצד האדם נמצא
רבוע ורבוע מורה שיש לו קצוות שנתרחק מנקודה האמצעית ורומז על פסיעה
לבר שכבר יש מקומות אצל האדם שיוכל לומר עליו שזה נתרחק מאוד מאור
ה'. ועל כוונה זאת ניתנה מצות ציצית בבגד שיש לו ד' כנפות שעל ידי המצוה
יזכיר אותו להחזירו לאור ה' שאף שרומז על פסיעה לבר עכ"ז יזכיר אותו
להחזירו להשי"ת.

In order to understand the Midrash, we must consider the shape
of the *tzitzis*, which is a square or rectangle. The *Yerushalmi*
(*Maasros* 5) explains that nothing square was created during the
six days of creation. What's the difference between a square and
a circle? In a circle every point is equidistant from the center;
in a square, the corners are the furthest place from the center.
To Hashem, the world is a circle; that's the way He made it.
Nothing is any further from him than anything else. However,
according to the *Yerushalmi*, a square is a man-made geometric
shape. This means that the distance between man and his
Creator is added by man. He "makes the world into a square" by
perceiving greater degrees of distance from the center.

To man there are unbridgeable distances, and points of no
return. It is for this reason that Hashem gave us the mitzvah
of *tzitzis*. The obligation to put *tzitzis* on each corner of the
garment allows a person to remember that there is no point
so far from Hashem that is irreversible, and therefore he must
return to Hashem, no matter what.

וזה העניין שטען קרח טלית שכולה תכלת פטורה מן הציצית וכמו שאיתא
במדרש נתעטף בטלית שכולה תכלת והיינו שטען שבאמת הוא מוקף באור
השי"ת שלא יוכל לעשות היפך מרצונו ית'. ועוד זאת טען שתפיסת האדם
יתבטל לגמרי ואין שום פסיעה לבר אצל האדם אם כן לא צריך כלל לעבודה.

237

Korach's *tallis* of *techeles* blue was a message to Moshe Rabbeinu. Korach's thought, was that the *tzitzis*, (meaning that Hashem would want man to do anything that man does not want to do) was irrelevant. Korach claimed to be "enclothed" in the will of Hashem, without any need to do anything else. He felt that anything he did was Hashem's will, and there was no need to do anything extra.

אכן על זה רומז מצות ציצית כמו שאיתא (תנא דבי אליהו) שמצות ציצית ניתן אחר חטא מקושש וזה לשונו (שם) אמר ליה הקב"ה למשה מפני מה חלל זה את השבת אמר משה לפניו רבש"ע איני יודע אמר לו הקב"ה אני אומר לך כי בכל ששת ימי החול יש לו לישראל תפילין בראשו ובזרועו ורואה אותם וחוזר ממעשיו אבל ביום השבת שאין לו תפילין לכן חלל זה את השבת א"ל הקב"ה צא ובירר להם מצוה אחת שיהיה נוהג גם בשבתות וימים טובים זה מצות ציצית וכו'. והיינו שזה רומז שהשי"ת נתן להם מצות ציצית לישראל שהן אמת שבשורשם הם מוקפים באורו של השי"ת אך יען שהשי"ת חפץ בעבודת האדם על כן הציב השי"ת שפעמים יתכן לאדם פסיעה לבר ויהיה מקום נסתר אצל האדם ועל ידי מצות ציצית תוציא יקר מזולל והיינו שהאדם העובד ה' מוצא אותו מתוך ההסתר ומגיע בחזרה לפני השי"ת אז יש לו חלק בעבודה והעבודה נקראת על שמו.

We can see this as well in a teaching of the *Tanna Dvei Eliyahu*, that the mitzvah of *tzitzis* was taught after the person who was gathering sticks on Shabbos. Hashem asked Moshe, "Why did the person gather sticks on Shabbos?" Moshe said, "Hashem, I don't know." Hashem said, "All week, the Jews wear *tefillin*, and this causes them to do *teshuvah*, but on Shabbos they don't; therefore this man desecrated Shabbos." Moshe said, "Hashem, please find a mitzvah for them to observe on Shabbos and Yom Tov as well." This is the mitzvah of *tzitzis*. Hashem teaches us through this mitzvah that it's true, we are in fact surrounded by Hashem's light, and we are surrounded by the garments that have *tzitzis* on them. Still, he wants us to serve him and hence put on *tzitzis* and act. Even though a person might err and walk away from what Hashem wants from us, through the mitzvah of *tzitzis* a person can return from that place. Then a person can choose to act, and it will be considered of his own volition.

The Izhbitzer Tradition

The Izhbiter seforim often discuss the fallacy of not wanting to change. See בית יעקב הכולל פרשת בא.

Practical Advice

So many of our problems are of our own making; Korach was not willing to see the world any other way but his own. He believed he was perfect, and everyone else was wrong. The tzitzis tell us that by seeking out Hashem, we can find the way out of our self-made problems. We only have to want to turn to Him, to want to leave our problem. We need to open our eyes to the possibility of another way of seeing things.

פרשת חקת

from Beis Yaakov ha-Kollel

וַתָּמָת שָׁם מִרְיָם (במדבר כ' א'). בזה"ק (חקת קפ"א ב'). כיון דאתעביד דינא
בהאי פרה לדכאה למסאבי. אתעביד דינא במרים לדכאה עלמא.

The בית יעקב cites the *Zohar* (*Chukas* 181b) explaining the
juxtaposition of death of Miriam to the red heifer. The *Zohar*
explains that Hashem's attribute of judgment, which was
awakened by the red heifer in order to clean *tumah*, was also
awakened with the death of Miriam. As they were to purify and
clean the world, they are both taught together.

כי באמת פרה מרמז על עתיד לחיים נצחיים. ומזה יובן כי בעולם הזה אין שום
שלם בכל ענינים. כי גם על משה רבינו עליו השלום היה טענה וקטרוג בעולם
הזה. כי בעולם הזה ההפסד שולט. וכן גם יתרו אמר למשה נבל תבל (יתרו י"ח
י"ח). ולכן מזה יפול תשוקת האדם בראותו זאת. ועל זה רומז מיתת מרים. כי
באר בזכות מרים (תענית ט' א'). ובאר רומז על חשק. וזה כי ניטל בזו הסדרה
החשק מישראל כפי שהיה בדור המדבר.

The בית יעקב explains this connection. The red heifer is a taste
of eternal life. Since the red heifer purifies a person from his
contact with death and its subsequent impurity, we understand,

240

therefore, that the red heifer combats death itself. Death is a symptom of the missing part of the world. The red heifer then allows a person to touch a world that is whole and perfect. But we know that there is nothing completely whole in this world. (Even Moshe Rabbeinu was disturbed by this world, as everything in this world is susceptible to the power of destruction. Yisro warned Moshe Rabbeinu about it, saying "you will surely fall" (*Shemos* 18:18), that everything inevitably is destroyed.) This fact causes a person to be depressed when they reflect upon it. Therefore, the *parsha* of the red heifer is followed by the death of Miriam. With her death, the well that supplied the Jews with water in the desert disappeared. The well, whose waters represent a desire for greatness and progress, existed in Miriam's merit. The significance of the well's disappearing in this week's *parsha* is that something was changing at this point in our history. The Jews had lost that desire for perfection that was representative of the generation of the desert.

והשי"ת נתן להם כח תשוקה חדשה כפי בחינת באי הארץ. ולפי שבזה הסדר התחיל כח באי הארץ להתגבר.

Hashem gave them a different new desire, though, the desire of those who were entering the land of Israel. In this *parsha*, we begin to feel the unique strength and desire of those who will enter the land of Israel. We will now understand the difference between these two ways of desiring greatness. The first is through grabbing onto something that is greater than where you are (the generation of the desert); the second is working to become great (the generation that entered the land.)

לכן אירע מכשול גם למשה. כמאמר תקוני זה״ק (תקונא כ"א מ"ד א'). דאלו הוה ממלל לסלע כברתא דמלכא לא היו ישראל צריכים להתייגע על דברי תורה.

As an example of this change of perspective Moshe Rabbeinu erred during this *parsha*. The *Zohar* (*Tikkun* 21 page 44b) says that if Moshe had spoken to the rock, the Jews would never have to struggle to receive words of Torah. However, the acquisition of Torah without struggle is the challenge of the generation of the desert, and was inappropriate for the generation of those entering the land.

כי ענין דור המדבר היה העיקר בחכמה ומחשבה. ובחכמה יכול האדם להשיג כל דבר שאינו שייך לו. ויוכל להפסיד על ידי זה. והנה דרך האדם שירצה בגדולות ממנו. ולהשיג ענין שצריך זמן רב רוצה האדם להשיג בזמן קצר. וזה יצמח מפני כי ימיו במספר קרוצים.

Let's understand the difference between those two generations in order to understand what transpired when the generations changed. The generation of the desert was characterized by *Chochmah* and thought. *Chochmah* means the gift of a flash or glimpse of understanding into a concept, even if the true comprehension is intellectually beyond the person's reach. However, this glimpsing can also be dangerous, because the person can misunderstand what really was being transmitted. The Jews of the generation that entered the land of Israel were possessed with a greater level of maturity. People who want to truly grow and attain things that are now out of their reach must accept that growth needs a lot of time. People are impatient and want everything in a short period of time because their days are numbered. The task of the generation of the desert was to grasp and glimpse holiness. The Jews who entered the Land were required to be patient in order to attain a goal. That's why they are called the "generation that entered the Land," because they are people who actually achieved their goal.

ולזה הביא הקב"ה כל ענייני קדושה לתוך מעשים ופעולות. כי במעשה לא יוכל האדם להשיג מה שאין שייך לו. כי כשיחטוף האדם דבר שאין שייך לו עוד. אז יוציא הקב"ה החיים מהדבר וישאר ריק בידו.

Only through acting with patience does Hashem bring holiness to a person's actions. These force a person to contend with reality, as you only can do what relates to you, what is relevant to you. When a person jumps to do that which does not relate to him, Hashem takes all of the life out of it, leaving him empty handed.

כמו שמבואר בנחש הנחשת שאח"כ בעת שעבדו לו קראו אותו נחשתן (מלכים ב י"ח ד'). כי נחשתן מורה על זה. כדאיתא (כלים ט' א') מנחושתו של תנור. והוא כי נתרוקן כח קדושה שנקבע בו אז. כי על ידי זה ניתן זה בפעולה. כי משה רבינו עליו השלום היה יכול ללמד לישראל תפלה שתוכל לפעול ככח נחש הנחשת אם היה רצון הקב"ה לזה. אכן לזה היה רצון הקב"ה להכניס זאת בפעולה. כדי שלא יוכלו ישראל להפסיד חס ושלום רק ישארו בקדושתם.

We see another example of this in the copper snake that was supposed to elicit prayers to Hashem, but instead became an idol that they called Nechushatan (*Melachim* II 18:30). The Mishnah (*Kelim* 9:1) explains that the word refers to the bottom of an oven. There was nothing of value left in it; it was like the ash on the bottom of the oven. Moshe wanted to teach the Jews a profound level of *tefillah*, but it was above their understanding. Therefore, they grasped the bottom, praying in front of the copper snake, which ultimately lead them to idol worship.

The Izhbitzer Tradition

Many times, a theme in Izhbitzer teachings is the importance of process, in growth and development.

Practical Advice

Many times in life when we witness greatness, we become despondent, thinking, "I can never achieve greatness." The problem is that we want to be great all at once. True lasting growth only really occurs when we take our personal growth step by step.

פרשת בלק

from Beis Yaakov ha-Kollel

וַיֹּאמֶר בִּלְעָם אֶל הָאֱלֹהִים בָּלָק בֶּן צִפֹּר מֶלֶךְ מוֹאָב שָׁלַח אֵלַי (במדבר כ"ב
י) . בבמדבר רבה (פ"כ ס' ו'). זה אחד משלשה בני אדם שבדקן הקב"ה
ומצא קרון של מי רגלים. קין חזקיה ובלעם. קין בשעה שאמר לו הקב"ה אי
הבל אחיך. בקש להטעות כביכול. היה צריך לומר רבונו של עולם הנסתרות
והנגלות לפניך גלויות ואת שואלני בשביל אחי. אלא אמר לו לא ידעתי השומר
אחי אנכי כו'. חזקיהו כשעמד מחליו שלח לו מראדך בלאדן דורון כו'. התחיל
מתגאה ואמר מארץ רחוקה באו אלי מבבל כו'. וכן בלעם הרשע כו'. בלק בן
צפר מלך מואב שלח אלי.

Bilaam responds to Hashem's question, "Who are those people
with you?" by saying that "Balak, son of Tzipor sent them to me"
(*Bamidbar* 22:10). The בית יעקב quotes the Midrash (*Bamidbar*
20:6) which says that "there were three people who were tested
by Hashem and were like a vessel filled with water to wash one's
self, but instead it was found to be full of urine."

What does this Midrash mean? Who are these people? They
are Kayin, Chizkiya and Bilaam. Kayin was asked by Hashem,
"Where is Hevel your brother?" It was as if Hashem was asking
to be misled. Kayin (*Bereishis* 4) should have said, "Master of
the world, all hidden things before You are revealed, and You

are asking me about my brother?" But instead, he answered, "I don't know; am I my brother's keeper?"

Chizkiyahu (*Melachim* II 20) recovered from his sickness, and Marduch son of Baladan sent him a present. He showed the messengers all of his treasures. Yeshayahu asked, "Who were those people and why were they here?" Chizkyahu demonstrated pride in responding, "They came from far away, to see me from Bavel," instead of saying, "Navi of Hashem, why are you asking me?" Bilaam answered the Hashem's question with a similar amount of pride that "Balak, son of Tzipor, sent people to me."

דהנה שאלת השי"ת בדרך נבואה אינה כשאלת בשר ודם.

The בית יעקב starts to explain this Midrash. He says when Hashem asks a question to a person through prophecy, it is not the same as another person asking. There is a purpose to the question, not merely to extract information. This is why the Midrash uses the phrase "like a vessel filled with water to wash one's self, but instead it was found to be full of urine." The question was an opportunity for the one being questioned to cleanse himself, and instead it was used to soil himself further.

כי כמו שהקב"ה שאל ליחזקאל התחיינה העצמות האלה (יחזקאל ל"ז ג'). לא היה רצונו יתברך בתשובתו. כי מה' תפעל תשובתו. אך רצון השי"ת היה כי יגיד לו. אם קבוע בלבו האמונה כי המתים יוכלו לחיות על פי רצון השי"ת. וכמאמר הגמרא (סנהידרין צ"א א'). דלא הוו חיי דהוי חיי לא כל שכן. או אין בלבו זאת האמונה בעומק. רק מאמין מגודל בטחונו בהשי"ת. ולא שיתאמת לו בשורש לבו. ועל זה השיב אדני ה' אתה ידעת (יחזקאל ל"ז ג') .

In a similar way, Hashem asked Yechezkel in the valley of Dura (37:3): "Could these bones live?" Hashem really was not interested in gaining information from Yechezkel's answer. What Hashem wanted Yechezkel to do was show that he had *emunah* that the dead could come back to life if Hashem willed it. This is demonstrated by Gemara (*Sanhedrin* 91a), which says that if those who weren't born yet, are brought to life, it is much less fantastic than someone died and then came back to life. However, we see that Yechezkel didn't have such profound *emunah* in the principle of *Techiyas Ha-Meisim*. How do we see this? Instead of saying, "If You will it, Hashem," he said, "Only You know, Hashem." He did not rely on Hashem's power. This showed that his *emunah* was not as strong as was required and need to be strengthened.

כי הכי בכח בן אדם להביט בנסתרות הלא ה' בוחן לבבות.

The purpose of Hashem's asking by means of a Navi is to allow a person to see into the depths of his heart, because we so often cannot see what's happening even in our own hearts.

והנה חזקיה המלך כשבאו אליו שלוחי מלך בבל. והוא הראה להם כל אשר באצרותיו. והם באו לדרוש את המופת. והוא סבר כי הוא מפאר שם ה' בזה שמראה להם כל אשר באוצרותיו. כי זה מורה שגילה להם דברי תורה יקרים. והוא לא הבין פן נמצא בלבו קצת התפארות מצד עצמו רק דימה כי עושה כלו לה'. ולכן כשבא הנביא אליו השיב לו מארץ רחוקה באו. ודימה כי פאר את אם ה' בזה. אבל היה לו להשיב מה יודע ה' מה הראיתי אותם. אם פארתי שמו או רציתי בכבוד עצמי. אך חזקיה לא הכיר ולא הבין לחשוב פן יש בזה נטיה מרצון השי"ת.

Let's see this concept now in the examples given in the Midrash. When Chizkiyahu was visited by the messengers of the king of Bavel, and he showed them everything in his treasure house, they came wanting to know about his miraculous recovery from his sickness. He thought that he was demonstrating the glory of Hashem by revealing to them secrets of Torah, the inner meaning of everything in his treasure house. He was not aware of the amount of pride that doing so contained. He thought that he was doing something entirely for Hashem. Therefore, when the Navi came to him and asked, "what did you show them?" Chizkiyah said, "I didn't do this for my own honor." But he didn't realize how much of himself he had invested, and how it could be taking him away from what Hashem wanted.

אבל קין ובלעם הכירו בשקרם. כי קין כשבא אליו השי"ת ואמר לו אי הבל אחיך והוא השיב לא השמר אחי אנכי. לא עלה על רעיונו לרמות את השי"ת. כי לא בשופטנא עסקינן. אך השיב כי לא יכול לשומרו. כי בא אליו כעס בלא בחירה. עד שלא היה ביכולתו להתגבר על כעסו. וזה שהשיב השמר אחי. וכי בי השמירה תליא והלא בך תליא היה לך ליתן לי כח בחירה להתגבר על כעסי. ובאמת ע"ז היה לו להשיב אתה ידעת. כי באמת היה לו כח בחירה. וזה שהשיב לו הקב"ה קול דמי אחיך צעקים (בראשית ד' י'). והוא באם לא היה בך כח בחירה אז לא היה דמו צועק.

But Kayin and Bilaam recognized that they were lying to themselves. When Hashem came to Kayin and asked him about the whereabouts of his brother, he responded, "I don't know; am I supposed to guard my brother?" (*Bereishis* 4:10). It never crossed his mind to try to fool Hashem. He just said he couldn't guard him. The בית יעקב explains that he had such rage that he could not control himself or stop himself from killing Hevel.

Kayin exclaimed that it wasn't his fault, but Hashem's fault for not giving him the ability to conquer his rage. But Kayin could have said, "Hashem, You know where he is." Kayin could have recognized the truth, admitting that he actually did have control, and that he killed Hevel, by saying "Hashem, You know." He would have been taking responsibility for his actions. This is why Hashem chastises him saying "that your brother's blood cries out to me from the ground." If Kayin really had no control, his brother's blood would not have been crying out, testifying to Kayin's guilt.

וגם בלעם כשרצה ליעץ רע על ישראל במצרים. כדאיתא בגמרא (סוטה י"א א'). וראה כי לא נעשתה עצתו חישב איך לקללם ויירא מאד. לכן אמר כי ישמור עצמו על המעשה שלא תצא מאתו שום דבר לפועל. ועל המחשבה אין צבא מעלה נזקקין לענוש. וחישב ופעל במחשבתו עד כי בלק שלח אליו. וכמבאור במי השלוח (חלק א' בלק). וכי הוא על ידי מחשבתו פעל אצל בלק. והוא השיב בלק בן צפר מלך מואב שלח אלי.

Bilaam wanted to give Paroh counsel against the Jews in Mitzraim, but he saw that it didn't work. Therefore he realized that he would not be able to curse the Jews. He took a different approach. He was careful not to act against the Jews directly, and he thought that therefore he would not be punished. He believed that a person is not liable for his thoughts. The מי השלוח said that he was hoping that some nation would come to him and be the instrument to destroy the Jews, as he realized that he could not. As a result of this hope, Balak approached him. Hashem asked Bilaam, "Who are these people," indicating that He knew that it was Bilaam's thoughts that brought Balak to him. Bilaam responded that Balak had sent them, trying to reject any responsibility for their plan, and his culpability in it.

The Izhbitzer Tradition

The Izhbitzer seforim often discuss the depths of a person's thoughts, their subconscious, and how to repair them. See מי השלוח חלק א פרשת בלק.

Practical Advice

David Ha-Melech said, "Hashem is good and straight; therefore he guides sinners down the path." The Rambam (Teshuvah 6:5) says that this means that Hashem gives us the opportunities to correct ourselves from the problems that are within a person. Hashem asks us questions, meaning He gives us the opportunities to fix the problems that are normally obscured from our view, because He loves us and entrusts us with a second chance.

פרשת פנחס

from Beis Yaakov ha-Kollel

לָכֵן אֱמֹר הִנְנִי נֹתֵן לוֹ אֶת בְּרִיתִי שָׁלוֹם (במדבר כ"ה י"ב). ומפרש ברבה במדבר (פי"א ס' ז'). דבר הקיים לעד. וזה רומז לתחיית המתים שבא על ידי אליהו זכור לטוב.

When Hashem intervened to save Pinchas from the mob, He said, "Pinchas turned away My anger; therefore, I'm giving him my covenant of peace" (*Bamidbar* 25:12). The בית יעקב quotes the Midrash (*Bamidbar Rabbah* 11:7) which explains that this covenant of peace means something that endures forever. What is it? *Techiyas Ha-Meisim*, the resurrection of the dead, which comes through Eliyahu Ha-Navi. We know he also was made a *kohen* and he never died. What is the association between being a *kohen*, never dying, and *Techiyas Ha-Meisim*?

וכדאיתא בגמרא (סוטה מ"ט ב'). זהירות מביא לידי זריזות כו'. והנה השי"ת זורע צדקות ומצמיח ישועות. ובמקום שהאדם יכול להפסיד משם יכול להבנות בנין עדי עד. כי אף במקום שנראה שהאדם מפסיד על כל זה נמצא בו נקודה קיימת אשר לֹא תתבטל ולא תלך לאבדון.

251

The בית יעקב begins his explanation with a brief introduction to reality and *avodas Hashem*. The Gemara *Sotah* (49b) explains how being careful leads to enthusiasm. When a person is careful not to get involved in things of an unseemly nature, he may become excited and enthusiastic in his *avodas Hashem*. This is a reference to Pinchas. By avoiding things that were inappropriate, he merited the *kehunah* as well as the enthusiasm of life and *avodas Hashem* (which is *kehunah*, as will be discussed later.) The Siddur tells us that Hashem "plants righteousness and salvation sprouts." What does it mean "to plant righteousness"? When Hashem places goodness in the world, then it can be repaired and attain perfection. A person has the choice either to destroy his life and ruin his own world or to be able to grow and mature. Yet, even though it looks as if a person can destroy the world, there is a point of goodness that never gets lost or destroyed.

וכמו שבעת השינה ישאר באדם קוסטא דחיותא שזה תעורר את כל הגוף. כן ישאר באדם עד לעת התחיה הבלא דגרמי. וכמבואר בזה"ק (שלח קס"ט א') וכמו שכל הזריעות שיזרעו בארץ לא יתבטלו לגמרי.

Just as when a person sleeps, there exists a little bit of life to awaken the entire body, so too, within a person there is something that stays alive until *Techiyas Ha-Meisim*. That part is never destroyed. The *Zohar* (*Shelach* 169a) says, "All of the things that a person plants are never lost completely."

וכמאמר הגמרא (סנהדרין צ"א א'). דלא הוו חיי דהוי חיי לא כל שכן. ואם יתבטל לגמרי מה הפרש וחילוק בין הוה ללא הוה.

The בית יעקב paraphrasing the Gemara (*Sanhedrin* 91a) explains the need for such a phenomenon, "Those who were never alive will come to life; those who were alive, how much more so that they will come back to life?" If the souls were to fade into nothingness after death, then what would be the difference whether someone had never been born or if they had been born?

והנה כמו שנמצא בכל נפש נקודה אחת הנשארת בחיים נצחיים מבלי שום שינוי ולא תאבד חס ושלום. כן בכלל ישראל המכונים לצורת אדם שלם מההכרח להשאר נפש שלם שלא יעדר.

The Jewish people are comparable to a single entity, and just as there is part of the person that never disappears, so too there is one person who never disappears.

והנה זה הוא פנחס הכהן בינען שלא רצה להכניס עצמו לספק. כי אין מיתה בלא חטא (שבת נ"ה א'). וחטא הוא הכנסה לספק. כי חטא מכונה לשוגג (יומא ל"ו ב').

This one person is Pinchas Ha-Kohen. He is the person who doesn't die or disappear. This is because he didn't want to enter into "an area of doubt." He didn't act without an explicit commandment from Hashem. Chazal record that he did not act until consulting Moshe and his court, to know that his actions were sanctioned by Hashem. This is because death, sin, and doubt are all intertwined. Death comes as a result of sin (as the Gemara, *Shabbos* 55a says) and because sin is the entrance into doubt (as sins are called *shogeg*—unintentional). We see this from the very first sin. When Adam Ha-Rishon ate from the tree of knowledge of good and evil, he drank the mixture of good and evil and everything became a question of "is it good or evil?" This is why the *Zohar* refers to the tree as the tree of doubt. This was also the beginning of the institution of death.

ושמר את הברית. וכמאמר זה"ק (וארא כ"ו ב') .ולא ישלוט ביה רע .כי יש
נפשות שעיקר עסקם להכניס עצמם לספקות. והם בספק אם יצליחו או חס
ושלום לא .ואם יעזור השי"ת להצליח אז זה גדול מאד.

This is reflective of the *Zohar* (*Va'era* 26b), which explains that
when someone keeps his end of the covenant, that evil never
rules over the person. There are souls whose purpose in life is
to enter realms of doubt, into enterprises that are not assured
of success. They are in doubt whether or not Hashem will
grant them success in their actions. When they remain true
to this purpose, even though the venture is dubious, Hashem
guarantees that He will not let them fall.

וכמו אברהם אבינו שהיה מדתו חסד. והוא רק להכניס את עצמו בספקות.
ויצחק היה מדתו פחד. והוא להשמר מכל ספק רק לילך בטח.

Avraham Avinu was one such person. His attribute was *chesed*,
which means to spread out. He brought himself into a doubtful
situation by going out, teaching people about the Master of the
world and interacting with the world at large. This interaction
made it certain that there would be ups and downs, causing
doubt whether Hashem would help him out of the difficult
situation. However, Yiztchak, whose attribute was *gevurah*
(which means to hold one's self back), guarded himself from
ever entering such a situation.

וגם פינחס בי ען כי לא הכניס עצמו לספק .לכן לא הכניסו הקב"ה לספק ההעדר.
כי ההעדר הוא ספק. כי אינו יודע מה יקום ומה יתבטל. ולכן ברית השי"ת היתה
אתו החיים והשלום. וזה תחיית המתים בא על ידי אליהו זכור לטוב. כי הוא
סימן לתחיית המתים. כי כשם שנשאר נפש מישראל חי וקיים.

Likewise, Pinchas did not want to enter into a dubious situation. As a result, Hashem did not subject him to the potential of doubt and decay. Decay is doubt, as we don't know what will endure and what will last. Therefore Hashem's reward to Pinchas was a covenant of life and peace. This is *Techiyas Ha-Meisim*, which comes through Eliyahu Ha-Navi. Eliyahu is the sign for *Techiyas Ha-Meisim*, because he is part of the soul of Israel that is always alive.

כן בכל נפש בפרט נמצא נקודה אחת מבלי העדר. והוא נקודת הכהונה האמתית כח העבודה. כי כל נפש מישראל נכלל מכהן ולוי וישראל. אכן הכהן יש לו כח הכהונה ביותר.

Just as there is one person of the Jewish people who is always alive, so too, in every Jew there is a portion of the person that exists without decay. This is truly what it means to be a *kohen*, to be the portion which is always alive and serving Hashem. Each soul from the Jewish people is comprised of Kohen, Levi, and Yisrael; however the *kohanim* have more of this attribute.

וכאשר נראה נראה שנפש אחד נשאר קיים. כדאיתא בזה"ק (ויקהל קצ"ז א') ואתלבש בההוא סערה וכו'. והנה מה שנצרך להתלבש בסערה הוא משום כח הישראל הנמצא בו. כי גם כהן נכלל מישראל ומלוי. אבל נקודת הכהונה האמתית אינה צריכה לשום לבוש רק תשאר בקיום מבלי שינוי וזה רומז לתתיה :

This is how that there is always one soul which always stays alive. This is what the *Zohar* makes reference to—that Eliyahu "wore a storm." Why does he need to "wear a storm"? Like we explained, there is a Yisrael portion to everybody as well. The Yisrael portion is the storm, then entrance into doubt, the need for change and as a result of their interaction. However, the *kohen* portion needs no garment, it is totally alive, requiring no change therefore, it hints to us of *Techiyas Ha-Meisim*. The Yisrael portion is the storm, but the *kohen* is the calm within the storm.

The Izhbitzer Tradition

The Izhbitzer speaks about entering into doubt (see (ב) מי השלוח
בית יעקב בראשית (כה) and (נח) and the notes in the new edition) as
part and parcel of most people's lives, that despite our best efforts,
we are in a world filled with doubt, and it is our struggle with
such a world which allows us to grow as people.

Practical Advice

There are times in the storms of life, that we encounter so many
doubts, and many times in the crash of those storms, much in our
life can be destroyed. Look to the kohen inside, of you, the Eliyahu
Ha-Navi, the pure part of yourself that is always inside. It is the
calm of the storm and through this calm, you can rebuild your life.

פרשת מטות

from Beis Yaakov ha-Kollel

וַיְדַבֵּר מֹשֶׁה אֶל רָאשֵׁי הַמַּטּוֹת לִבְנֵי יִשְׂרָאֵל לֵאמֹר (במדבר ל' ב'). זה
שאמר הכתוב אם תשיב משבת רגלך עשות חפצך ביום קדשי וקראת לשבת
ענג לקדוש ה' מכבד וכבדתו מעשות דרכיך ממצוא חפצך ודבר דבר. אז תתענג
על ה' והרכבתיך על במותי ארץ והאכלתיך נחלת יעקב אביך כי פי ה' דבר
(ישעיה נ"ח).

This *parsha* begins, "Moshe spoke to the heads of the tribes,
saying," (*Bamidbar* 30:2), and continues with the laws of
nedarim, vows, and their annulment. The בית יעקב explains this
pasuk by quoting one from *Yeshaya* (58), "If you withhold your
feet (*raglecha*) on Shabbos, from doing your wishes (*chafatzecha*)
on my holy day, and you will call Shabbos a delight, and honor
it by refraining from your matters and from speech of weekday
thing—then you will delight in Hashem, and he will set you
upon the land, so you may partake in the limitless inheritance
of Yaakov your father, as the mouth of Hashem has spoken.

שבת שמא דקודשא בריך הוא (זה"ק יתרו פ"ח ב'). ובאם האדם ישוב בחפציו
המסתירים והמשכיחים ממנו קדושת השי"ת על זה רומז שנאמר רגלך. כי
בהרגלים נקטן הדעת כי הם ביותר ריחוק מהראש משאר האברים. והאדם צריך

257

לדעת כי אף העסקים היותר גדולים אצלו שנראים בעיניו כדבר הקיים. מכל
מקום בעיני הקב״ה אינם אלא כדברי חיי שעה. כי קדושה הוא דבר הקיים לעד .

What are the implications of this quotation and why does it
explain the beginning of this week's *parsha*? The *Zohar* (*Yisro*
88b) says that Shabbos is the name of Hashem. What is the
connection? Yeshaya says that when a person restricts himself
from the things that are "your feet," which is a person's *regel*—
meaning, their regular everyday affairs, then he will delight in
Hashem. Through Shabbos you can meet Hashem. However,
regel, the word for "feet," which also can be translated as "ordinary,
everyday actions," can make him forget Hashem. Therefore, the
term "your feet" is really relevant, as the feet are furthest from
the head, meaning the furthest from understanding.

וזהו עשות חפצך ביום קדשי. וקראת לשבת ענג הוא שהאדם יזמין את עצמו
מצדו לקבל קדושת שבת. אף כי קדושת שבת אינו נתפסת בגבול גדר שכל
האדם. כדאיתא בסנהדרין (ס״ה ב׳). שאל טורנוסרופוס את רבי עקיבא אמר
לו ומה יום מיומים על יום השבת.

This is what the Navi means "doing your will on My holy day."
"And you will call Shabbos a delight," means that a person
will prepare himself to accept the *kedushah* of Shabbos. Even
though *kedushas Shabbos* is outside of the realm of the intellect
of a person, a person prepares himself to receive it. The Gemara
(*Sanhedrin* 65b) discusses a story in which Turnus Rufus asked
Rebbe Akiva, "Who said today is Shabbos?" To which Rebbe
Akiva responded, "Who made you a general?" Turnus Rufus
said, "The king did" Rebbe Akiva responded, "The same with
Shabbos; the King said it is special." The nature of Shabbos is
above us; only Hashem's decision makes it Shabbos.

כי קדושת יום טוב אשר ישראל מקדשים אותו זה נתפס בגדר שכל תפיסת
אדם. אבל קדושת שבת אין ביום הזה שום יתרון לקדושה על פי שכל אדם. אך
להנפש מישראל המכין את עצמו מצדו זה יזכה כי ירגיש אף מקדושת שבת. ואז
והאכלתיך נחלת יעקב אביך נחלה בלי מצרים (שבת קי"ח א'). שיוכל להמשיך
קדושת שבת אף על דברי חול.

The holiness of Yom Tov, which the Jewish people sanctify,
is within our intellectual grasp. But the holiness of Shabbos
is above any understanding that man could have. The soul
prepares itself, and through this, feels *kedushas Shabbos*. "You
will eat from the portion of Yaakov your father, a limitless
inheritence." So you can find the holiness of Shabbos even in
the mundane days of the week.

כמו שמאי הזקן שכל ימיו היה אוכל לכבוד שבת. והלל הזקן שכל מעשיו לשם
שמים (ביצה ט"ז א'). וכן זהו קדושת נדרים שיוכל להכניס לו גדר תחת מצות
השי"ת. וכל זה כשהאדם הוא תחת עול השי"ת ודומה כמי שיש לו אלקי אז
יכול להמשיך קדושת ה' אף על דברי חול.

This phenomenon is seen in relation to Shammai (*Beitzah* 16a),
who "ate all week in honor of Shabbos." He would find some
nice food and say, "I'm saving this for Shabbos." If he would
find something nicer, he would eat the other portion and
save that one. By restraining his regular everyday actions, he
honored Shabbos. The בית יעקב contrasts this approach with
that of Hillel, all of whose actions were for the sake of Heaven.
One does not only find Hashem by restraining your weekday
activity. Hillel actively transformed his daily life into a life of
kedushah and awareness of Hashem. This theme connects with
the first mitzvah in our *parsha*, the mitzvah of *nedarim*, oaths.
The holiness of oaths makes anything a mitzvah from Hashem.

וכמבואר בספרי (עקב פנ"א). כל המקום אשר תדרך כף רגלכם בו לכם יהיה
כו'. אמר להם כל מקום שתכבשו חוץ מן המקומות האלו הרי הוא שלכם כו'. הרי
שכבשו חוצה לארץ מנין שמצות נוהגות שם. הרי אתה דן נאמר כאן יהיה ונאמר
להלן יהיה. מה יהיה האמור להלן מצות נוהגות שם אף כאן מצות נוהגות שם.

The בית יעקב returns to the imagery of feet to discuss the concept
of making our daily life filled with awareness of Hashem.
Avraham Avinu was told that "anywhere your feet shall tread,
it will be yours." The Midrash (*Sifri Ekev* 51) says based on this
that Hashem's promise to Avraham, that everywhere the Jews
will tread in the conquest of the land, the *mitzvos* of the land
(*challah, shmitah, terumah, maaser*) will apply. The conquest—
bringing *kedushah* to the land—is done with one's feet.

ואם תאמר מפני מה כבש דוד ארם נהרים וארם צובה ואין מצות נוהגות שם.
אמרו דוד עשה שלא כתורה. התורה אמרה משתכבשו לארץ תהיו רשאים
לכבש חוצה לארץ. הוא לא עשה כן אלא חזר וכיבש את ארם נהרים וארם
צובה. ואת היבוסי שהיה סמוך לירושלם לא הוריש אמר לו הקב"ה סמוך
לפלטירים שלך לא הורשת היאך אתה חוזר ומכבש ארם נהרים וארם צובה.

There seems to be a caveat to this rule. The Midrash asks, how
is it that David Ha-Melech conquered Aram and yet the *mitzvos*
don't apply there? The Midrash explains that it is since he did
not conquer the Yebusi, who were right next to Yerushalayim,
his palace. Hashem said, "How can you conquer Aram, when in
your own backyard is the Yebusi?" As a result the *mitzvos* did
not apply fully there.

וכן כתב הרמב"ם (הלכות תרומות פ"א ה"ג). ארם נהרים וארם צובה אין להם
דין כארץ ישראל. ומפני מה ירדו ממעלת ארץ ישראל. מפני שכבש אותם קודם

שיכבוש כל ארץ ישראל. אלא נשאר בה משבעה עממים. ואלו תפס כל ארץ
כנען לגבולותיה ואח"כ כבש ארצות אחרות היה כיבושו כלו כארץ ישראל.

The Rambam (*Terumos* 1:3) records that Aram does not have
the halachic status of the land Israel. Because David Ha-Melech
conquered it before conquering all of the land of Israel, there
still remained a stronghold of the seven nations there. If he had
reversed the order, then it would have had the status of Eretz
Yisrael.

ועל זה נאמר אל ראשי המטות כי להיות בשוה עם כל ישראל די להתנהג על
פי כללי דברי תורה. אבל להשיג התנשאות זהו כפי שיקדש האדם את עצמו
במותר לו כן יהיה מנושא.

The *parsha* begins by indicating that the laws of *nedarim* were
given to the heads of the tribes (the *nesi'im*). Doesn't the Torah
apply to everybody? However, to reach greatness (the word
nasi means a "prince" or a "leader," but it also means "uplifted")
one must live in an elevated state, making himself holy even in
mundane matters.

והנה זו הפרשה ניתן להם קודם שנכנסו לגבולות העמים. כי נגד ישראל די
בגדרי התורה. אבל מפני שיצר האומות יסתעף בין ישראל לזה צריך תוספות
קדושה.

Why was this taught now? This *parsha* was taught before the
Jewish people entered the territory of the nations. Normally it's
enough just to follow the Torah to live a fulfilled life. Now as they
were about to enter into the Land, the spirit of the idolatrous
people of the land could sway them; therefore it was necessary
that they learn how to take upon themselves more holiness.

וכדאיתא בגמרא (ב"ב ק"כ ב'). רבי יוסי הגלילי אומר מועדי ה' נאמרו שבת
בראשית לא נאמרה. בן עזאי אומר מועדי ה' נאמרו הפרת נדרים לא נאמרה.
כי שבת הוא קבוע וקיימא. ויום טוב הוא דישראל מקדשי ליה. וכמה שיברר
האדם את עצמו מצדו בפרשת נדרים שהוא בינה בלבו לגדור לו גדר פרטי
השייך לו לנפשו. כן יזכה בקדושת יום טוב. ועל ידי זה יתברר בקדושת שבת
שהוא נבחר מהשי"ת אף בלא מעשיו.

The Gemara (*Bava Basra* 120b) recounts a conversation
betweeen Rebbe Yosi HaGelili and Ben Azzai. Rebbe Yosi
HaGelili said when the *pasuk* records, "These are the holidays
of Hashem," Shabbos was not taught. Ben Azzai argues that the
removal of vows was not taught, and Shabbos exists and is set
with us forever; whereas Yom Tov depends upon the Jewish
people. What does this conversation mean, especially in light
of what we have been discussing? Both sets of laws—vows and
Yom Tov—are dependent on a person's own personal exertion. A
person through his understanding of his own situation, through
the laws of *nedarim*, creates the proper personal mode for him
to serve Hashem. This state that a person reaches has an aspect
of the *kedushas Yom Tov*. Through a person's own experiences
of growth, he becomes further aware of the spiritual gifts that
Shabbos brings, as Shabbos is always present, and requires a
person not to create it, but to connect to it.

The Izhbitzer Tradition

See א מטות פרשת השלוח מי *and* א וביום עצרת שמיני הכולל יעקב בית *who
deal with similar topics.*

Practical Advice

A person's lifetime is a search for themselves. Throughout our lives we find different experiences, feelings, and opportunities to react to them. Through the parsha of nedarim we try to uplift all of the facets of our life.

פרשת מסעי

from Beis Yaakov ha-Kollel

וְלֹא תִסֹּב נַחֲלָה מִמַּטֶּה לְמַטֶּה אַחֵר כִּי אִישׁ בְּנַחֲלָתוֹ יִדְבְּקוּ מַטּוֹת בְּנֵי יִשְׂרָאֵל (במדבר ל"ו ט'). הנה בפ' ויקרא נכתבו כל קדושות ועבודות ישראל על סדר קרבנות. וגם נכתב קדושת ישראל על סדר מקומות הרבה פעמים. ובפרשת פינחס נכתב על סדר זמנים. ובסדרה הזאת נכתב קדושת ישראל על סדר המקרים שהקרה לפניהם.

In *Parshas Masei* after we learn about the travels of the Jewish people in the desert, we hear the heads of Shevet Menashe voicing concern, that if inheritance of land passes to daughters, and the daughters marry into another *shevet*, then the original *shevet* will lose land. Moshe reassures them saying (36:7), "The inheritance will not pass to another, because everyone will cling to their inheritance." What's the connection between the travels in the desert and question of losing the tribal inheritance?

The בית יעקב explains that in *Parshas Vayikra* we see all of the *kedushah* and *avodah* that come to the Jews as a result of the *korbanos*. We see the *kedushah* of the Jewish people many times in *Chumash* in different places. In *Parshas Pinchas* we see the *kedushah* of time. In this *parsha* we see the *kedushah* of the

Jewish people in everything that happens to them, throughout the forty-two different stops that the Jews made in the desert. As a result of all of the journeys in a person's life, he arrives at his own personal *kedushah*, with its significance, holiness, and self development.

ולכן סיום הסדרה כי איש בנחלתו ידבקו. כי לכל אדם שייך מצוה אחת בשורשו.

Therefore, in this week's *parsha*, the *pasuk* says, "Each person will cling to his inheritance." Each person has a mitzvah that is intrinsic to his soul. This means that each person has a uniqueness and significance all his own.

וכל הנסיונות שיבאו לפני האדם הם לטובתו. כדי שלא יגע אחר במה שמוכן לו.

Understanding this in context, there are so many travel, travails, and challenges that a person must overcome, (expressed by the forty-two desert stops). We are told that we will arrive at our personal spiritual significance (as expressed by the portion regarding inheritances, and the assurance that we never will lose them). Therefore, every challenge that a person has is for his own benefit. Only that specific person can have those challenges and grow from them. No one else in the world could have the benefit of your challenges except for you.

וכמו שמבואר בגמרא (שבת י' ב'). הנותן מתנה לחברו צריך להודיעו כו'. מכאן אמר רבן שמעון בן גמליאל הנותן פת לתינוק צריך להודיע לאמו. מאי עביד ליה. אמר אביי שאיף ליה משתא ומלי ליה כוחלא. והאידנא דחיישינן לכשפים מאי. אמר רב פפא שאיף ליה מאותו המין.

The בית יעקב continues to explain the notion of these challenges through a teaching of the Gemara (*Shabbos* 10b), which says that a person who gives a present to his friend must tell him. Rabban Shimon ben Gamliel says, "Therefore, a person who gives bread to a child must alert the child's mother." The Gemara asks, "What should he do? Abaye says put some oil on his nose and a little blue on his face." The Gemara responds, "But nowadays when we are concerned about magic, and that the child might have somehow been involved in something of the sort, what do we do?" Rav Pappa said, "Wipe a little bit of whatever you gave him on his face."

כי כשפים רומז על חוצפא כלפי שמיא.

Let's understand this puzzling Gemara. Any time you give someone a present, you need to tell him. So too, if you feed someone else's children, you must let the parents know. We used to put a little color on their face, but now that there is a concern of magic, we leave whatever they ate on their face. What is magic? The Gemara tells us that magic is chutzpah against Hashem. Why? Hashem made the world in a certain way and the sorcerer has the gall to try to change the natural order of the world's function!

והנה באם היה נותן הקב"ה טובה לעולם הזה בלבוש תפארת אז היו הכל קופצין עליו. לכן שאיף ליה מאותו המין וממילא נראית בעולם הזה כצמצום.

What is the danger of chutzpah, then, and what does this have to with spiritual growth and achievement? If Hashem were to give a present to this world in a beautiful garment, meaning in a way that everyone could access it, everyone would jump on it. Think about it, fulfillment, growth of self and personality; it's readily available, how many people would rush for it?

Therefore, the Gemara says, wipe a bit of the item (like bread crumbs) on their faces. You can glimpse a little bit of the spiritual treasures that await you, but it's hard to see.

כמו שבת שרומז על לעתיד שלא יצטרך האדם למעשה ידיו ובעולם הזה נראה כצמצום. ואם יאמר האדם אם כן איך יגיע האדם השייך להטובה איך יגיע לה מאחר שנראית כצמצום.

The בית יעקב explains the concept of magic, using the reason for the prohibition of work on Shabbos, which alludes to the world to come, where a person will not need the work of his hands. At that time, anything you possibly could do doesn't measure up to what is being given there. Work becomes "bread crumbs" as compared to what Shabbos has to offer. So, a person might think, "What's the point of doing anything if it is not comparable, if it's just bread crumbs, in comparison to what the spiritual and personal attainment is?" Magic means to jump over the reality that you must work for attainment and the chutzpah to want to receive something now that should take years to achieve.

לזה נסמך בגמרא (שם). מילתא אלבישייהו יקירא. כי זה ששייך לה יבקע כל חומות ברזל המבדילים והמסכים המסתירים. ואחר כל הצמצומים יבא אל הטובה. וכמו שנתבאר בפרשת כי תשא:

Therefore, the Gemara connects this previous statement with the story that when Rav Chisda would hear a teaching in the name of Rav, he would put on an expensive garment. Rav

Chisda explained that every teaching despite its smallness, had the ability to break down walls that separate us from seeing the true value of things and keep us from attaining our potential. This reminds us that when we "follow the trail of bread crumbs," we get past the smallness into a world of achievement.

The Izhbitzer Tradition

See מי השלוח ובית יעקב הכולל פרשת כי תשא which deals with this concept of your spiritual heights and kedushah which it is accessible only to you.

Practical Advice

During your most trying times, remember that no one can steal your heritage. This week's parsha tells us that through all of your travels, you will arrive at the place you need to be to grow and use the opportunities given you—to reveal your personal spiritual strengths.

פרשת דברים

from Naos Deshe

אֵלֶּה הַדְּבָרִים אֲשֶׁר דִּבֶּר מֹשֶׁה אֶל כָּל יִשְׂרָאֵל וגו' (דברים א' א'). יש
לדקדק מפני מה לא מנה כסדר החטא ועוד בכולם מנה על שם המקום והאחרון
אמר ודי זהב. וגם כל מקום שנאמר אלה פסל את הראשונים.

The *parsha* begins with the phrase, "These are the words that
Moshe spoke to all of the Jewish people" (*Devarim* 1:1). Let's
explore why the Torah counts the sins of the Jewish people by
the places instead of their chronological order, why this order
ends with Dei Zahav, and why the *pasuk* starts with the word
eleh, which usually means to reject the previous information.

אך הענין הוא כי המדרש מתחיל הלכה אדם מישראל מה שיהא מותר לכתוב
ספרים בכל לשון וכו' ומסיים שם שדברי תורה מרפאין את הלשון. עיין שם
באריכות. ויש לדקדק מה ענין הפתיחה לכאן וגם מה שאמר שמרפאין את
הלשון. כי משה קודם שלמד את התורה אמר לא איש דברים אנכי ועכשיו
שלמד את התורה התחיל לדבר דברים שנאמר אלה הדברים.

The נאות דשא explains that the keys to understanding are found
in the beginning of the Midrash (*Devarim Rabbah* 1:1), which
asks an halachic question: Is one allowed to write the Torah in

any language, and then concludes with "the words of Torah heal the tongue." Why is does the Midrash start like that? What is the relevance of the notion that Torah heals the tongue? The Midrash explains that Moshe Rabbeinu, before learning the Torah, said, "I am not a man of words." Now that he has learned it, the Torah says, "These are the words that Moshe spoke."

ויש לתמוה וכי עד עכשיו לא דבר והלא כבר אמר כל התורה.

We may wonder: Did Moshe never speak until now? How could it be? So why, only at the beginning of *Devarim*, does the Torah explain that Moshe spoke these words?

אך הענין הוא כי איתא בתקוני זוהר הקדוש (קלב ע"ב) פומא וליבא דא
אורייתא דבכתב ואורייתא דבעל פה והם לוחות שניים כדאיתא במדרש
(שמות רבה מז:ז) שהם הלכות ואגדות ספרי וספרא וכתיב כתב לך ואיתא
במדרש כיון שהטריח הרבה אמר לו הקב"ה לך אני נותנה ומתוך טובת עין
שהיה בו במשה נתנה לישראל. וזה הספר משנה תורה הוא אורייתא דבעל
פה שמשה קבל תורה מסיני ומסרה ליהושע וזה משנה תורה שאמר הקב"ה
ליהושע לא ימוש ספר התורה הזה מפיך כדאיתא במדרש (בראשית רבה
פ ו:ט) זה אורייתא דבעל פה שכתוב בו שמור כי התורה שבכתב הוא זכור
כדאיתא בזוה"ק (ח"ב דף קיח ע"ב).

The נאות דשא cites the *Tikkunei Zohar* (132b) to explain the connection between the Book of *Devarim* and Moshe's ability to speak. He says that the most intimate way to connect to the Written Torah is through the heart, while the mouth is the way to connect to the Oral Torah—the second set of tablets. The Midrash (*Shemos* 47:7) says that the second *luchos* are *halachah*, *aggada Sifra*, and *Sifrei*. They were meant to stay oral, while the

Torah, Neviim, and Kesuvim were to be written down. The Midrash says that since Moshe toiled intently to understand the Torah, Hashem gave it to him as a gift. Then due to Moshe's generosity, he gave it to the Jewish people. *Sefer Devarim* is the gift of the Oral Torah, as it is the record of Moshe's teaching to the Jewish people. It is also called "*Mishneh Torah,*" the second transmission of the Torah. But it could also imply the combination of Mishnah and the Torah, making it the Oral Torah and Written Torah together. This Oral Torah is what Moshe received on Mount Sinai, and passed on to Yehoshua. Hashem told Yehoshua, "Don't let this book of the Torah leave from your mouth." Hashem calls *Sefer Devarim* "a book which is in your mouth." This tells us that *Mishneh Torah* is more than just a regular text. *Sefer Devarim* is *Torah Shebal Peh*, even though it's *Torah Shebichsav*.

This fundamental difference in *Sefer Devarim* also accounts for differences in the Aseres Ha-Dibros. (They are written once in *Parshas Yisro* and once in *Va'eschanan* in *Devarim*.) For example, the *pasuk* in *Yisro* says "*Zachor* (remember) the day of Shabbos." In *Va'eschanan*, it says, "*Shamor* (guard) the day of Shabbos." What accounts for this difference? *Sefer Devarim* is *Torah Shebal Peh*, and we were commanded, *shamor*, as the function of *Torah Shebal Peh*, which is the obligation to guard the words of Torah. The Written Torah says *Zachor* regarding Shabbos (*Zohar* 2:118b).

ונתן להם התורה שבעל פה אחר החטא כדי שיוכלו לתקן החטא כי חיים ביד הלשון וכן כאן נתן להם משה הספר משנה תורה הזה כדי שיכלו לתקן הכל.

Therefore, to correct all of their sins in the desert, Moshe Rabbeinu gave the Jewish people the *Torah Shebal Peh*. Since "life is in the hands of the tongue," so too, through the Oral Torah, which also possesses the power of speech, one can repair everything. Therefore, it was no coincidence that the second *luchos* were given to the Jewish people. Additionally the thirteen attributes of *rachamim*, which are an appeal for the chance to do *teshuvah*, are correspond to the thirteen rules of how to explain the Torah (which are recited at the beginning of Shacharis, according to *Rebbe Yishmael Omer*).

וזה שנאמר אלה פסל את הראשונים כי מקודם לא כתיב רק החטא ולא התיקון וכאן נתן להם עצה איך יתקנו את החטא כסדר הזה.

For this reason *Parshas Devarim* and *Mishneh Torah* begin with the word *eleh*, which means to throw out the old version. Previously we only saw the sins in places of the desert and the old failed way of life; now we are going to learn how to live in a new way. Instead of the path of destruction and failure, we see a new route, a way to fix ourselves.

במדבר בערבה היינו במדבר שאמרו בשבתנו על סיר הבשר ואחר כך בערבה בשיטים היינו מלא כריסא זיני בישא אלה השנים הולכים יחד ואם תברר עצמך באלה השנים אזי תוכל להתבונן מה יהיה התכלית שלך כמה שכתוב באור החיים. ומקודם שתברר עצמך באכילה ובתאווה לא יפנה לבבך לחשוב על התכלית ואם תחשוב על התכלית אזי תוכל לשמור מלשון הרע וזהו פארן במרגלים. ותופל ולבן היינו במן שתסתפק במועט תענוג. וחצרות היינו מחלוקת שתברה ממחלוקת.

The נאות דשא explains Moshe Rabbeinu's teaching of a new path through the desert of life, through the episodes that took place in the actual *midbar*. There, in Arava, the Jews complained how they wanted to sit by pots of meat, the way they had in Mitzraim. It was in Arava in Shittim, where many people succumbed to the temptation of the Midianite women. These two places go together. If people can straighten out their priorities and overcome physical temptations, they can have the clarity of thought to consider their purpose in life. They can then triumph over the desire to speak *lashon hara*, as its insidiousness is to take the focus off of themselves and decimate those around them, so they don't have to change. Therefore, the stop that is included next on the list in this week's *parsha* is Paran, where the *meraglim* spoke *lashon hara* about Eretz Yisrael. Tofal Lavan, where they complained about the *man* (manna), teaches us about being able to live life with less of the luxuries. If *man* can taste like almost everything, then what else do you need? The next stop is Chatzeros, which is where the rebellion of Korach took place, teaches us to keep away from divisiveness.

ודי זהב פרש"י ז"ל בשביל רוב זהב ובדבר זה אין כאן לישראל שום טענה כי למה השפיע להם הקב"ה רוב זהב וזה מרמז אם תתקן מה שכתוב מקודם אזי כל הטובות שתתקבל לא יתן הקב"ה פתחון פה לשום מסטין לקטרג עליך כמו במצרים שהענן קבל כל החיצים ואבני בליסטרא היינו כל הקיטרוג שאמרו או"א עובדי ע"ז הקב"ה קבל על עצמו ליישב הכל. וכמו בשעיר ר"ח על שמעטתי את הירח היינו שאמר הקב"ה אשר הרעותי (מיכה ד' ו').

Regarding the last place mentioned, Dei Zahav, Rashi explains that it means "enough gold." If Moshe Rabbeinu is rebuking the people based on their complaints, why mention this, as the Jewish people didn't have any complaint about having too much gold. What is the message here? Moshe is telling the Jews that, if you repair all of the aforementioned problems, then there will not be any complaint in the Heavenly Court about the material goods that they have.

ולכן מתחיל המדרש (תנחומא וירא ה') מה שיהא מותר לכתוב בכל לשון דאיתא במדרש ילמדנו פ' נח שצפה הקב"ה שאומות יכתבו התורה יוונית ויאמרו אנו ישראל לפיכך ניתנה משנה בעל פה שהם מסטורין של הקב"ה עיין שם פירושו.

The Midrash (*Tanchuma Vayera* 5) begins with the question of whether or not it is permissible to write the Torah in Greek. The Midrash says Hashem foresaw that the nations of the world would translate the Torah into Greek and say that they are the Jewish people. It is for this reason that the Mishnah was given orally, for it is Hashem's secrets, demonstrating the relationship between Hashem and the Jewish people.

לתת לאדם עצה לתקן החטא זה הוא סוד בפני האומות רק לישראל שהם עמו וסגולתו וזה המשנה תורה שבזה יהושע הדמים החמה ואם האדם יגע בה אזי מאירה לו הספר הזה לתקן הכל ולכן בתחילה אמר לא איש דברים ולפי שלא שמעו לו בני ישראל כמו שכתוב ולא שמעו אל משה ועכשיו שקבלו תוכחתו כתיב אלה הדברים שרפאו את הלשון ששמעו לו בני ישראל וזה תורה שבעל פה כדאיתא בזוה"ק פומא ולבא.

What are these secrets? The route to fixing sins that are hidden from the nations is in the *Torah Shebal Peh*. It is only given to the Jewish people. When a person toils in *Sefer Devarim*, then it will illuminate everything and grant him new perspectives in life. Through it, he can repair all of the facets of his life. For example, at the beginning of the Torah, Moshe said, "I am not a man of words," and complained that he had a speech impediment, so that the Jewish people would not listen to him. But now at the end of his life, they listened to and accepted the rebuke in his month-long discourse. This was only made possible through *Torah Shebal Peh*, the Torah of repair.

The Izhbitzer Tradition

See בית יעקב הכולל פרשת ואתחנן, which discusses Shamor and Zachor and their implications.

Practical Advice

The sefer of Devarim is the beginning of the Torah Shebal Peh, the process of how the dvar Hashem descends into our lives to heal us, and presents us with the vision of a better life. It endeavors to repair the broken hearts, of the broken luchos, and our broken lives. It is no coincidence that this week, Shabbos Chazon is Parshas Devarim. Chazon—when (according to the Berdichover) we are given the vision of the third Beis Ha-Mikdash, a vision of how life could and should be. We also acquire the tools of the Torah Shebal Peh, the thirteen Middos how to activate Torah Shebal Peh, which are the thirteen attributes of the tefillah to rebuild our lives. This Shabbos, dream and make plans how do rebuild your live, receive the present of Mishneh Torah and the vision of the third Beis Ha-Mikdash.

פרשת ואתחנן

from Beis Yaakov ha-Kollel

אָנֹכִי ה' אֱלֹהֶיךָ (דברים ה' ו'). ענין ההפרש שבין לוחות הראשונות לדברות
האלו. כי אלו נשתיירו בשלמות. כי בהראשונים כתיב זכור את יום השבת
לקדשו (יתרו כ' ח'). ובאלו כתיב שמור. כי מצד השי"ת היינו הזכירה הוא
באור גדול. ואין האדם יכול לקבל אור כזה שיטיב לבו להתמשך אחר השי"ת
בעומק. אכן שמור הוא שישמור את עצמו על המעשה וזה בכח האדם. וממילא
מצד השי"ת היה הדיבור זכור. אכן מצד האדם לא קבל רק שמור.

What is the difference between the first set of tablets and the
second set? What changed so that they were not shattered as
the first ones were? It's because the first ones said, "Remember
Shabbos to make it *kadosh*" (*Shemos* 20:8) and the second *luchos*
said, "Keep the Shabbos." What does it mean to "remember"
Shabbos, and what does it mean to "keep" Shabbos?

A brief word of introduction. In everything in the world
there are two dynamics: light and vessels. Light involves giving,
and vessels are about receiving. In this physical world, we see the
personification of giving and receiving in the male (who give in
the reproductive process) and the woman (who receives). The
comparison is only in terms of anatomy. The most traumatic
experience in the history of the world was the moment when

light and vessels were split from each other. This was called the *nesirah*, when Adam and Chava were split from each other; in *Bereishis*, light and vessels were split forever.

Hashem wants to give the Jewish people the mitzvah of Shabbos in all of its spiritual depths. This is contained in the mitzvah of *Zachor*. But a person can't receive the greatness of Shabbos and absorb its message to change himself. Therefore, the mitzvah of *Shamor* is to enable us to guard something we have to until you are able to make use of it. Hence on the first *luchos*, which are from "Hashem's perspective," it speaks of Hashem wanting to give the Shabbos. However, we're incapable of receiving it like that. Therefore on the version of the second set of *luchos*, which describe the Torah from our perspective, it says, *Shamor*, "Guard."

וזהו זכור ושמור בדיבור אחד נאמרו (ר"ה כ"ז א'). ושניהם נכללו בזכור. אכן האדם לא קבל רק השמירה. וכמו דאיתא בזה"ק (אמר צ"ב ב'). זכור לדכורא. ושמור לנוקבא. וענין הנוקבא הוא צמצום אור אין סוף ברוך הוא. וכמו שנאמר יפל ה' אלקים תרדמה על האדם (בראשית ב' כ"א). וממילא נשאר אצלו נקבה. וכמבואר בכתבי האריז"ל (עץ החיים שער הנסירה פ"א). כי נתנסרה אשה מהסרה אור ממנו. וממילא נשארה נקבה גם כן:

The Gemara says that both "remember" and "guard" were said together, and both sets of *luchos* really said "remember" and "guard." The *Zohar* (*Emor* 92b) says that "remember" is masculine, and "guard" is feminine. To understand the meaning here, we must return to the *nesirah*. When light was separated from vessels, man was separated from woman. In order to receive Hashem's eternal light, it must be compressed. Hashem caused sleep to fall on man, and upon his awakening, he awoke to find Chava as a separate entity from him.

וגם בלוחות הראשונות נאמר טעם השבת. כי ששת ימים עשה ה' את השמים
ואת הארץ את הים ואת כל אשר בם וינח ביום השביעי (יתרו כ' י"א). וכאן
כתיב וזכרת כי עבד היית בארץ מצרים ויצאך ה' אלהיך משם ביד חזקה ובזרוע
נטויה על כן צוך ה' אלהיך לעשות את יום השבת. כי בדברות הראשונות היה
כתיב זכור מצד השי"ת ורומז על לעתיד. כי שבת רומז על לעתיד שלא יצטרך
האדם למעשה ידיו. וזה שנאמר כי ששת ימים עשה ה' את השמים.

Both sets of *luchos* present reasons for Shabbos. The first
indicates (*Shemos* 20:11) that Hashem made the heavens and
earth, and then rested on the seventh day. The second *luchos*
say, "Remember that you were a slave in Mitzraim and Hashem
took you out from there with a strong hand and outstretched
arm; therefore Hashem commanded you to keep Shabbos." The
first set of *luchos* say, "remember," referring to the world from
Hashem's perspective, and giving a glimpse of the future. How
so? Despite the fact that we believe so much depends on our
efforts, in the future when we won't have to act, we will have
moved in the phase of reward.

כי כמו שאצל השי"ת שהכל שלו לא נמצא בו שום טירדא. וכמו ששאל
טורנוסרופוס את רבי עקיבא. מפני מה הקב"ה מוריד גשמים. והשיב לו כי מי
שיש לו שתי חצרות מותר לו לטלטל מזה לזה (מדרש תנחומא תשא סל"ג).
כי אצל השי"ת לא נמצא שום טירדא ושכחה. ועיקר שנאסרה מלאכה בשבת
הוא בכדי שהאדם יזכור את השי"ת. ועל זה רומז כי ששת ימים עשה ה' כמו
שאין שכחה לפניו.

Hashem owns everything and there is nothing that is an
exertion for Him. Rabbi Akiva had this same debate with
Turnus Rufus (*Tanchuma Ki Tissa* 33). He asked Rabbi Akiva
why can Hashem make it rain on Shabbos? Isn't there a problem

of carrying without an eruv? Rabbi Akiva responded, but if you own two areas, then you can carry between them. For Hashem, there is nothing that is a burden and He never forgets. The reason why *melachah* is prohibited on Shabbos is so that man will remember Hashem. Therefore the *pasuk* says, "For Hashem made Heaven and earth" meaning that He owns everything; and in His Presence, there is no forgetfulness.

אבל בהשניות כתיב שמור מצד האדם. ועל זה צריך להזהיר וזכרת כי עבד היית בארץ מצרים. ולכן בלוחות האלו נאמר במצות כבד את אביך ולמען ייטב לך. כי הדברות האלו נאמרו לטובת האדם.

But the second set of *luchos* it is directed to us. Therefore, it says to remember that you were a slave in Mitzraim, indicating that to us, there is the possibility of our forgetting. The *pasuk* also says that the mitzvah of respecting your father and mother is for our own good.

ולא באור הקב"ה שאין האדם יכול לסבלו. וכמבואר בגמרא (פסחים ח' א'). החילוק בין אבוקה לנר. כי אבוקה נקרא אורו של הקב"ה. ונר הוא אורו של בשר ודם. וכמו שמבואר (שם) למה צדיקים דומין בפני שכינה כנר בפני האבוקה ועל אורו של הקב"ה נאמר שהוא אורו לאחריו ובעית ומיקטף איקטופי.

This is not the case when Hashem brings all of His good and light into the world. Man cannot tolerate it. This is what the Gemara (*Pesachim* 8a) means when it asks, "What is the difference between a torch and a candle?" A torch is Hashem's light, and a candle is man's light. Why are *tzaddikim* compared to the Shechinah in the same way a candle is compared to a torch? Hashem's light is a great torch, and the candles are small bursts of that light.

ועל ידי זה נאמרו כאן כל הדברות בהוספת וי"ו שמוסיף על ענין ראשון (שם ה' א'). לא תרצח ולא תנאף ולא תגנב. כי צורת אדם נמשל בזה"ק (אחרי ס"ו ב') לאות וי"ו. וכמו שמבואר בגמרא (ברכות ל"א ב'). גברא בגוברין כו'. ולא חכם ולא טפש.

The second five *Dibros* begin with the letter *vav*, meaning "and," which is to say that each one adds to what we started from. This is why the *Zohar* says that person is compared to a *vav*. Why? On a simple level, a person is shaped like a *vav*. A person is a composite, a mixture of many things, hence the *vav ha-chibbur*. The Gemara (*Brachos* 31b) explains what Chana davened for in a son: he should be not overly wise, but not stupid either, not to any one extreme. (This methodology is described by the נאות דשא earlier in this *parsha* as giving the Torah in "a feminine, composite or guard way.")

כי דברות הראשונות היה כל דבור בהתפשטות. כמו שהם מצד השי"ת כל דיבור בגודל הסתעפות. ולכן באם היה דבר מה בהאדם נגד השי"ת היה חס ושלום מתבטל והאדם אינו יכול לקבלם.

The first set of *Dibros* presented everything in absolute terms. When every command was "spoken," had there been any opposition, the power of Hashem would have destroyed everything that had been created. The *Zohar* describes this way of giving as masculine, as "remember."

כי לא תרצח מצד השי"ת היינו שלא ימצא בהאדם שום כעס. ומצד האדם אין
זה ביכולת. שבאם לא ימצא בו שום נטיה לכעס אז לא יוכל להשמר מאהבה
יתרה. וכמו שנתבאר במי השלוח (חלק א' נח). על פסוק ישלח את הערב. ולפי
שאלו נאמרו שאחד צריך לחברו לכן הם כפי דעת האדם שיוכל לקבלם. והוא
שנזהרו לא תרצח שלא יהיה בהם שום כעס. ומכל מקום ולא תנאף שבמקום
שנצרך מעט ממדת הכעס נגד מדת לא תנאף. יוכל האדם להכניס את עצמו מעט
בזה וכן כלם. ועל ידי זה נתקיימו:

The בית יעקב explains the composite nature of the second
luchos. For example, the other side of "do not murder" is that a
person should not retain any anger. However, that is impossible,
because without the ability to have anger, there could not be the
ability to balance too much love, or love which is inappropriate.
The בית יעקב demonstrates this idea from a teaching of the מי
השלוח. When Noach sent out the raven, he wanted to send
away all anger. But the raven came back. This taught Noach
that he couldn't live without anger, because there are some
circumstances where it is needed.

This is the reason why all of the commandments in the
second *luchos* are linked with a *vav*. Each one seems to be an
ideal, but it would be impossible for a person to maintain that
ideal level. Rather, it is the blending together of the different
attributes that creates a whole person. When we say "do not
murder," we mean that a person should relinquish his anger.
However, sometimes we need a little anger, to fight against a
desire for things that are prohibited. Therefore, the next of the
Dibros prohibits adultery. By finding the proper balance of each
middah, a person will be able to live as he should.

The Izhbitzer Tradition

The Izhbitzer seforim often talk about finding a way through impossible contradictions, within the world and within one's self, to understand a person's obligations in this world. See מי השלוח פרשת נח regarding the balance in a person's midos. Also בית יעקב פרשת שמיני הכולל about the mix of love and awe, and פרשת ויקהל about the power of nonaction.

Practical Advice

Often we are pulled by our impulses to react in certain extreme ways. While there is a time for extremity, most of the time, life is walking a tightrope, and extreme movement will knock you off. When you feel pulled to act with any middah in an extreme fashion, wait a little bit, and think a little more objectively if this will truly accomplish what you had in mind.

פרשת עקב

from Beis Yaakov ha-Kollel

וְהָיָה עֵקֶב תִּשְׁמְעוּן אֵת הַמִּשְׁפָּטִים הָאֵלֶּה וּשְׁמַרְתֶּם וַעֲשִׂיתֶם אֹתָם וְשָׁמַר ה'
אֱלֹהֶיךָ לְךָ אֶת הַבְּרִית וְאֶת הַחֶסֶד אֲשֶׁר נִשְׁבַּע לַאֲבֹתֶיךָ (דברים ז' י"ב). והיה
באחרית הימים נכון יהיה הר בית ה' בראש ההרים ונשא מגבעות ונהרו אליו
כל הגוים (ישעיה ב' ב'). והיה הוא לשון שמחה (פתיחתא דאסתר רבה סי"א).
באחרית הימים מורה כשיסתלקו כל ההסתרות וכל הספקות ויתברר הטוב מן
הרע. וכמבואר בזה"ק דא אלנא דטוב ורע שיתבררו ויתחלקו לעתיד וכמבואר
בכתבי האריז"ל.

The *pasuk* says, "And it will be because you listen to these
mishpatim-laws, guard them and do them that Hashem will
keep the covenant and the kindness that He swore to your
forefathers" (*Devarim* 7:12).

The בית יעקב explains that the word *ve-hayah*, "and it will
be," refers to the vision of Yeshayahu the Navi (2:2), that the
Beis Ha-Mikdash will be sitting atop the hills and the nations
will stream to it. The Midrash (*Esther*, introduction 11) explains
that the word *ve-hayah* also means "happiness." The בית יעקב
says both explanations are complementary. The Navi Yeshayahu
says that "in the end of days" refers to the future when all doubts
and hesitations will disappear, and good will be distinguished

283

from evil. The *Zohar* says that "One day the tree of good and evil will be separated, and then there will be much happiness." The בית יעקב will explain this fascinating statement of the *Zohar*.

ויום מורה על ראיה ברורה ומפורשת. ואז נכון יהיה הר בית ה' בראש ההרים. כי הר הוא בליטה מפורשת והכרת אור השי״ת מפורש לעיני האדם.

"Day" means being able to see things clearly. Yeshayahu is prophesying that the Divine ideal, Hashem's will, will become as apparent as the Beis Ha-Mikdash over the mountains, and it will be as clear as day.

כי בעולם הזה נמצא דומם צומח חי מדבר. והמדבר מדוגל במעלתו שהוא בעל בחירה. וכן החי מנושא על הצומח. והצומח מנושא על הדומם. כי בו גם כן ניכרת מעט תנועה. אבל הדומם חייו הם בהסתר גדול. והנה בעולם הזה אף בהמדבר שנמצא בו בחירה. מכל מקום ישאף לסגל רכוש להסתר מפני ה' מאחר שהרכוש הוא בלי בחירה. אבל לעתיד ינהרו הכל אל הר בית ה'. כי זאת תהיה הרכוש מה שהאדם יכיר כי לה' הכל.

The classical texts of Jewish philosophy describe the creations in terms of four categories: inanimate matter, plants, living creatures, and speaking creatures. There is a hierarchy that exists based on their complexity and our ability to see the spark of life and the divinity within them. The speaking creatures occupy the highest status as they have the ability to choose. Living creatures have the advantage of mobility over vegetation. Vegetation can grow, but inanimate objects, whose vitality is hard to detect, don't. Despite the fact that the speaking beings have free choice, they wish to have the ability to hide from that choice. They do this because they think that a person's lot is given to him in this world without his imput. So Yeshayahu prophesies about when everyone will stream to the Beis Ha-Mikdash, at that time when man realizes that everything depends on his ability to recognize Hashem as the source of all creation.

והנה האבות פעלו בתפלתם כשהאדם יפנה להתבונן לכח השי"ת. אז יגע בהאור ההוא שהם טעמו ממנו. וכמו שכתוב אשר יאמר היום בהר ה' יראה (וירא כ"ב י"ד).

How does a person have the ability to get past his apathy and be able to see through the mixture of good and bad to see Hashem? The Avos accomplished with through their *tefillos*. When a person turns to think about Hashem's power as the source of everything, then he will experience that understanding in a palpable way. This is why Hashem promises, "On the mountain of Hashem, they will see" (*Bereishis* 22:14).

וזהו תשמעו את המשפטים האלה. שהאדם יתמשך בדעתו אחר המשפט. כי משפט הוא דבר ברור. כי באמת כל מה שהאדם שואף לסגל רכוש נצמח מפני שיש בכל דבר חקים טובים.

Now we can have a clearer understanding of Moshe's statement, "because you have listened to these *mishpatim*-laws." A *mishpat* is a law whose reasoning is clear. We assume that when a person works, what he accomplishes is the result of that effort. However, this natural rule of cause and effect is only because Hashem has set up the world in such a way (this is referred to as *chukim tovim*, "good laws").

כמו שכתוב מלפנו מבהמות ארץ (איוב ל"ה י"א) אך החוקה שנטבע בברואים הוא בלי טעם שאינה מרגשת בזה.

This is opposite of the way in which the animal kingdom and laws of nature function. Nature works without the assumption of meaning and accomplishment that come as a result of work. Animals can't fathom why; they just do.

Hence, the *pasuk* in Iyov (35:11) says, "Teach us to be smarter than the animals."

אבל לעתיד ירצה אדם באור מפורש שגם הוא ירגיש מחיים אמתיים כי לה' הכל.

Man feels that it would be easier not to have to think and make choices and thereby avoid pain and frustration. In the future, a person will want to be able to live in a mindful way; to live with the awareness that Hashem is the source of everything in his life.

זהו והיה עקב תשמעון וגו' ישמר ה' אלקיך לך את הברית. כי השי"ת ישמור כל מעשים ומחשבות ישראל לבלי ידח מהם נדח. כי בפרשת ואתחנן (ז' ו') כתיב. בך בחר ה' אלהיך להיות לו לעם סגלה. והוא כי על ידי זה בחר השי"ת בישראל לפי שהם מצמצמין עצמם לעת הצורך. כי סגלה מורה על זה.

This is the meaning of the phrase, "and it will be (*ve-hayah*) because (*eikev*) you listen and Hashem will keep the agreement with you." Despite man's desire not to choose, he will do so as a result of an agreement with Hashem. This will ultimately be the cause for *simchah*.

Moshe says that Hashem will guard the agreement between Him and the Jews. He does this by guarding all thoughts and actions of the Jewish people so that no good thought or feeling will ever be lost. This is because Hashem chose us to be his treasured (*segulah*) nation. The Jewish people are described by the word *segulah* (as the *Tikkunei Zohar* states above). The word *segulah* has to do with knowing the appropriate action in each situation.

וכמבואר בתקוני הזהר סגל אימא רביע על בנין. כי סגל הוא תלת נקודין. כל נקודה יש לה עוד שנים לכל צד. וכשירצה להתפשט יוכלו להתפשט עד אין שיעור. כי לכל נקודה הנוספת יתוסף עוד. וכן כשירצה בהסתר יוכל לקבץ כל כחותיו לתוכו עד דלא ישתכחון לה. וזהו עיקר בעולם הזה כי השמירה מעוטה והרכוש רב. ולכן בעולם הזה הבחירה בעידית. לפי שהוא מעט הכמות והתפשטות תוכל להתפשט לרב. אבל לעתיד תהיה הטובה כשתתפשט כי גם ההתפשטות הוא טובה גדולה. אכן בעולם הזה הטובה הוא ההתכנסות.

The בית יעקב explains the meaning of the word *segulah*. He says that it comes from the concept expressed in a *segol*. The *Tikkunei Zohar* explains that a *segol*—three dots as a musical note or vowel—is employed to describe the ability to either expand, contract, or choose which is most appropriate in this situation. *Segol* and *segulah* are cognates, they both describe the ability to find the appropriate for course of action for each situation.

Therefore, in this world, a person's choices are of prime importance. There will come a time in the future when reaching out and touching everything is appropriate, when we'll understand that everything is from Hashem. But for the time being, not everything that is in our grasp should be taken, not everything that we can do, we should do.

והנה השי״ת בחר בישראל על ידי צמצומם. והשי״ת נתן את האדם לעולם הזה כדי שיברר את עצמו. והאמנם כי כל הבריאה הוא מהשי״ת ולמה יצרך

לבירור. אכן כי השי״ת ברא את העולם בדברי תורה. ובכל דבר נמצא מוצא
פי ה׳ שהוא המחיה. וכמו שכתוב החכמה תחיה בעליה (קהלת ז׳ י״ב). ולולא
שהוא נסתר בכולם היה די בכל דבר המוצא פי ה׳ בלי התלבשות בדבר גשמי.

Hashem gave us this world so that we should be able to process
and separate good from evil. Why should we have to do this
if it's all from Hashem? Since Hashem created everything
through *divrei Torah*, all of reality is given its existence through
Hashem's words.

אך בעולם הזה לפי שהוא נסתר לכן אינו ידוע למה האדם שואף. אם לחומר
הגשמי או לחכמה הנמצאת בו. ולכן כל הצדיקים נתנו לבין האומות. יעקב
ללבן ויצחק היה אצל אבימלך. כי הם היו אז הגדולים שבאומות והטובים
שבהם. והיה נראה על הגוון שעושים מעשים טובים. לפיכך נתנו ביניהם כדי
שהם יצמצמו עצמם ביותר. וכדי שאף בעולם הזה יראו כי הם יכולים לצמצם
עצמם ביותר.

But in this world, where the word of Hashem is hidden, we
don't know what people really want. Do they want the physical
thing, or the wisdom within? We need to be able to see through
the mixture of good and bad and reach the truth.

It is for this reason the *tzaddikim* were scattered amongst
the nations, as Yaakov was with Lavan and Yitzchak was with
Avimelech. Even though on the surface Avimelech and Lavan
seemed to be doing good things, the *tzaddikim* were sent there to
seek out the truth, to find and choose what's good, right, and true.

כן כל נביא כשראה איזה מאומות העולם מצמצם עצמו. אז התחיל הוא להתנהג
ביתר צמצום. וכן הזהיר גם לכל ישראל. וכל הצמצום אין צריך רק בעולם
הזה שצריך בירורים. אף שהכל נברא בדברי תורה מכל מקום לפי שהם בגוף

ונכללים בפעולות בהם צריך בירורים. כי אחר חטא אדם הראשון נתערב הטוב
בהרע. כמבואר בכתבי האריז"ל.

Therefore, every Navi was able to remove a little falseness from
the world. The Navi then taught the Jewish people what they
themselves had accomplished, in order to help them see what
was good and what was bad in the world. Even though the world
was created through words of Torah, now that these words have
been passed down into the physical world, they need to be
clarified. This is due to the sin of Adam Ha-Rishon; as a result
of the sin, the world became an admixture of good and bad.

כי חטא אדם הראשון היה שאכלה פגה. כדאיתא בבראשית רבה (פי"ט ס' ה').
סחטה ענבים ונתנה לו כטועם את התבשיל לידע מה צריך. ועל ידי זה ניתן
בגוף שצריך בירור. וכמבואר בזה"ק שבתחלה לא היה במדרגה שפלה הזאת.

Adam Ha-Rishon partook from the world too early. The
Midrash (*Bereishis Rabbah* 19:5) said that Chava squeezed the
grapes (from the tree of knowledge) and gave it to him to taste.
When Chava did so, it was in order to know what was missing,
implying that the grapes and the world wasn't ready for man's
consumption. As a result of taking from the world too soon,
everything was given incomplete physical bodies. Therefore,
mankind's mission in the world is to penetrate through the
confusing mixture of reality in order to repair the world.

כי כל המצות הם כתיקונום. כי באמת מה איכפת ליה להקב"ה למי ששוחט מן
הצואר. או ממי ששוחט מן העורף (בראשית רבה פמ"ד ס' א'). ואף במצות
המשפטים מצד השי"ת מה איכפת ליה וכל שכן החקים. אבל לעתיד יהיו כלם
משפטים. והוא שהאדם יבין עומק כל טובה בשורשה ומוצא פי ה' המחיה

אותה. וזהו ושמר ה' אלהיך לך את הברית. זהו ההתקשרות עם האבות. ואת החסד. זה אור השי״ת שהיה פתוח להאבות יהיה לנו גם כן.

Each mitzvah is a way of fixing something in this incomplete world. Each one of the details is important in enacting this repair. Why does it matter to Hashem whether we perform the *mitzvos*—even those that are *mishpatim*, the ones we understand? In the future, Hashem will give us the reason for each mitzvah, making it abundantly clear how it fixes the world. Every mitzvah penetrates the fabric of creation to find out how Hashem is giving it life. This is why the *pasuk* says, "Hashem will keep his promise." When we fix the world, searching for Hashem through the *mitzvos*, we are connecting with the Avos, who also searched for Him in this world.

The Izhbitzer Tradition

Many Izhbitzer teachings deal with the motivations within a person and the conflicts that arise for an oved Hashem.

Practical Advice

Many times we have to fight that inner voice that tries to convince us not to excel. The בית יעקב reminds us that, because we make the right choices, we will reach the simchah of closeness to Hashem and the clarification of the world.

פרשת ראה

from Beis Yaakov ha-Kollel

אַחֲרֵי ה' אֱלֹהֵיכֶם תֵּלֵכוּ וְאֹתוֹ תִירָאוּ וְאֶת מִצְוֹתָיו תִּשְׁמֹרוּ וּבְקֹלוֹ תִשְׁמָעוּ וְאֹתוֹ תַעֲבֹדוּ וּבוֹ תִדְבָּקוּן (דברים י"ג ה'). בזה הפסוק יבואר כל דינו של אדם. כמבואר במסכת (שבת ל"א א') .על פסוק והיה אמונת עתיך.

In this week's *parsha*, Moshe Rabbeinu tells of the challenge to a Jew who is faced by a false prophet who tells him to serve idols. Moshe Rabbeinu is *mechazeik* (encourages) the Jews, "Follow after Hashem, your G-d, and you shall be in awe of Him. Do His *mitzvos*, and listen to His voice; serve Him and attach yourself to Him." The *pasuk* hints at the potential each person has. The Gemara (*Shabbos* 31a) explains that every person is asked six questions at the end of his life to determine if he lived up to his potential. Each one of these ways is hinted to in the *pasuk*. The questions are, "Did you do business ethically? Did you set aside time to learn? Did you try to bring children into the world? Did you yearn for *Geulah* and Moshiach? Did you involve yourself in deep understandings of wisdom? Did you understand one thing from another?"

אחרי ה׳ אלהיכם תלכו הוא נגד נשאת ונתת באמונה. כי אחרי מורה בשעה
שהקב״ה נסתר מאד מהאדם. כמו שנתבאר על פסוק לכתך אחרי במדבר.
ובשעה שהאדם נפנה מדברי תורה אז גם כן צריך להיות הקב״ה נגדו וילך
אחר מדותיו.

The phrase "You will follow after Hashem," corresponds to the question at the end of one's life, "Did you do business fairly?" The word "after" describes a mode of Hashem's interaction when Hashem is hidden from man, and man's response to follow after Him despite it. This is like Yirmiyahu's description of the Jewish people's following after Hashem into the wilderness without plans for sustenance. When a person closes the *sefer* for the day and goes to work, then he needs to chase after Hashem in the physical world and follow His ways.

ואתו תיראו הוא נגד קבעת עתים לתורה. כי יראה מורה על קביעות מורא בלב
אדם .

"And be in awe of Him," corresponds to the question, "Did you set aside time for Torah study?" The בית יעקב says that real awe means that the experience should be set deep into your heart. You should not allow it to be something that happened to you once, but as time passes from the experience, its impact upon you wanes. Therefore we are enjoined to take steps to preserve our inspiration.

ואת מצותיו תשמרו הוא נגד עסקת בפריה ורביה. כי כשיבוא כל מדות האדם
למעשה וליותר בהולדת נפש שם צריך ליותר שמירה.

"Guard His *mitzvos*" corresponds to "Did you engage in having children?" While our attributes are fundamental to our personalities, they don't affect this world until they find their expression in the *mitzvos* that we perform. This process of translation requires that we be careful that our ideals translate into our actions. The same applies with giving birth to and raising children.

ובקלו תשמעו הוא נגד צפיתה לישועה. כי דיבור היינו כשיצא מפורש. אבל קול מורה על פנימית הנסתר. ולזה רק ציפוי וקיווי.

"Listen to his voice," is the question "did you await Moshiach and *Geulah*?" What's the difference between Hashem's speech and His voice? Speech is straight out and particular, it means the words which are beginning to be expressed. However, voice is a much more nuanced and understated. Hearing it requires that a person long to hear and listen much more carefully. You can say the same phrase and depending on the voice derive alternative messages. Therefore, the person must long to hear the message of Mashiach, and it's a message which requires that we listen carefully.

ואתו תעבדו הוא נגד פלפלתה בחכמה. כי כשאדם סובר ומבקש לידע טעם ההלכה נקרא משמש תלמידי חכמים. וכשירצה להתבונן בטעמי ההנהגה שהעולם מתנהג נקרא שמשמש השי"ת. כי כל מה שהאדם מתבונן בזה יותר יקשה לו. וכדאיתא במדרש תנחומא (יתרו ס' ז'). משה אמר הצור תמים פעלו וגו'. אלו אמרו אדם אחר היו אומרים מנין הוא יודע. אלא למשה נאה לומר דבר זה כו'. לפי שלמשה היה יותר קשה מכל העולם כי הוא הבין יותר.

"Serve him," corresponds to the question, "Did you delve into wisdom." When a person thinks about the *halachah* and wants to know the reasoning behind it, he is called a person who serves Torah scholars. When they want to know the way the world works, they are called serving Hashem. The more a person thinks about how Hashem runs the world, the harder it is to understand. Moshe Rabbeinu said, "Hashem is the Rock Whose ways are perfect." If anyone else said it, we would say, "How do you know?" But because it's Moshe Rabbeinu, it is fitting and proper that He could say something like this, as He had arrived at a deep understanding how to serve Hashem and the way the world works. To Moshe, understanding the world was even harder because he knew more.

ובו תדבקון הוא נגד הבנתה דבר מתוך דבר. שהאדם יהיה דבוק בהשי"ת. ויבין את השינויים מה שהשי"ת מחדש בכל יום תמיד מעשה בראשית במה יעסוק עתה.

"And you shall cling to Him," is the question, "Did you understand one thing from another?" When a person looks at the world and realizes how Hashem is everything, then whatever he sees brings him to the awareness of how Hashem is always renewing everything. There is no other choice but to connect to Hashem; what else will they dwell on?

The Izhbitzer Tradition

Izhbitzer teachings often deal with the contradictions and complexities of life. See נאות דשא פרשת. See מי השלוח פרשת אמור. בית יעקב הכולל פרשת ואתחנן and דברים which discuss Sefer Devarim as the premier book of mussar and ethics.

Practical Advice

In the time most laden with contradictions, when a prophet says to serve idols, Moshe Rabbeinu tells us that we can become great. Sefer Devarim, the ultimate mussar text, reminds us of the potential we have and what we can achieve. We know we can achieve this potential, as this is what we will be asked at the end of our lives by the malach who taught us Torah in utero. This means that we were born with this potential for greatness and we have it all our lives. Moshe Rabbeinu tells us in this most challenging of times who we can be, because it's who we are.

פרשת שופטים

from Beis Yaakov ha-Kollel

שֹׁפְטִים וְשֹׁטְרִים תִּתֶּן לְךָ בְּכָל שְׁעָרֶיךָ אֲשֶׁר ה' אֱלֹהֶיךָ נֹתֵן לְךָ לִשְׁבָטֶיךָ **(דברים ט"ז י"ח)**. שעריך הוא במקום שהאדם הוא מקבל טובה. צריך משפט ומשטר איך לקבל טובה מבוררת שלא תזיק לך. ולשבטיך היינו במקום שהאדם משפיע טובה צריך ליותר משפט. כי כשהאדם מקבל טובה והטובה היא תחת האדם. אז אין האדם עומד רק תחת יראת ה'. כי צריך שהשי"ת יעיד עליו כי קבל טובה ברורה.

The בית יעקב explains the commandment to place *shoftim* (judges) and *shotrim* (enforcers) in all of the gates that Hashem gives you for all of your tribes. "Your gates" means any place where a person interacts with the world. Anywhere something can enter or leave a person's body needs a *shofet* and a *shoter*. The places where a person gives and receives need to be kept safe. What is the danger? Even something seemingly good that a person experiences can cause damage. How so? A person can believe everything is under his control and as a result, he loses track of Hashem. He can have delusions of grandeur brought about by the apparent ownership of the things he was given.

והשי"ת נקרא רב חסד. כי על המחשבה אינו דן הקב"ה. אף כי נגד הקב"ה אין
הפרש בין מחשבה למעשה כי לפניו הכל גלוי. מכל מקום כי על המחשבה אינו
מבין שום בריה רק השי"ת לבדו. והוא נקרא רב חסד.

Hashem is called "great in kindness," though, because he doesn't
judge us based on our thoughts. Even though to Hashem, there
is no difference between thought and action, to everyone else,
thoughts are imperceptible. Yet, Hashem doesn't judge us
regarding them, even though He could. For that reason, He is
called "great in kindness."

אבל כשיחל לפעול מה נגד עיני בשר ודם אז צריך ליתר משפט. פן יראה זר
בעיני אחרים. וליותר צריך משפט כשאדם משפיע להוליד נפש חדש. שאח"כ
יעשה הנפש מעצמו אף בלי דעתו. ואיך יתראה מעשיו בעיני האדם. והנה כל
מה שאדם גדול מחברו כח השפעתו גדול ממנו לכן צריך ליותר שמירה.

However, once a person interacts with the world at large, then
people will judge the decisions that he makes. He must act
carefully regarding what he lets in and what he lets out. The
greater a person is and the more powerful his choices are, the
more those choices need to be guarded.

ונגד זה צריך שופטים ושוטרים בדעת האדם. שופטים היינו בהתחלה שהאדם
נכנס לדברי תורה. וכוונתו להשיג יתרון התעלות.

A person needs both *shoftim* (judges) and *shotrim* (enforcers)
in his mind. Let's understand how. When a person starts out
to learn, he wants to reach the heights of growth and personal
refinement.

ואח"כ יראה שאין לו שום קיום אף בעולם הזה בלא דברי תורה זה נקרא
שוטרים. כדאיתא במדרש תנחומא (נצבים ס"ג). העבר בך קללה. וזהו הגערה
שהאדם גוער בעצמו .כמו שאיתא בהקדמת זה"ק (ו' א') מחלליה מות יומת.
מאן מחלליה מאן דעאל לגו חלל דעגולא ירבועא.

Afterwards he sees that without words of Torah, there is no
existence, even in this world. This is function of the *shoter*,
the enforcer of the law. The Midrash (*Tanchuma Nitzavim* 3)
explains that his job is to exhort and pronounce a curse, "If you
do this you'll be in trouble." This threatening keeps everyone in
line. The inner *shoter* (enforcer) threatens the person, not to not
do things that would be self destructive. The *Zohar (introduction*
6a) says in the introduction, that "those who profane it will die."
Why does the *pasuk* use the word "profane" (*mechalleleha*)?
Anyone who exposes their internal spiritual essence to the
outside (as *challal* means "hollow") will, as a result, die.

והנה שופט מורה על שכל האדם. כי בו האדם שופט על כל גופו. ומזה צריך
ליקח לו מדת השוטר היינו גערה. כמו שמבואר העבר בך קללה. ומחמת כי
השכל נקי וברור מבלי שום סיג נגיעה. בזה יוכל האדם לגעור בעצמו.

While a judge refers to a person's intellect, which makes the
decisions regarding what enters or exits his entire body, a
person also needs to be his own enforcer, making certain the
decisions that have been made are carried out. Since the intellect
is divorced from the physical, there must be something much
more tangible to enforce those decisions.

אף כי אכל שום וחזר הנגיעה אשר תדרכהו לחזור ולאכול שום. אבל מצד
השכל אינו כן. כי הראשון יעבור בזמן קצר ואח"כ ישאר נקי. כי לא סילף דרכו

298

בשורש. כי עוד נמצא בו נקודה טובה. כי התאוה לחזור ולאכול שום הוא מפני
שידמה לו כי אין ישועתה לו באלהים חס ושלום. ובזה צריך שהאדם יהיה נקי
מאד שיוכל להבין זאת.

Let's say, for example a person ate something, what was his
motivation? What caused the thought to stay long enough to eat
it? If we discuss the *middah* of a *shofet* then the idea came in,
but quickly went out, because he in his essence is good. Where
does the desire to eat come from? From the thought that
Hashem is not going to be the source of his salvation, a person
has to be very pure to understand this.

וכמו שמצינו במדרש תנחומא (שפטים ס"ג) שרבי חנינא בן אלעזר קצץ תחלה
את אילנו. ואח"כ צוה לקצוץ את אילן חבירו. כי באמת בהשוטר נמצא אהבה
יתרה מה שלא נמצא בשופט. כי במלחמה כתיב. ויספו השטרים לדבר אל העם
ואמרו מי האיש הירא ורך הלבב וגו' (שפטים כ' ח'). וזה היה מאמר השוטר.

The Midrash (*Tanchuma Shoftim* 3) says that Rebbe Chanina,
son of Elazar, cut his tree, then cut the tree of his fellow. This
speaks of the nature of the *shoter*. The *shoterim* gather when the
Jews assemble for war, and ask, "Who is the man who is faint
of heart?" (*Devarim* 20:8). What they are asking is, who does
not have the strength to live with their convictions and needs
prompting by the *shoterim*.

The Izhbitzer Tradition

*Many Izhbitzter teachings deal with the nature of choice and how a
person's latent urges and thoughts arrive at decisions. The בית יעקב
also continues on the theme of Devarim, the premier mussar sefer.*

Practical Advice

Many times we have to fight about that inner voice which tries to convince us not to excel. The בֵּית יַעֲקֹב reminds us that because we make the choices we will reach the simchah of closeness to Hashem, and the clarification of our doubts in the world.

פרשת כי תצא

from Beis Yaakov ha-Kollel

כִּי תֵצֵא לַמִּלְחָמָה עַל אֹיְבֶיךָ וּנְתָנוֹ ה' אֱלֹהֶיךָ בְּיָדֶךָ וְשָׁבִיתָ שִׁבְיוֹ (דברים כ"א
י'). זה שאמר הכתוב כי בתחבולות תעשה לך מלחמה ותשועה ברב יועץ (משלי
כ"ד ו'). כי בתחלת כניסת האדם לעבודת ה' עוד אין לבו מזוכך להישר דעתו
ורצונותיו לרצון השי"ת. רק בתחבלות יסבב את עצמו להטות רצונותיו מרע.

This *parsha* opens up by telling us about wars: "When you
go out to war against your enemies, Hashem will place your
enemies into your hands and you will bring back prisoners"
(*Devarim* 21:10). The בית יעקב adds that Shlomo Ha-Melech
(24:6) advised us that in order to make war, "You should have
tachbulos, tactical plans, and you'll be saved with much advice."
The בית יעקב explains these *pesukim* to mean that in life, when
a person starts to serve Hashem, his heart still has things that
need to be worked out, and he must think clearly in order to
want what Hashem wants. The only way for him to fight against
his baser desires is by using a cunning strategy.

ולא שיוכל להטותם לטוב כי עוד אין לבו מזוכך לזה. רק יוכל להטות רצונותיו
מעניין לעניין. אף כי העניין שיבא לתוכו גם כן אינו טוב בשורשו ולא יוטב לפניו
לשהות בו. אכן לפי העת היא עצה לפניו להנצל מהדבר שעומד בה. וזה נקרא
תחבלות. מלשון רב החובל.

301

What is this strategy? As we said, people aren't ready to mount a frontal attack and turn their lives around to always be good, because they still have issues to work through. Therefore they cannot always maintain their changes. But they can take a moment of challenge and turn it around. The בית יעקב says: to use a strategy (*tachbulos*). The word comes from the word *rav ha-chovel*, "captain," the person who turns the steering wheel on the ship. (*See Ibn Ezra, Yonah 1:5, Radak, Yonah 1:6 who explain this further.*)

כמו שרב החובל כשתטה הספינה לצד אחד אז ימהר להטותה לצד השני. ואף כי כשיאריך בנטותה לצד השני אז תוכל לנפול גם לצד השני ולטבוע שמה כמו בצד הראשון. אכן לפי העת טוב לפניו להטותה כי תנצל משאיתה כעת. וכמו שמבאר הרמב"ם ז"ל בשמונה פרקים איך יציל האדם את נפשו ממדות רעות בהטותו מן הקצה אל הקצה. ואף כי לאחוז בקצה האחרון ולעמוד שם גם כן אינו טוב. וכן הוא בדברי תורה. נגד תאוה העצה להכניס את עצמו במדה הכעס. אף כי לא טובה היא המדה. וכן להפך. אך לא לעשות דבר פעולה למעשה כי זהו הרע הגמור. וכמו שמבואר במי השלוח (חלק א' נח). בפסוק וישלח את הערב.

The *rav ha-chovel* turns the ship's wheel to one side, and then needs to adjust it to the other side. If he were to leave it turning to any one side for too long, the ship could tip, hit something, and sink, and everyone aboard might drown. Therefore, he has to turn the wheel at the right moment. The Rambam says in the *Shemonah Perakim* that you can be saved from bad *middos* by going to the opposite extreme, but remaining there is also not good. The בית יעקב gives an example, a person who is dealing with desire should use the *middah* of anger to counterbalance it, even though anger is also not a good *middah* (and a person should definitely not act in anger), but the one will balance out the other.

ותשועה ברב יועץ. היינו אחר גודל עבודה אז יראה הקב"ה לאדם את קו
האמצעי לאחוז בו ולא ירפנו. ויברר לנגד האדם כי תמיד עשה רצונו מבלי
נטיה אף במחשב ה. וזה יראה הקב"ה לאדם אחר שישיג כל הטובות המעלות
והמדות בשלמות. ויראה לו כי כי החשק הוא מותר כי הוא רק מהשיי"ת. אכן
בעולם הזה צריך להשמר ממנו כי יוכל לבא לידי מעשה. אבל כשלא בא
לפעולה אז החשק טוב מכל הצדדים:

The בית יעקב explains the end of Shlomo Ha-Melech's advice,
"And with much advice, man will be saved." After a person
grows in serving Hashem, after a lot of adjusting the wheel, he'll
open your eyes to find a happy medium. There will come a time
that he will no longer have to keep "adjusting." Hashem will
show the person how to use all of the *middos* properly. At this
stage, he'll see how all of the *middos*, which come from Hashem,
are beautiful and holy, each in their own context, as the word
middah also means amount.

The Izhbitzer Tradition

*See Parshas Noach in the מי השלוח which talks about Noach trying
to rid himself of anger, but seeing how he really needed it to offset
inappropriate love. Also look in בית יעקב פרשת ואתחנן where we
discuss this concept of the necessity for all of the middos.*

Practical Advice

*One of the greatest challenges to personal growth is the fear that
you will not be able to sustain it and the tremendous feeling of
being overwhelmed by it. Think, "What can I do in the 'right now.'
How can I positively affect the next five minutes?" It's great to*

have a big plan, but when feeling overwhelmed, think, "How can I change this little corner of my life." Finally, daven for the time when you can merit to see how all of the little changes made you a big person.

פרשת כי תבוא

from Naos Deshe

וַיְצַו מֹשֶׁה וְזִקְנֵי יִשְׂרָאֵל אֶת הָעָם לֵאמֹר שָׁמֹר וְגוֹ' (דברים כ"ז א') וְאחר
כך כתיב וַיְדַבֵּר מֹשֶׁה וְהַכֹּהֲנִים הַלְוִיִּם אֶל כָּל יִשְׂרָאֵל לֵאמֹר הַסְכֵּת וּשְׁמַע
יִשְׂרָאֵל (דברים כ"ז ט'). ופרש"י ז"ל על שמור לשון הווה כלומר שאינו
לשון צווי. להבין כוונת רש"י בזה. וגם אצל הסכת פרש"י ז"ל היום הזה
נהייתה לעם כאילו היום נכנסת עמו בברית. ויש לדקדק למה דוקא בזו הפרשה
כאלו נכנס עמו בברית. גם יש לדקדק למה שינה בזו הפרשה מכל התורה
שכתוב וידבר משה וזקני ישראל וגם אצל הסכת כתיב והכהנים הלוים מה
שלא כתיב כן בכל התורה כולה ולמטה גבי אלה יעמדו לברך את העם כתיב
משה לבדו כמו בכל התורה.

The *parsha* says, "Moshe and the elders spoke to the people
and said, 'Guard the *mitzvos*'" (*Devarim* 27:1). Afterwards, the
pasuk tells us that Moshe, the *kohanim* and Leviim said, "Listen
Israel. Today you have become a people" (ibid. 27:9). What
does that mean? The נאות דשא quotes Rashi, who says the word
"guard" should be understood as the present tense and not the
command form.

Rashi also says that similarly: when Moshe and the Leviim
say "Listen," it means "today you are a nation," not that they
commanded the nation to listen to know that then they became

a nation, rather, that this process is a constant one. Every day, "Listen," today you are a nation and enter into a covenant with Hashem. The נאות דשא asks, why add that Moshe and the elders spoke to the Jewish people, and that Moshe and the Leviim, spoke to the people. We have never seen such a thing mentioned in the Torah before.

ועוד יש לדקדק כי צוה לבנות מזבח בהר עיבל ולעלות עולות ולזבוח שלמים ולשמוח שם לפי הנראה היה צריך לעשות אלה הדברים בהר גריזים בהר ברכה ולא בהר עיבל. ועוד כתיב באר היטב בשבעים לשון למה נכתב בשבעים לשון ואיתא שהיו אומות העולם באים וקופלים את הסיד וזהו תימא שהרי באותו היום עצמו הרסו את האבנים וקפלו את הסיד והביאו את האבנים לגלגל במקום שלנו שם הלילה. ואם תאמר שהסיד נשאר בהר עיבל ויכולים האומות לקרותו זה אינו בדרך הטבע כי בשעה שמהרסים האבנים אזי הסיד נשבר ולא יצלח. ועוד האיך אפשר שיכתוב על המזבח שהוא קטן שבעים פעמים כל התורה כולה.

The נאות דשא continues with questions. Why were they commanded to build an altar on Har Eival, offer sacrifices and rejoice there, if that was the mountain where they would be warned about transgressing the *mitzvos* and hearing the curse? It should have been on Har Gerizim where they would receive blessings that they should celebrate!

Also why did He command them to write the Torah in seventy languages on the Altar. What was the use of putting lime on a stone and writing on it if the nations would only come and pull the lime off of the stones later that day, anyway? This is strange also, because the Jews took apart the altar and moved the rocks to the place where they would sleep that night. If you say that the lime stayed together, this isn't natural because when they'd take apart the *mizbeach*, then the lime would fall apart. Finally, how could they write the whole Torah 70 times on such a small area?

אך הענין היא כך דלכך פרש"י ז"ל שומר לשון הוה ואינו לשון צווי דרש"י ז"ל מתרץ למה שינה כאן לכתוב וידבר משה וזקני ישראל להודיע שאינו לשון צווי כי בכאן צוה אודות האבנים להעמיד בירדן ובהר עיבל והצווי הזה לא היה צריך לומר לישראל רק ליהושע לבדו כי יהושע היה הראש לכל ישראל ואצלו שייך הצווי כמו שכתוב בספר יהושע שהוא עשה את כל הדברים האלה ומה שייכות לומר לישראל הפרשה הזו. לכן פירש"י ז"ל שאינו לשון צווי רק לשון הוה ולכן כתיב וזקני ישראל להודיע שאינו לשון צווי ככל התורה רק לשון הוה וכן פרש"י ז"ל גבי הסכת כתרגומא והתרגום פירש אצית כוונת רש"י ז"ל בזה שהפרשה הזו שנאמרה לישראל היא רק שיטו אזנם לדבר זה כי היום נהיתה לעם ופירש"י ז"ל כאילו עמו בברית.

The answers to all of these questions lie within Rashi's explanation. The word "guard" was not a command, rather a statement of what will occur on that day. This also explains why we changed from the normal formula of "Hashem speaking to Moshe." What is recounted on that on that day, is that Yehoshua, as the new head of Israel, would be the one to take the two tablets at the Yarden to the top of Har Eival. Therefore it says that the elders of Israel repeated it too, to show that this is not a commandment, but a statement. This is why Rashi says that you will look back everyday as if were the day when you entered into the covenant with Hashem.

להבין זה כי הפרשה הזו יצאה מילין מנרתקא כי כתיב י"א ארורים כנגד השבטים כפרש"י ז"ל. ויש לדקדק למה פרט דוקא אלה הי"א דברים יותר מכל התורה תרי"ג מצות. וגם לבסוף כתיב ארור אשר לא יקים ופרש"י ז"ל

כאן כלל כל התורה כולה וקבלוה באלה ובשבועה. ויש לדקדק כיון שכלל כל
התורה כולה למה כתיב פרטים.

To understand this matter, let us delve more deeply into this
covenant. We see that there are eleven curses that are invoked,
one for each tribe of the Jewish people. Why pick specifically
those eleven *mitzvos* as opposed to any of the others? Then
it concludes by saying, "Cursed is he who does not keep the
Torah." Rashi says that this includes all of the Torah, which is
received with an oath, and the people say *amen ve-amen.*

אך בכאן לפי שקבלו עליהם באלה ובשבועה שנאמר ואמר אמן כמו שמשביעין
הסוטה ואמרה האשה אמן לכן גילה להם משה רבינו חסרונם בפרט היינו לכל
שבט ושבט חסרונו מתולדתו האיך יתחיל לתקן השורש החסרון אף שכל ספר
משנה תורה הוא דברי מוסר אך הם בכלל לכל ישראל וכאן פרט להם כי זה
הוא כל האדם שידע לאיזה דבר הוא נשלח לעולם הזה לתקן כי האדם בעצמו
אינו יודע שורש החטא אף שיודע בעצמו שחטא אבל השורש אינו יודע למשל
מי שאינו בבריאות בקל יוכל להזיק אף שיאכל מאכלים טובים לגוף אם אך
יאכל מעט יותר אזי יזיק לו מה שאין כן בבריא. כן היא בנפש כל זמן שלא
יתקן השורש אזי בקל יוכל לידבק לו כל הרעות שבעולם. למשל למי שיש
לו מכה אף שנרפא לו קצת מהיסורין דהיינו שהתחילה להוציא דם וליחה על
כל זה אם לא יתחוב לתוכה פתילה להוציא השורש הרע אזי תוכל תיכף מכה
אחר בצדה לצמוח אבל כשמוציא השורש אזי נרפא לגמרי. כן היא בנפש כל
שלא יתקן השורש אף שעושה מעשים טובים ולומד תורה והקל לו מעט אך
אינה רפואה גמורה כי בקל יוכל עוד להתפתות כאשר אנחנו רואים בעינינו
בכל יום אבל כשמתקן השורש זו היא רפואה גמורה שלא יתפתה עוד בתאוות
עולם הזה.

What is the nature of this oath? The statement *amen ve-amen*
is similar to the case of the *sotah*, who says *amen*, accepting

her curse if she goes against the oath. The connection here is that each tribe, in responding *amen*, was accepting Moshe Rabbeinu's scrutiny, to reveal what was lacking in each one of them and how they could repair that lack. It is well known that *Sefer Devarim* is the ethical instruction for the entire nation and for each individual. The essence of man is to know why we were sent to the world and what to repair. A person might know that he sinned, but not know why he sinned, and what makes him sin. For example, someone who is not healthy can easily cause damage to his health by eating a little more than normal, whereas a healthy person would not. A person who is not healthy spiritually, who has not repaired his soul at its root, will easily be drawn to all that's bad in the world. A person who has an injury, even though it has partially healed, will need to have it drained, so that it does not become infected. If it is not, even after the wound has disappeared on the outside, it is only a matter of time before it returns to cause him pain. In matters of the soul, despite the fact that the person with the infected soul can perform good actions and learn Torah, it isn't a complete recovery. He can easily be swayed back to his old ways, as there is an "infection" in his soul.

ולכן כאן מחמת שקבלו עליהם באלה ובשבועה גילה להם משה רבינו שורש החטא בפרט כמו שמצינו בזה"ק אצל נפילת אפיים בשביל דמסר גרמי' באתר אילנא דמותא לכן יש לו תיקון אף במקום שנאמר אם יכופר העון הזה לכם עד תמותון (ישעיה כ"ב י"ד) ולכן גם כאן בשביל שקבל על עצמו אלה ושבועה אם ח"ו יעבר על דברי תורה לכן מגלין לו שורש נשמתו האיך יתקן. ולכן היה המזבח והעולה והשלמים בהר עיבל כי הפכו כלפי הר עיבל ופתחו בקללה ומזה זכו לשלימות הגמור לכן ילמד אדם לעצמו שמזה שלומד מצות אנשים מלומדה לא יוכל לבוא לשלימות אף שהוא דבר טוב אבל יצפה שיוכל

לטרוח אחר דברי תורה באגר שלים אזי יקנה דברי תורה בשלימות הגמור.
וזהו בשבעים לשון פירשה להם היינו לכל מקום שיגלו לשם לא יכלו האומות
להתפתות אותם כמו שנאמר שובי שובי השולמית כי לא ישמעו להם.

Therefore, Moshe Rabbeinu gathered the people together with an oath and revealed to them the root of their sins in their souls. The *Zohar* (*Chadash* 52:1) says regarding *nefilas apayim*, that when we put our head down during *Tachanun*, it is through that descent, that it is revealed to us what must be repaired in our souls. Similarly, when the oath was administered to the Jews, should they go against the Torah, Moshe Rabbeinu revealed to them how to repair their souls. As a result, Har Aival was a place for rejoicing, and why there was an altar, the *olah*, and *shlamim*. Through their accepting the curse if they break their oath, there they reached completion. We learn from this that a person cannot allow their involvement with the *mitzvos* to be casual, for it will not allow them to reach completion even though they are something good. *Avodas Hashem* requires that we accept that it will be intensive, but it will be equally rewarding. The point of writing the Torah in seventy foreign languages is to protect the Israel from being seduced by foreign ideologies. By writing the Torah into a foreign language, it sends Torah to all of these foreign places. This means that there is no place where we can be pulled away from the Torah, as it is already there.

The Izhbitzer Tradition

In Izhbitzer seforim, Sefer Devarim is known as <u>the</u> sefer of Mussar. Moshe Rabbeinu, as our teacher, can open our souls to help us to repair ourselves. See נאות דשא דברים. See also בית יעקב הכולל פרשת לך לך, which discusses the blessing of knowing one's faults.

Practical Advice

It is so important to pursue our Yiddishkeit with an open heart. How many times do we sit in a situation and say, "been there, done that, not interested." Before doing a mitzvah, especially one we have done before, try to prepare, open your heart, say to yourself, "If I have an obligation to do this mitzvah, then there is something more that this mitzvah is supposed to do for me; how can I enter into it?"

פרשת נצבים

from Beis Yaakov ha-Kollel

אַתֶּם נִצָּבִים הַיּוֹם כֻּלְּכֶם **(דברים כ"ט ט')**. הטו אזנכם ולכו אלי שמעו ותחי
נפשכם ואכרתה לכם ברית עולם חסדי דוד הנאמנים (ישעיה נ"ה ג').

In explaining this week's *parsha*, where we read, "You are all
standing today before Hashem" (*Devarim* 29:9), the בית יעקב
quotes a *pasuk* in *Yeshaya* (55:3): "Turn your ears and go to Me;
listen and give your souls life. I will make a covenant with you
forever, the trustworthy kindnesses of David."

הטו אזנכם היינו הטיה בכח לילך אחרי השי"ת. ושמעו היינו הבנה כשהאדם
מתחיל להבין עמקי דברי תורה אז תחיה נפשו ואכרתה לכם ברית עולם חסדי
דוד הנאמנים. כי לדוד המלך עליו השלום היה האהבה בהתגברות. כי תכף
בשובו נאמר לו גם ה' העביר חטאתך לא תמות (שמואל ב' י"ב י"ג).

Let's understand the words of the Navi: "Turn your ears." This
means to direct one's talents and strengths towards Hashem
and his dictates. "Listen" means to understand that when
a person begins to hear the depths of Torah, then his soul is
revived. What is the "covenant of the trustworthy kindnesses
of David"? David Ha-Melech was a person whose love for

312

Hashem was constantly gaining strength. We know this to be immediately, for when David Ha-Melech did *teshuvah*, Nasan Ha-Navi (*Shmuel* II 1213:) said, "Hashem has removed your sin; you shall not die."

והנה בפרשה הלזו מבואר מצב ישראל איך התקשרו כלם במצב חזק. כי התחיל למנות כל נפשות ישראל מן רום המעלות עד שפל המדרגות אחד מול אחד והראשים נגד הטף. כמבואר במי השלוח (חלק א' נצבים).

In this *parsha*, there is an explanation about how all of Israel can connect to Hashem in the strongest way. The *parsha* starts by counting the Jews from the highest in level to lowest. By discussing them all together, the Torah is explaining that all of them are connected. Even those on the most extreme ends of the spectrum—the heads of the community are connected to the children. Regarding these extremes, the *parsha* describes different modes of their relationship with Hashem. The heads of the community must "listen and turn your ears," but to the children, who can't make such choices yet, Hashem tells you that, "I will make a covenant."

כי אמת כשאדם בא על דברי תורה מעבודתו בשכל יוכל להשיגם גם כן. אכן שיקשבו בו עד למדרגת טף במקום שהחיים נקטן גם שם לא יסיר מהם. לזה צריך כי יקשר הראש והשכל בקשר גדול באלה ובשבועה. כי באמת החסרון בטף יגיע עד להראש. וכן בפרטי נפשות כשאדם ממליך בבוקר את השי"ת ואח"כ יאונה לו חס ושלום נטיה מרצון ה'. אז יבין כי בעומק לא המליך את השי"ת.

Sometimes we serve Hashem as "leaders," other times, we serve Him as "children." There are times when a person reaches Hashem through his own exertions and understanding of

Torah, which is called, "the heads of Jewish people." There also times when we serve Hashem on the level of "children," when we cannot serve Him on this level. This situation describes someone who is feeling that something is missing in serving Hashem. How does he create a relationship with Hashem? This person enters into an oath; it keeps him committed even when he is not as engaged. When there is a lack "in children," the problem reaches to "the head," as the entire nation is connected. People at first try to accept Hashem as their King, themselves, but then revert to sin. They have not made Hashem King in their world in any meaningful way.

כי בלעם הרשע בעת שחפץ לקלל את ישראל אמר תחלה אשר ישים אלהים בפי אתו אדבר (בלק כ"ב ל"ח). וסבר בדעתו שממליך את השי"ת בשלמות וממילא יוכל חס ושלום להמשיך את רצון ה' כפי חשקו. אבל השי"ת הראה לו אח"כ כי באמת אף בעת ההוא היה זדון בלבו. כי זה ענין כל טעותם של אומות העולם כמבואר בגמרא (מנחות ק"י א'). מאחר שבכל מקום מקטר מגש לשמי ומנחה טהורה מהו התעלות ישראל. ומבואר שם שהם קוראים את השי"ת אלהא דאלהא. כי אומרים שלהם גם כן יש כח וכן בהטבע יש כח אך השי"ת מושל עליהם. ואם בהתחלה ימליכו אותו אז יוכלו כביכול להמשיכו לרצונם.

We see this regarding the wicked Bilaam, who started by saying (*Bamidbar* 22:38): "Only what Hashem places in my mouth, I will say," but he planned to curse Israel afterwards. He felt that that he could say Hashem is truly King, and then he could make Hashem do what he wants. But Hashem showed him afterwards that He was aware of Bilaam's plan. This concept underscores the error of the nations of the world. The nations call Hashem the G-d of gods (*Menachos* 110a). They say that there is power in nature, and Hashem rules over nature. If at first they say He is King, then, so to speak, they can do what they want.

אבל באמת אינו כן כי כי בישראל נמצא זאת המבינות כי לעולם השי״ת נמצא. ואף כי דוד המלך עליו השלום אמר גם כן הודו לאלהי האלהים (תהלים קל״ו ב'). אכן כי בישראל באם נמצא חסרון אז מכירים כי אין להם כח מצדם. וכמו כן באם נמצא חסרון בטף אז אין שום ראש כי מאחר שהטף נברא לצוות להראש. וזה שנקשרו פה במשה רבינו עליו השלום שהוא הראש את אשר היה אז וגם אשר ישנו שם. ולפי שעל משה רבינו עליו השלום סמך הקב״ה את ידיו וממילא יתחייב שלא יהיה על שום נפש מישראל שום דבר חס ושלום כי כלם טובים:

Of course this isn't true; Hashem is everywhere. And even though David Ha-Melech (136:2) himself said, "Praise Hashem, G-d of gods," he clearly didn't mean it the way the idolators do. David Ha-Melech meant to express that Hashem rules over all of reality, and there is nothing separate from Him. One could think that if you notice something lacking in any person of Israel, then there must be something faulty in the source. To put it in terms of the *pasuk*, if there is something missing in the children, then there is something missing in the heads of Israel, as well. However, Moshe Rabbeinu connected everyone back to their source. He said, "Each person is standing before Hashem," meaning they are connected, no matter how far away they might seem. As the *pasuk* said, "those who were here," and "those who are not here." This means that even if it seems that they are not connected, they in truth are and will be inspired by the power of the *bris* to make that connection palpable once more.

The Izhbitzer Tradition

See מי השלוח חלק א נצבים, who discusses the interconnection of Israel, and נאות גשא כי תבוא, which discusses "oaths" as brisos. See

בית יעקב הכולל פרשת בא, which deals with the fallacy of lip service to Hashem's rule over the world.

Practical Advice

Many times when our resolve is challenged and we feel we will not be able to achieve, we want to give up. The truth is that we need to remind ourselves, that our failures are only a small portion of the picture. Hashem has greater plans for us. Our job is to hold on as the next portion of the story is about to unfold.

פרשת וילך

from Beis Yaakov ha-Kollel

וַיֵּלֶךְ מֹשֶׁה וַיְדַבֵּר אֶת הַדְּבָרִים הָאֵלֶּה אֶל כָּל יִשְׂרָאֵל. וַיֹּאמֶר אֲלֵהֶם בֶּן מֵאָה וְעֶשְׂרִים שָׁנָה אָנֹכִי הַיּוֹם וגו' (דברים ל"א א'-ב'). בזה"ק (וילך רפ"ג ב'). מאי וילך לאן הלך אלא וילך כגופא בלא דרועא. הענין בזה כי הזרועות הם מנהיגי הגוף שהאדם יכול להגביה אותם למעלה מראשו. והוא כי האדם יכול להגביר בכח עבודה שיגיע למעלה ממקום תפיסת חכמתו.

Moshe went and spoke all of these things to all of the Jewish people. He said, "I am one hundred and twenty years old today" (*Devarim* 31:1-2). The *Zohar* (*Vayelech* 283b) asks, "What does it mean and 'Moshe went?' He went like a body without arms." What does this mean? Let's understand. The בית יעקב explains that the arms figuratively refer to a person's direction in life. There is an expression in English, when something is within your reach or grasp. He notes that because a person can raise his hands over his head, his reach is figuratively greater than his intellectual grasp. Through the course of his service of Hashem, a person can rise even higher than he ever thought he could. So long as a person is alive, Hashem conceals things from his grasp, to enable him to achieve even more than he ever imagined.

317

וזהו כל זמן שהאדם בגוף שנתן שנתן הקב"ה כח הסתר בעולם שהאדם ירעיש בעבודה. ועל ידי זה יתגלה לו למעלה מכח חכמתו שנחלק לו. אכן כעת נשלם משה רבינו עליו השלום. ועיקר השלמת מנהיג הדור הוא שיכניס כל כח חכמתו ובינתו ועבודתו ללבות ישראל.

Now let's return to the concept of not having arms. At this point Moshe Rabbeinu had reached the completion of his task in this world. It is the function of the leaders of the Jewish people to instill the power of his knowledge, understanding, and spiritual achievements into the hearts of the Jewish people.

ואחר שנשלם והשי"ת ייחד שמו עליו שכל מה שהשיג הוא נקי וברור בלי שום פסולת יכול למסור זאת ללבות ישראל. והם ינהגו את כח חכמתו. והם ינהגו בכחם את חכמתו.

After Moshe Rabbeinu had completed a lifetime of service to Hashem, he could then pass on all of what he had learned to the hearts of the Jewish people, so they would be able to act based on this wisdom.

כי כל מה שתלמיד ותיק עתיד לחדש הוא נכלל בתורת משה (ויקרא רבה פכ"ב ס' א'). והוא שמנהיג תורת משה רבינו עליו השלום שיכניס לתוך גדר תפיסת התלמיד.

So much so that the Midrash explains that any new idea in Torah that a student comes up with could be found in the Torah that Moshe received. Therefore the Torah of Moshe entered into the life of that student and all other students.

וזהו וילך שהלך ומסר עצמו לתוך לב כלל ישראל. ובאמת גם בימי הנהגת משה רבינו עליו השלום היו ישראל נכללים בזרועותיו. אכן ההנהגה היתה מסורה

בידו. ועכשיו ניתן ההנהגה ליד ישראל והם המנהיגים וחכמתו נכללת בהם. כי
עד עתה היה הוא הראש וישראל הזרועות. ועכשיו ההנהגה נתן להם.

This is the meaning of "and Moshe went." He passed on the Torah
to the entire Jewish people. During the lifetime of the generation
that left Mitzraim, Moshe Rabbeinu guided the Jewish people
with his wisdom. Now he was speaking to the second generation,
those who would enter the Land. They would make their own
choices, but his wisdom would guide them.

The Izhbitzer Tradition

See תפארת יוסף וילך and תפארת החנוכי וילך, which deal with these
concepts in greater depth.

Practical Advice

What is the legacy that you are passing on to the coming
generation? What avodah is so part of yourself that it will make
a contribution to the future? All of us have certain connections to
different concepts in Torah and avodah, which we favor. When we
speak about them, work on them, daven for them, and live them,
whether we know it or not, we pass it on to later generations.

פרשת האזינו

from Tiferes Yosef

זְכֹר יְמוֹת עוֹלָם בִּינוּ שְׁנוֹת דֹר וָדֹר (דברים ל"ב ז'). זה מורה שהשי"ת ציוה
לזכור השקליא וטריא שהיה אצלך קודם שבאת אל ישוב הדעת. והדיעות
שהיה אצלך מקודם שבאת אל גודל ישוב הדעת ולא היה אצלך עבודתך בסדר
מסודר. בינו שנות דור ודור זה מורה אחר שבא האדם על סדר עבודה. וכבר
הוא אצל בני אדם הסדר מסודר בקביעות.

In this week's *parsha*, Moshe Rabbeinu says, "Remember
bygone days; contemplate the years of passed generations"
(*Devarim* 32:7). תפראת יוסף explains "Remember bygone days
(literally, 'the days of the world')" as teaching us that Hashem
commanded us to remember the back and forth that existed
before arriving at clarity. Remember the ideas that prevailed
before settling into a course of serving Hashem. "Understand
the years of each generation." After a person has arrived at a way
of serving Hashem, then it can become an established order.

וזה הוא נמי החילוק בין שב מיראה לשב מאהבה כדאיתא בש"ס (יומא פ"ו
ב') האי עון מזיד הוא וקא קרי ליה כשלון אלא שב מיראה זדונות נעשות לו
כשגגות שב מאהבה נעשות לו כזכיות.

This is also the distinction between a person who returns to Hashem through fear versus one who returns through love. The Gemara expounds that if a person committed a willing sin and does *teshuvah* from fear, it will be considered as if he stumbled. Through the greatness of *teshuvah*, willful sins become like unintentional sins; with *teshuvah* from love, they become merits. How does that work?

ואמר בזה כבוד אזמו"ר זללה"ה ששב מיראה אין פירושו ששב מחמת יראת העונש אלא מרמז שכבר קנה והשיג אור בשלימות ורק שלא נקבע עוד אצלו בקביעות גמור ועוד יכול לפסוק ממנו זה האור. וזה מרמז ששב מיראה שעוד יש לו יראות גדולות שמא יופסק ממנו אור השי"ת מחמת שלא השיג עדיין בסדר מסודר ושב מאהבה מורה שכבר קבע קדושה אצלו בקביעות כיתד בל תמוט וכבר השיג אור השי"ת בסדר מסודר.

My grandfather (the Radziner) said that that someone returning through fear does not mean he is afraid of punishment. It means that a person has already understood the spiritual implications of a level of *kedushah*, but has not been able to make it a part of his life. This fear, that he can at anytime be separated from his spiritual level, is operational in *teshuvah* from fear. The fact that he has not returned through love indicates that he has not set it as a foundation in his life and cemented it in his *avodas Hashem*.

The Izhbitzer Tradition

See סוד ישרים זכור ימות עולם ד"ה ב *who explores this concept in greater depth.*

Practical Advice

In this time of introspection, we aspire to look for the parts of our lives and avodas Hashem that are shaky. The fact that we don't feel settled in them, means that we have not conquered them yet. We don't feel so comfortable in our own skin. During this season of teshuvah and of self-discovery, think about what needs to be accepted with more love and make concrete and real in our lives.

www.ingramcontent.com/pod-product-compliance
Lightning Source LLC
Chambersburg PA
CBHW031236090426
42742CB00007B/216